MW00943140

A Star to Sail Her By

A FIVE-YEAR ODYSSEY OF COMING OF AGE AT SEA

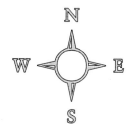

Alex Ellison

iUniverse, Inc.
Bloomington

A Star to Sail Her By
A Five-Year Odyssey of Coming of Age at Sea

Copyright © 2011 Alex Ellison

All rights reserved. No part of this book may be used or reproduced by
any means, graphic, electronic, or mechanical, including photocopying,
recording, taping or by any information storage retrieval system
without the written permission of the publisher except in the case
of brief quotations embodied in critical articles and reviews.

iUniverse books may be ordered through booksellers or by contacting:

iUniverse
1663 Liberty Drive
Bloomington, IN 47403
www.iuniverse.com
1-800-Authors (1-800-288-4677)

Because of the dynamic nature of the Internet, any Web addresses or
links contained in this book may have changed since publication and
may no longer be valid. The views expressed in this work are solely those
of the author and do not necessarily reflect the views of the publisher,
and the publisher hereby disclaims any responsibility for them.

Any people depicted in stock imagery provided by Thinkstock are models,
and such images are being used for illustrative purposes only.

Certain stock imagery © Thinkstock.

ISBN: 978-1-4620-1832-1 (pbk)
ISBN: 978-1-4620-1833-8 (cloth)
ISBN: 978-1-4620-1834-5 (ebk)

Library of Congress Control Number: 2011906658

Printed in the United States of America

iUniverse rev. date: 5/17/2011

Author Photo by Brian Crowley, courtesy of Phillips Exeter Academy

Dedicated to my parents and sister Lara,
without whom the voyage would neither have been
possible nor worthwhile, and to Don Treworgy, who
taught me the stars when I needed them most.

I'd like to thank both the people who made the story and who made the book. To my parents and Lara, thank you for being my crew. To my entire family, thank you for your support; especially my sister Kristin, whose expertise and effort has been invaluable, and to my Grandmother, who has kept every article I've generated along the way. Thank you to the sailing community for participating in my saga. Finally, may the brave sailors we loved and lost to the sea rest in peace.

Contents

Preface

The sea called to all of us in our family and captured our imaginations. This version of the story is my son's to tell: it is a coming-of-age story at sea, which began when he was eight years old, and ended when we returned to the United States when he was almost fourteen to enter high school. But it is also our family's story, our journey together; for without my husband and me casting our fortunes and lives to the wind, my son never could have embarked on this path that measured more than 25,000 nautical miles.

My husband, Lee, and I are both physicians and have both lived off the beaten path at various times in our lives. He was a Peace Corps doctor in Malawi for two years, and I coordinated and worked on a project in Ghana for the National Institute of Health. We have seen children suffer and die in myriad circumstances, from the tragically preventable to the result of careless avarice from the powers that be. We both had been touched deeply by the words of Elie Wiesel who states, "No child will be safe unless everyone comes to view every child as their own"—so simple, but profound. Having children is the ultimate leap of faith: you will love them more than life itself, yet have such little control over their fate. When we had our children, we vowed to try to help them live differently, to help provide them with a unique and balanced perspective. We wanted them to see the tapestry of humanity in all its varied hues and become citizens of the world. As a parent, I also hoped to offer some small degree of inspiration for those who may dare to live differently. Modern American culture often defines our roles and dictates our transitions with alarmingly little choice at times. To live outside the box of "2.2 children and the Volvo wagon," as we refer to it in our family, takes a certain self-reliance and conviction. The rewards, however, are immeasurable.

My husband and I have sailed for pleasure throughout our lives, and we've owned a series of sailboats since we've been married. I had been primarily a coastal sailor, whereas he had done more blue-water sailing, and participated multiple times in racing to Bermuda. We often took off for a few weeks each summer to the islands of Cuttyhunk, Martha's Vineyard, and Nantucket, but the snippets of time never seemed long enough. Just as we would all fall into the lovely rhythm of life on the water, we would be due back home again. As we watched the world around us grow more materialistic and pull us away from what we held dear, we conceived of escaping for a longer period of time. We felt the keen pressure of working in two medical careers, doing important work that, unfortunately, kept us from our own children—who were growing so quickly, as all do—for long and often unpredictable hours. In my role as pediatrician, I would often quip to a parent, "Your children are the most important things in your lives," and then think to myself, *Yet mine are home with the nanny.*

My husband and I discussed our options for spending more time with our family. We envisioned a one-year sabbatical, a one-year voyage during which we could sail down the Atlantic from New England to Bermuda, then through the Caribbean to South America and back again. We surmised that the most auspicious time in our children's lives would be when they were old enough to swim well and have an adventurous spirit, yet still young enough that we were the center of their social lives, so as not to disrupt the all-important friendships that are the hallmark of the early teen years. Complicating this was our daughter, who had several developmental delays; we were concerned, along with her physicians, that her shyness and language delays may have signaled a mild form of autism. The fear of the unknown can be paralyzing to any parent, but somehow having a child who has special needs, and therefore seems more vulnerable, made the decision more poignant and difficult for us. However, her speech therapist kindly teased us, what better therapy for a child who tends to self-isolate than to be on a forty-seven-foot sailboat with three talkative and motivated groupies to tend to her education and stimulate her growth? It was the type of immersive therapy that would shape all of our lives.

The reality of financial burdens also came into play, but fortunately,

I had recently finished paying off my student loans from medical school. With some creative financing, we realized if we could rent our house, which was small but lovely and on the water, we could cover both the house mortgage as well as that of a newer sailboat. The boat we had at the time was a classic Sweden 38, over twenty years old, and a former racer. She had an exceptionally tall rig, but even more daunting, a very deep keel at almost seven feet. Knowing that we would want to go into reef-strewn shallow coves and around tiny cays, we felt the draft would be a serious liability. We also knew that most (if not all) of the sailing would be short-handed, with just ourselves and two young children for most of the passages; at the time, Alex was eight and Lara, seven. We needed lines from the sails on deck to reach into the relative safety of the cockpit, so if one of us were on a night shift alone we did not have to go up on deck to adjust a line or reef the main. We looked at several different models, and decided that a Beneteau, which was originally a French-held family company that produced seaworthy hulls, was the best fit for our family. We previously chartered several different versions of these sailboats in the Caribbean before, so we knew they had a user-friendly transom and manageable sails. We also felt that we'd have a lower risk of problems with a newer vessel and the price difference was negligible.

The children were the most concerned with having their own cabin or space. Luckily, this was easily accomplished on the Beneteau 473, which also had a large main salon and ample galley space. One of our favorite family activities is cooking, especially baking, and we knew that we wanted to be able to sample and prepare local produce wherever we went. We also knew we would be homeschooling, so we needed spaces large enough for white boards, colorful posters, and the myriad of art projects I envisioned decorating the cabin between ocean passages.

One of our first tasks was naming the boat, and on that subject we all agreed. We had *promised* we would always sail away on a grand adventure; one of our favorite books *The Owl and the Pussycat*, by Edward Lear, had a version illustrated by Jan Brett, with the name *Promise* painted on the hull of the characters' illustrious boat. So *Promise* it was, from our hailing port of Essex, Connecticut.

Lee, a veteran of four previous Bermuda races as captain, felt that it would be prudent to start with the Bermuda Race, which in 2003 was leaving from Marion, Massachusetts (the race alternates each year, with the other starting point in Newport, Rhode Island, our local sailing capital). There would be no shortage of able-bodied seamen willing to help, and it would expedite our herculean efforts to ensure that we had all the proper gear, training, and procedures to sail offshore. Our preparation had actually started the previous year, when we enrolled in review seamanship classes at Mystic Seaport, and a year-long program in celestial navigation.

Celestial navigation is an elegant and yet often forgotten art. Using a handheld, non-electronic sextant, one can measure the height of a given star, or its angle of inclination, from the horizon. A steady hand is required to do this, especially on a rolling ship at sea. It also requires an encyclopedic knowledge of stars in order to utilize them as lighthouses of the sky. Finally, it requires spherical trigonometry and mathematics skills to complete the complex calculations required to determine your position. The sailor must know a variety of other mathematical techniques for sun sights and moon sights, short sights where there is no horizon, and a plethora of other confounding variables. Fortunately for us, we had the great pleasure of studying the historical mixture of art and science under Professor Don Treworgy, whom everyone referred to as Don. Don was brilliant, kind, and generous with his time and talents. He had the enviable skill of making these obtuse concepts crystal-clear; he also explained in detail the mathematics behind the science, which proved his awareness that our, and our children's, lives depended on us getting it right. Trying to find Bermuda in the middle of the Atlantic, not to mention the other tiny islands spread out over thousands of miles between there and South America, was daunting to even a skilled practitioner; still, failure was not an option. The risks were highlighted by the fact that our class textbook had been written by a friend of Don's, Susan Howell, who had gone down with a ship while navigating in the North Atlantic, leaving three young children behind.

We enrolled in the Bermuda Race in the celestial navigation class, and would only use that mode of navigation from Massachusetts to that tiny coral island, backed up by low-tech but valuable techniques, such as dead reckoning. After Bermuda, once we were on our own, we obviously could use our electronic navigation systems and GPS, but we had heard so many stories regarding failure of these critical systems that we knew we needed an ironclad back-up plan to ensure our safety. We both took the course, and I became certified to serve as the official navigator for *Promise*.

As we prepared for the trip itself, we had ample help from incredibly competent and generous friends willing to augment our skills and crew. Bill Clapp, who had accompanied Lee on several previous trips, headed up the list, along with Lee's daughter Kristin; her friend, Fritz; and a sailing buddy, Mark. For the race we needed two on a shift, and three shifts of crew for optimal performance and safety. The race starts in the cool waters of New England, crosses the treacherous Gulf Stream, and then enters tropical waters with their plentiful squalls. Ships were regularly lost on the Bermuda race, and in this stretch of the Atlantic in general, so preparation and vigilance would be our allies.

Vessels embarking on this voyage have to be inspected, and the captain and crew exceedingly well prepared. Attendance at a seminar at MIT was required, as were multiple layers of documentation of competence. Although we thought we paid a fair price for the boat, we spent an additional $50,000 on safety equipment, such as an eight-person inflatable life raft. We had additional stays put on and specialized storm sails custom made. All sails and equipment had to be labeled with our official International Yacht Register (IYR) number for identification purposes, should we be lost at sea. We installed a single side band radio (SSB) over which we could contact or receive messages from people half way around the world. This was especially essential as we were moving south during hurricane season which officially began on June 1st. During the race, special weather updates, as well as information regarding the Gulf Stream, were supplied to all crews via the SSB. The Gulf Stream courses through the North Atlantic like a superheated river; it meanders along its course at a temperature several degrees warmer than the surrounding water. Special satellite imagery shows the Gulf Stream to be actually several inches higher than the surrounding sea, which unfortunately is not evident to the eye. Sailors have specific strategies linked to this forbidding stretch of water which can produce significant squalls and treacherous weather very quickly. Circulating eddies of warm water often pinch off and spin to the side of the main current. This is of significant benefit and provides a boost in speed of a few extra knots, if one caught them in the appropriate southerly direction. As our hull speed was often only six to eight knots, every knot of speed expedited our journey.

Unfortunately for our boat speed, we were also well prepared for our life during the upcoming year. While some race boats are stripped down to bare hulls with minimal comforts (to keep the vessel's weight down), ours was laden with goods. We carried books for a year's worth of schooling for both children, for learning every ancillary skill related to boating, and for pleasure; blank notebooks and journals; and a huge stock of art supplies, paint, crayons, paper, and everything needed for any conceivable project. We had a medical supply station with everything from intravenous fluids to a defibrillator, and we possessed spare parts to handle every possible emergency from engine failure to hull breach. We carried aboard enough food and water to last the crew for several weeks in case of a worst-case scenario. We did, however, spare weight when we thought it appropriate: the boat had come with a brand new flat-screen television, which I had them promptly remove. We were not sailing down the ocean carrying the idiocy of that medium, much to the children's dismay.

We set sail under a clear sky from Buzzards Bay, an uninspiring name for such a beautiful expanse of water: Massachusetts to its north and a string of tiny jewel isles, the Elizabeth Islands to its south. High-tech boats with crews in matching uniforms sprinted past us with the latest gear and sleek hulls, some as large as eighty-five feet. It was amazing to see hundreds of boats at the start of a race—yet a few hours later, as darkness fell, to find no other ship for as far as the eye could see. As night set in, we rejoiced that food had an amazing way of transforming into a magical feast on a lonely, cold, dark ocean. We had hearty fare prepared and frozen before we embarked, and each night thawed and served a potluck feast of a variation of casserole confection.

The first night south of New England's fishing grounds was frigid; the crew on watch stood bundled in full foul-weather gear pants, jackets, gloves, and boots. Those who were off-duty tried to sleep to the constant rocking of the hull, while tucked into center-line berths. At least no one aboard was seasick, all of us veterans of the sea, and the sea and wind comfortably off our beam.

Five days of sailing passed quickly, with variations in temperament of the sea and sky. We were initially lulled into complacency with a gentle downwind run; but, we then suddenly encountered tempestuous seas and squalls, which blew out our first spinnaker before we could even react. A tiny bluebird, more brown than blue, became our constant companion in our quest for land. We first noticed it circling and returning to the mast our first day out, and it continued to amaze us with its persistence. On day three when I was on deck taking a sun sight, I noticed straw and dried grass by a slot in the forward side of the mast, and realized that a tiny nest protruded from the opening—we had a stowaway aboard! We named him Eddie, and he provided us with delightful hours of voyeurism as his world literally rocked and he tried to adjust. We claimed we would write a children's book one day, *Eddie the Bluebird Goes to Bermuda*, but, alas, we never did. (Neither did we claim him at Customs and Immigrations.)

We arrived at midnight to the welcome strobe of the lighthouse off of St. George's Harbor; we had found the tiny island in the sea navigating only by the stars. Miraculously, after travelling days without sighting another vessel, all of a sudden, sails and hulls appeared out of the night mist and accompanied us over the finish line. As we crossed and they announced our time, a flying fish dove with great accuracy and speed into Kristin's lap, a gift from the sea god.

The docks of the Royal Bermudian Yacht Club were festooned with colorful pennants waving in the breeze. The intrepid vessels whose crews had braved the North Atlantic and safely come to rest on Bermuda's coral-strewn shores filled the berths.

Alex and Lara had flown to Bermuda with my mother, Helen, and my niece, Kirsty. We had decided before the race that the stressful, chaotic world of ocean racing, along with the chameleon and unpredictable Gulf Stream, was no way to begin their year aboard the boat. They would earn their sea legs as we headed toward the balmy waters of the Caribbean. Sailing south from this point had its own variables, especially as it was now late June—hurricane season. We would not be covered by marine insurance until we reached the waters of 12 degrees north, or southern Grenada, but that was the least of our worries; gambling with our children's lives was a much more sobering proposal. By all expert accounts, we could get a fairly accurate eight- to nine-day window on weather, as most storms were born off the west coast of Africa before spinning westward. With professional meteorology reports and our own calculations, we felt secure that we could reach safe harbor and be out of harm's way in that interval of time. We also had additional able-bodied crew aboard, including Ken Corson, a capable and charming sailor in his early twenties from Massachusetts, and my nephew Justin, recently out of high school. They were both incredible assets and excellent shipmates as we ventured off in a direction that no other ship was travelling.

Before that departure, however, we enjoyed the festivities and rituals that accompany the end of the race. From the bagpiper playing at sunset on the docks each evening to the lyrical reggae bands each night, the camaraderie of those who had completed the passage was genuine and reciprocally enjoyed. We were notified that we had been awarded the Cook's Prize. Captain Cook is well known to all of us navigators, I was thrilled, thinking our acumen and prowess in celestial navigation surely was the foundation of this prize. We all laughed uproariously when we learned that we were so honored for having the worst adjusted completion time in our class; hence, the one who "cooks" the longest (sails the slowest boat) garners the honor. Since I was both navigator and cook, the distinction was mine regardless, and Alex and I triumphantly accepted the engraved silver trophy with peals of laughter.

Alex turned to me and said with zeal, "Gee, I sure am glad *Promise* didn't come in second-to-last. They didn't get anything!"

I smiled and replied with one of my favorite Willa Cather quotes, "It is not the destination but the journey that is important," as we celebrated with our crew.

That aphorism brought strength the next day, during tearful good-byes on the docks with Helen, Kristin, and dear friends. My mother, with her unspoken fear that this may be the last time she would see us alive, watched us head off into the proverbial abyss and sail off the edge of the world. The clear skies and calm winds belied our own hidden fears as well, as we cast our fates literally to the wind.

Although the first days out were sunny and warm, they also brought little wind, five to ten knots. *Promise* was twenty-three tons empty, and had additional stocks of heavy equipment adding to her weight. She liked twenty knots or more, which we would not see until day four out of Bermuda—halfway through our original eight-day window of relative safety from tropical storms.

Rewards big and small graced our watery path, however, as we traversed the waves. Flying fish in huge numbers provided hours of entertainment, especially with the children rushing forward, tied on of course, to cast any school members stranded on deck back into the surf. Our second night out, we were also becalmed under a near full moon, sailing along at a mere two to three knots, when I noticed large islands appearing in front of us like a mirage. The islands began to roll and splash and, most amazingly, sing. Humpback whales dancing in the moonlight! It was a scene of profound beauty and could not help to provoke awe. Lee and I woke Ken and Justin, but chose not to wake the children, a crime for which I have still not been forgiven all these years later.

Alex, having gotten his sea legs and being able to read and write again without a trace of nausea, began his methodical journaling of the travails and triumphs of *Promise* and her crew. He zealously wrote in his daily journal for almost five years. At times, we all kept journals, and the varying perspectives on any given event or adventure changed tremendously with the author. The ship's log, however, was meant to be objective, so whichever one of us was writing the details and events of the previous shift as we were signing off—even if it was 3:00 a.m.—did so in as factual a way as possible, recording conditions and major events as they impacted the ship and its course. The remaining accounts, however, are Alex's alone.

Signing off.
Marybeth Ellison

Chapter 1

Off to the Caribbean in Hurricane Season

Although extraordinary and utterly foreign to me, life at sea was one I adapted to quickly. For my sister Lara and me, this first ocean passage was easy; we had little to offer in the way of actual help, so we stayed idle. Mom blocked me in to help Ken for the noon-to-three shift each day. This hardly kept me busy; we were moving along at about three knots, which is slower than walking speed, on flat seas and under a glaring blue sky. The incandescent, smooth blue above us merged at the horizon almost seamlessly with the cool dark of 20,000 feet of water. Water four miles deep over the Mid-Atlantic Trench, a hot day and low boat speed was an invitation to swim. Putting on harnesses, Lara and Justin leapt from the boat, towed along at two to three knots as we went. Mom did the same, much to my father's dismay. I overcame my trepidation about the possibility of sharks (which, honestly, was minimal) and followed suit. When back safely onboard, Dad, who had snapped some dramatic photos, recounted how it could not have more closely resembled trolling, with lines trailing behind the stern and live bait on the ends. Fortunately, no one bit.

When at sea, meals circumscribe the daily schedule. One lives for mealtime; while the food is rarely special—in fact, usually inferior to one's standard diet—it is always very much appreciated. All of us would cram into the cockpit for spaghetti one night, a deformed pizza the next. While the sea was still calm, we were even able to treat ourselves to a couple of veritable feasts, including a honey-baked ham and a stuffed roast turkey. Still, supper did not mark the end of the day. Every other day after dinner, we would bring the trash can up on deck, and sitting over the transom, we would sift through and make a pile of cans, cardboard, and the little food waste we had not already thrown overboard. Cardboard was torn into small bits, and cans were punctured so they would sink into the crushing abyss below. Plastic was always stored to dispose of in port.

On about the fourth day out from Bermuda, the wind and waves picked up—as did our speed. The blazing sun was finally obscured by clouds, and the cockpit was thermally bearable. About noon, Justin called from behind the wheel, "Hey, Uncle Lee! I think your GPS thing is broken. I don't know why, man; it just stopped working."

Dad walked over to the GPS. The monitor and keys worked, so the unit was fine; it just gave us no coordinates. Dad pursed his lips and said, "Well, we can do celestial navigation later, but for now let's pull out the handheld GPS." Opening the special watertight abandon ship bag with the flares and other emergency equipment in it, Dad procured the Garmin handheld unit. He flipped it on and waited for it to generate our location as I peered over his shoulder. After a moment, a dialog box popped up: *Coordinates not available.* Southeast of Bermuda ... we were in the Bermuda Triangle.

Mom and Dad laughed, hiding the unsettling situation from Lara and me. We were fine, because we could perform celestial navigation, but it was still concerning. Several shifts, about 24 hours later, the main GPS beeped; service was back. Coincidently, the handheld unit was suddenly working again, too. The Bermuda Triangle is an inexplicable but apparently real phenomenon, an area of ocean that appears intermittently not to exist. We fortunately had alternate methods of navigation and sailed under fair weather, so it had no consequences for our voyage.

However, *Promise* succumbed to maladies that did not fit the traditional description of Bermuda Triangle problems. Our sixth evening out, Mom and Justin were sitting on deck watching the sun set over the growing waves, holding onto the lifelines for stability. Justin commented, "Auntie Mary, do you have this weird electric feeling? I get it in my upper body."

The following day, our pristine white hull had gone orange at the bow; the bow stanchion had nearly rusted through, the oxide having run onto the deck below it, and then in two ribbons down each side of the boat, where the water had flushed it along the gutters. Although ugly and worrisome, the discoloration did not affect our performance, and the seas and speed only continued to grow. While rocketing along at a healthy nine to ten knots, the conditions passed ideal to become mildly concerning. We were now nine days out, and had reached the end of the safe sailing window previously determined by my mom and her meteorological guru back home. A tropical wave had developed from a trough moving westward off the coast of Africa; it was organizing and could become a tropical storm within twenty-four hours. Most ominously, it was moving northwest from its position briskly, and would intersect with our course around Antigua in approximately 24 hours. This was unbeknownst to me at the time, however, and I simply commented with glee how much more "fun" the rolling waves had become. As Lara began to voice her concerns about the increasing seas, my mother launched into one of many songs and chants she would invent to keep our anxiety to a minimum. This particular one became a standard that we still teasingly use today: "Up and down, uuuuuuupppp and dooooowwwwn!"—sung to a tune from Kindermusik class we had taken the previous year.

The next morning, our tenth since leaving Bermuda, Justin bellowed into the sky, "Land! Land ho!" In days past this sort of feat, being the first to spot land, would have earned the vigilant sailor an extra ration of grog (not a tradition we maintained on *Promise* though). Sure enough, a small, dark wrinkle barely visible on the horizon: Antigua! We careened toward it as conditions continued to escalate. By the time we sailed down Antigua's east coast and made our way along her southern shore, careful to stay far enough out so that we did not get pushed onto her coral strewn coast, fifteen foot swells rose well above the decks. The bitter wind howled at forty-five knots as some intrepid porpoises leapt along with us. Dad, our current helmsman, exuded grace under pressure, methodically trimming the reefed sails and guiding the vessel through the towering surf that was the approaching edge of Tropical Storm Claudette.

Promise tacked behind the colossal old fort that bars off most of the serpentine English Harbor. As we entered the sheltered area, the waves vanished, the wind abated, and a sparsely used anchorage and mooring field spread out before us. This naturally strong hurricane hole, which had served the British admiralty for more than two centuries, had been our original destination; we had no idea how appropriate and fortuitous it would turn out to be. We navigated through the small collection of boats and made our way to the quay where, although it was a Sunday, sailors scurried about the wharf making their vessels fast during the imminently approaching storm.

Tying the dock lines and pulling the keys out of the ignition was the most gratifying moment! I leapt from the deck, the solid impact of concrete jarring joints that had become accustomed to a moving surface. A brief tropical deluge found Ken in his underwear on the docks, a bar of soap in hand. For Lara and me, the hiatus of hygiene had been awesome, but for most civilized individuals, ten days was a long time to go without a shower, especially in the salty, grimy environment of an ocean passage. Getting clean was nice, but there were some drawbacks: Lara's impenetrable mat of hair could have been used as a replacement for Kevlar, and Mom's attempts to comb it out were met with blood-curdling screams for a full thirty minutes. Later, however, even Lara admitted that the sensation of cleanliness was wonderful.

Now ashore and presentable, I was able to appreciate the harbor. The British had constructed the buildings a few hundred years prior from coarse grey stones the size of my eight-year-old torso. The quaint architecture and grass were tremendously inviting, and we lounged on the wet turf ten feet from *Promise*, ecstatic for a change, and nearly oblivious to Claudette whipping around Antigua. We were nestled behind substantial hills to shelter us from the wind, while several twists down the narrow harbor subdued the waves. It was not until later when we visited a museum on local history that we learned that one of the hills sheltering us from the wind had been moved to its current location, back in the 1800s at the command of the British Royal Navy. Extensive chains had been wrapped around the hill at three altitudes, and armies of enslaved people, who were at the other end of the chains, managed to drag the hill into a position better suited for sheltering the harbor.

Our own exhausting work, pale in comparison, had been done, and we were able to relax—at least in part. Dad never left the phone booth as he called the maritime insurance company covering us, and then our boat's manufacturer, Beneteau, and finally a local electrician. This was the start of something I was to learn about sailing: not everything always works the way it should. The other thing I had started to learn about sailing was that change really was about the only thing you could count on. After Claudette swept past, we pushed on southward, heading toward the safety offered by the lower latitudes. One tempestuous brush was enough. We were going to Grenada.

Justin aloft under light winds at sea south of Bermuda

Sextant- A noon sighting in the Bermuda triangle

Trolling along over the mid-Atlantic trench
at a depth exceeding 20,000 ft

Skipper steering us into our first port of the
Caribbean: English Harbor, Antigua

Chapter 2

Pirate Lairs

To call it "rain" would be misleading. "Deluge" also fails to be even remotely accurate. According to the GPS, we were off the coast of St. Vincent. Although we were theoretically only a mile from shore, we couldn't even see the front of the boat through the downpour. Not one to miss out on the activity, I sat in the rain with my self-inflating lifejacket, filled with perverse glee, hoping the rain would accidentally trigger the CO_2 cartridge to explode and inflate the lifejacket. Mom was onto me, though: "Alex, get out of the rain before that thing inflates!" She needn't have bothered; I was moving in under the canvas cover anyway, because hailstones had begun to fall.

The winds, which had been a boisterous thirty knots, accelerated to over fifty, a "strong gale" on the Beaufort scale. Although bursts of squalls were a frequent occurrence at sea, this batch was particularly ferocious.

Ken shook water out of his short hair and pondered, "Do we want to head into a harbor on St. Vincent, maybe? I doubt this is going to lighten up any time soon." The adults all looked at each other. Within moments, Mom was navigating through the digital chart by the helm. She tried but sputtered over the harbor's name a couple of times before correctly pronouncing, "Waliabou."

We pulled into the wind, toward the island allegedly there. Our sails were already reefed due to the high winds, and we now rolled them up completely to prevent them from flogging and getting damaged against the rigging. Suddenly, the mountains of St. Vincent appeared out of the mist, looming ominously. The island's features did not become well defined until we were a mere few hundred feet away. I assumed the duty of bow watchman, calling out in the event of lobster pots, moorings, boats, or any such surprise, "Something ahead!" I really had not expected a rowboat to be rocketing out of the harbor toward us—no one had—but the minute skiff was easily outpacing *Promise*, and pulled alongside within moments of coming to our attention.

The pilot was a tall, powerful looking man with long dreadlocks that he shook as he called, "Hello there, skippa! If you ha' a long line I can tow you asho' … trus' me, you no a gon' see much in dis rain and I know the bay good." He was right; we were functionally blind and, as our handy travel guide had indicated, nearly all the harbors on St. Vincent required an intricate mooring system. So, we threw him our longest line; one end of the black line was secured in his rowboat, and I knelt at the bow to cleat the other end down.

He wriggled momentarily on the oarsman's seat as he adjusted the oars in their locks. Then, bending forward, he dipped his blades into the water and heaved: we were off. I felt the hull's vibration change as someone put the engine into gear, to give our rower less weight. But he called out, "No! It's fine! Put it back in neutral." His voice did not even sound strained as he propelled us toward shore. The folds of the peaks sharpened; to our left, a rocky arch spanned a fair expanse of water. The shoreline also became clearer; I could see long wooden docks extending into the water. At the end of one was a small coconut thatched hut; at the end of another stood a wooden crane, a thick hemp rope dangling from it. The oarsman called up instructions. We were to spin the boat so the bow was facing the sea, and drop an anchor into the eighty feet or so of water. Normally when anchoring, one wants a 7:1 ratio of line, or scope, to the depth of the water; we only had 300 feet of stainless steel chain, insufficient here. A longer scope secures the angle of the anchor and reduces the chance of it dragging across the bottom. Dragging in this small, rock-strewn harbor in the middle of a gale with night approaching would be terrifying at best, and a disaster in the worse, more likely scenario.

Our tow service islander ordered us to drop the anchor and then back in toward shore. Coconut trees. We tied stern lines to two coconut trees ashore with an anchor out in the bay. None of our ropes exceeded twenty-five feet in length, so, even when we tied them together to make a single long line, we were still really quite close to shore. In this harbor, however, that hardly mattered; it turned out that the bottom was bizarrely steep. Our anchor, out with all 300 hundred feet of our chain, hung straight down. The throttle was pulled back to neutral, and the key turned. *Promise* finally came to a rest.

"Thanks for your help, sir!" Dad called.

"No problem, man. Dat a be twen'y dollars though."

As Dad gratefully shelled out the cash, I looked around. The buildings along the wharf were all stone with thatched grass roofs. None stood more than two stories tall. Wooden placards hung from the front of some; I saw "Cooperage" and "Blacksmith." I was amazed; these were terms for establishments that belonged in a museum dedicated to maritime history, such as Mystic Seaport, not in my real life in 2003. No people walked about. With the docks and architecture like that of the 1700s, and no solid human proof that it was still the twenty-first century, it began to feel like the storm we had outrun had sent us through a time warp. The rain had diminished, and mist hovered eerily over the surface of the water; our helpful local guide had silently disappeared. Looking out at the harbor, was unsettling, as if we'd sailed back in time.

"I'm going to go ashore and see if I can do customs," Dad said. As the captain, he was the individual required to find the customs and immigrations office and officially clear both the vessel and her crew in and out of every nation we visited. In addition to paying port fees and duties, this also required significant paperwork, copies of the boat's documentation, insurance policies, and passports of all crew members. Even when we had visitors, they were always labeled "crew", since the designation "passenger" carried even more onerous requirements. Dad zipped over the short distance by dinghy and returned a long thirty minutes later, with an ear-to-ear grin. He was eager to recount his tale.

After beaching the dinghy on the black sand, he found his way onto the waterside street. All of the buildings were sealed, windows dark and dusty. He passed a deserted bakery and the blacksmith, bales of hay stacked in the attic visible through the open windows. Several horses were gated in a pasture behind a barn. Not seeing anyone, he went the length of the street, finally coming to a building of similar architecture, low and of massive grey stones. This one building had a warm orange glow in the window, and a placard over the door bearing the words, "Customs and Immigration." Once inside, the office was standard with lamps, leaves of paper, a computer, and best of all, a person. Dad inquired, "Hey, as cool as this place is… it's a bit odd, isn't it? With no people, and hey, what's up with having a blacksmith?"

The woman behind the desk laughed. "They just finished filming *Pirates of the Caribbean* here! They left the set up," she added. We'd just sailed into the set of a hugely anticipated movie with awesome commercials we'd seen; the area served as the false Jamaican harbor, Port Royal. When we all went ashore later, I ran a hand along the walls of the blacksmith's shop. The stone felt weak, too dry. I patted it; it emitted the hollow echo of *papier-maché*. But it certainly had been convincing visually, which was all a camera required.

At the opposite end of the street from Customs, a bridge (this time of real stone) spanned a rustling creek (the same bridge Johnny Depp ran over while soldiers shot at him). Of course, I was not to realize that until I saw the movie the next summer in Grenada. A large wooden crane, the sort for lifting cargo off old ships, was mounted to the edge of the wooden dock. This was where Jack Sparrow swung around as the hapless British soldiers fired. In the same, less exotic light as the reality of clearing customs, there was also a restaurant, the patio embalmed in more papier-maché to maintain a level of continuity for the set. The external features belied the popcorn and TV inside, where Lara happily joined the owner's children in watching a Pixar movie, *Monsters, Inc.* I was too engrossed with my own meal to watch, or even participate in the dinner conversation, which revolved around our speculation about the movie and its set.

The following morning dripped with sunshine; having dried out thoroughly, we were ready to leave the port—perhaps the first boat in months to leave without a camera trained on it. As we sailed out, we studied the glorious natural arch with nothing dangling from it. We would later learn it was where they hanged the pirate skeletons in the film; they were taken down at the townspeople's request, lest they scare off any actual sailors and potential customers passing by.

Chapter 3

GRENADA

After our brief respite in St. Vincent, we continued our hasty course to Grenada. Its southern harbors were at twelve degrees north of the equator, theoretically providing protection in the event of a hurricane. Expert meteorologists designated that Grenada was farther south than the course of most hurricanes; data revealed that hurricanes usually raged through the Caribbean at a latitude of twelve-and-a-half degrees north or higher. We called harbors south of that "hurricane holes," and most marine insurers and their actuaries called them safe zones—which meant they were insurable.

Grenada is no small island, and our time following the leeward shore south was scenic and calm, a paradigm shift from the tumultuous seas I had known for the past two weeks. A ragged road ran the length of the coast, connecting the infrequent towns. This tortuous ribbon of dirt and asphalt snaked its way along the shore; right behind that, the land rose in undulating ridges and valleys with stilted houses perched on their verdant slopes.

As we followed the coast south, the imperious mountains dwindled to foothills that eventually became the flat, arid Parish of St. Georges, where the identically named country capital was located. When we rounded Point Saline, the most southern tip of the island, and escaped the wind shadow of the island, we relished the newfound breeze and waves. We passed by the first two harbors, True Blue and Prickly Bay, and then came to the cove best fortified against hurricanes, Mt.

Hartman. A reef formed a gate across the entrance to the bay with a narrow slit permitting entry and exit. There was one lone mark off a prominent reef (nautical marks are notoriously erroneous or nonexistent in many Caribbean ports).

Lining ourselves up with the angle of the cut in the reef, we motored in, sails down, slowly. Though we had corroborated data from our GPS chart and our paper charts, there was no substitute for good daylight overhead and a person on the bow with polarized lenses when entering an unfamiliar, coral-strewn harbor. Mt. Hartman Bay, also called Secret Harbor, was a long, deep bay, and from the mangroves at the far end almost all the way out to the reef, the entire extent of the harbor was crowded with anchored boats waiting out hurricane season. We passed through the mooring field, and I gazed at a hill conservatively sprinkled with terracotta-roofed cottages that stood at the western edge. In sinking rows the cottages pointed to a marina, its docks our destination.

Dad held the VHF, a short range (20 miles) radio, in one hand and the helm in the other. He hailed the marina with standard protocol, "Moorings base, Moorings base; this is sailing vessel *Promise*, come in please."

After a moment they responded, *"Promise,* this is the Moorings base. How can we help?"

Scanning the dock for a free slot, Dad said, "I see a free space on the dock. Can we get some help for getting in?"

"Sure, we'll have guys down there in a moment," replied the operator.

We were going to back into the dock, referred to as Mediterranean-style mooring. We would be stern to the concrete dock, our bow tied to pylons on either side. This arrangement allowed many more boats to be kept on the dock, yet could be tricky to maneuver if the wind or current were coming perpendicular to the vessel. As we approached, moving backward, Ken and Mom deftly lassoed the pylons, keeping plenty of slack. The dock hand caught the line tossed to him and said, "Okay, stop backing now." Then, when the boat kept moving, he yelled, "You're getting close! Stop!" Dad had thrust the throttle into the forward position but it had no effect; the boat was still moving in reverse, and we continued to hurtle toward the concrete dock. The boat shook and a resounding, sickening crunch ensued. An evaluation later would reveal that the cable from the shift lever to the transmission had failed below deck. The fiberglass of the stern was damaged, but we were still afloat and no one was injured. We would end up lingering in Grenada for several months awaiting completion of repairs to the transmission, fiberglass, an extensive electrolysis problem, and, of course, the end of hurricane season.

Sitting in the cockpit, I surveyed the dock and harbor, still a bit dazed from our dramatic entry. Having seen very few boats since leaving Bermuda, I was amazed to see so many different types of crafts. Some of the boats at the dock were sealed tight, hatches battened and the companionway bolted; their owners were not coming back any time soon. However, most of the boats were clearly occupied: people scurrying about, laundry hanging from the lifelines to dry, hatches open. Many of the decks were adorned with paraphernalia indicating other children, such as inner tubes, smaller bicycles, and water toys. This made me ponder a conversation we'd had with our parents before we had even left Connecticut. They sat us down and my mom said, "Okay, kids. We know you're both used to having a bunch of friends over for your birthdays, lots of games, all that stuff. We'll probably be alone out sailing, and we probably won't find any other kids. But, you know what? It'll be fine; we'll have fun as a family."

Two months later, it was August twenty-first, my ninth birthday. Since our arrival, our floating home had not left Grenada. The Moorings base here included not only the marina, but also the resort and pool atop the hill. We had pool rights, and that's where I wanted to spend my birthday, with my family, and, amazingly, every other kid from the boating community in the bay, about thirty kids between the ages of three and seventeen. Living on a boat was a unique experience; we children stuck together. Age differences that would have seemed vast on land disappeared in this environment. Nationality, language, cultural background: all vanished, and every child was welcome at every event. Tolerance, acceptance: it was childhood at its best. Everyone participated in the lime-and-spoon relay race, pin the nose on the pirate, water balloon toss, and piñata. Older teens purposefully sought out toddlers as partners in races just to bolster confidence and ensure success for all. My friend Dylan participated, a guy younger than I with whom I'd grown fairly close. We'd had multiple sleepovers on each others' boats—his was *Navigator*. Lauren, who was our babysitter when my parents went on dates, was also there, along with Adam and Warren from *Scud*, who were incredible sailors and had lived on a ship for years; they were amazing role models for us new recruits. It was one of the best birthdays ever, and a fantastically far cry from the lonesome celebration promised by my parents.

As it is for most children, at the end of the summer, school became a daily reality. This was part of a new rhythm for life aboard, a rhythm we would sustain for years. Nothing was set in stone, everything subject to change. Basically though, sailors are early risers and everyone was awake by seven o'clock, voluntarily or otherwise. Breakfast was varied, but usually involved cereal with long life milk, which as the title suggests, has a long shelf life, so it's fine after months without refrigeration. Sometimes we'd cook something warm for breakfast—pancakes were a favorite although we always defaulted to the ease of using premade mix. The first time we tried this though, after pouring the powder out, we found ourselves with a bowl of weevils. After bitterly complaining to a veteran cruising family, they smiled knowingly and said, "Bay leaves." With our next box we put two or three bay leaves in, shook it up, and put it back in the cupboard. Amazingly enough, we never had a problem with weevils again.

With breakfast behind us, we would commence home schooling for the day. Posters decorated the main salon: world maps, the food pyramid, parts of a sentence, and the like. Having two parents for two kids worked pretty well, especially for subjects such as math and English, for which my sister Lara and I were at different levels. For some other subjects, in which Lara and I were equally inexperienced (such as geography), we were taught together. For most of the conjoined classes we were taught by our mom, a pediatrician with a mania for education. She often wove the curriculum together so that we were studying the geography, history, and literature of a given region concomitantly. There were some subjects that Dad taught, such as math, art of all kinds, and music. Music filled an important niche for our crew, and included an array of instruments which varied amongst guitars, recorders, a keyboard, or a locally acquired steel pan. These subjects were in whatever order suited us on that particular day; however, given the exclusive attention of the teachers, we were efficient with time and were usually done by noon. The rest of the day would then be ours—sort of. Afternoons would be spent on "learning excursions." Our parents felt that the world was now our classroom, and in order to take full advantage of that, interaction with the peoples and cultures we were visiting was essential. This was a core tenet throughout our entire journey. Beginning in Grenada, but continuing through every island or country we visited, we had to do an immersion project. This resembled a multifaceted report, wherein we had to interview indigenous people, observe and learn about their traditions, and profile their occupations. We'd describe flags and symbols, statistics regarding population, the geography of the landmass, and capitals. The most popular section for us was the flora, fauna, and other natural wonders, which fascinated my sister and me, as it would most children. One of our initial forays into making the world our classroom was our first of many trips into the lush mountains of the rainforest.

We travelled up the circuitous road with precipices and verdant peaks around every stunning turn to Grand Etang, the national park in Grenada's central rainforest. Our first stop was the information center, where I became enthralled with the various species listed and pictured on the walls, including boas, three-banded armadillos, and wooly opossums. One of the rangers was idling in the building, so I bombarded him with questions about the animals I had seen on the information boards.

"So, how often do you see the three-banded armadillos?"

He laughed. "Not often, my friend. I've seen maybe two in the past few years here. But you'll probably see a Mona monkey; they're everywhere."

This was somewhat consoling, but I really wanted to see an armadillo. To my nine-year-old brain, rainforests and monkeys were synonymous. However, I learned that these monkeys were not indigenous to Grenada; rather, they had arrived on ships from Africa— another casualty from a darker time in human history. As I walked into the parking lot, I could scarcely contain my shout of, "Oh my gosh! It's a Mona monkey!" One was sitting on the trunk of a parked sedan. The driver, leaning against the other side of the car, volunteered, "He's a friendly one. I've known him for a while. You can pet him, too." Tentatively I reached out, brushing my hands over his scruffy fur. He looked at me with his translucent orange eyes. I scratched his cranium some more. "Make sure you wash your hands, Alex," said Mom with a smile that belied her serious intent.

Following the path away from the paved road, we delved into the surrounding jungle. We became utterly enveloped by the foliage within a few steps. This was the way toward Grand Etang, the lake and namesake of the park. It was actually an ancient volcanic crater, long ago filled with water. The path was more easily distinguished than expected given the density of the growth, since it was a winding clay streak, a vibrant orange stripe down the steep slope. The recent rain had turned the path into a putrid water slide, treacherous if you did not watch your footing. I constantly looked to either side of the path in hopes of finding a three-banded armadillo, and frequently imagined them peering back at me. Unfortunately, I never did spy one of the rare creatures; so ultimately, I turned my attention to tamer ones.

Crewmates of the non-human kind fascinated and captivated all of us, and my sister and I soon became obsessed with expanding our crew. We'd seen boats with parrots living aboard, dogs of every conceivable breed, captured geckos, and the most traditional and beloved pet, the proverbial ship's cat. One of our friends' boats, *Surface Interval,* had a huge, fluffy Golden Retriever named Snowflake. Incidentally, people are always referred to in the sailing and traveling community by their boat name; that is, it's Dave-*Surface-Interval* or Alex-*Promise*. Hence, a pithy, pronounceable name is the most welcome when communicating between ships or filling out cumbersome immigration and customs documents which are required every time one either enters or leaves a port; their subsequent boat is named *Zing!*

Snowflake had been the family's pet long before leaving their Florida home, and this particular family had removed Lauren, their fourteen-year-old daughter, from her friends and normal teen environs. Needless to say, it was a daunting prospect of getting her to buy in to sailing away for a year to the Caribbean and South America. To soften the blow, they knew they must take their beloved pooch. When we met them, Snowflake had been aboard their thirty-six-foot double-ended sloop on and off for a few years, but had never embarked on a major cruise. The captain of *Surface Interval*, Dave, had proudly trained Snowflake to do his business on a small 2 x 2-foot square of AstroTurf, which he had cleverly affixed to the foredeck of the boat. Twice daily, Snowflake became a regular biological clock and did his business on command without fail. The crew would then simply hang the AstroTurf off the side of the boat by a line as they travelled. This cleaned it off beautifully and was quite practical when travelling at sea and out of reach of land. In fact, this method has been employed by many sailors during voyages for cleaning everything from pots and pans to dirty crew members: simply hang them off the back of the boat from a sturdy line, and let the "churning of the salty brine, give 'em a shine." Of course, since you never actually want to lose anything that skitters along behind the boat, this was best done in fairly calm waters while travelling at a speed of less than five knots. Unfortunately, for even the most diligent of crews, weather conditions can change fairly rapidly at sea. Hence, one fateful trip when Snowflake's AstroTurf was in the saline scrubber, it came loose and was lost at sea in a squall somewhere south of the Dominican Republic. Now, a lesser crew may have panicked, but *Surface Interval*—knowing that the bonds of friendship at sea require tenacity seldom necessary on dry land—called out to all the boats in the area to keep a look-out for the fateful piece of turf. Most boats looked conscientiously for their friend's poop-pad, despite knowing it would be difficult to discern in a bouncing blue-green sea. Sadly, the turf could not be found, and Snowflake had become such a literal creature of habit that he simply refused to defecate for the rest of the journey. Five days later, upon landing in Puerto Rico, the poor creature waddled miserably off the boat to find the relief of a deserted tract of beach.

Once we had heard this tale of woe, our captain vetoed the adoption of a pooch. We had oceans to cross and he felt we had enough responsibility keeping our human crew healthy and regular. Moreover, having researched it, we found that many countries simply would not allow a foreign canine to step ashore. Often there were complicated rules of quarantine and herculean tasks of documentation necessary to even enter coastal waters with a dog onboard. Many nations that were rabies-free had an additional level of bureaucracy simply to prevent that catastrophic disease from touching their shores. Countries were often suspicious of one another as well. For example, Nevis, another Caribbean island, did not accept animals certified as rabies-free in France or any of its territories, simply because they felt that the French did not have enforceable policies. This is especially amusing as often the nations casting aspersions on the other were markedly less efficient, and had a much poorer infrastructure. Nonetheless, a dog aboard would have added another layer of complexity to an already daunting journey.

We had friends on ships who had little pets, such as hamsters and rodents of various kinds. These kept children entertained and could remain on the ship at all times, and hence not run afoul of the local authorities, as long as their escape was deemed impossible. The thing about cute furry animals and children, however, is that they often get together for skin-to-fur contact; hence, there are also tales of these tiny animals going on walk-about aboard. Trying to find a two-inch dwarf hamster as it scurries about in crevices behind paneling and in wiring conduits is nearly impossible; plus, there are stories of them nibbling critical wiring, such as navigation lights, GPS leads, and other features that are essential to one's life aboard. Captain Dad vetoed this prospect as well.

By far the most common pet was the darling ship's cat. In days gone by, ships had cats for the very practical reasons of keeping mice and rats to a minimum. For long journeys at sea, it was often necessary to store large quantities of food and dry goods such as flour, grains, rice, and more, and these were often tucked in various spaces below decks. In these dark crevices, vermin of all kinds could also thrive. A ship's cat was invaluable for keeping these critters at bay, to protect the food supplies from being contaminated, and also to avoid potential disease vectors. On the practical side, cats have great balance and agility, which is essential for any creature's survival aboard a ship. They also cuddle and snuggle—when they choose to, of course—and are private and neat regarding their toileting needs. We thought we had the winning idea for our pet. Looking around at the new leather settees in the main saloon, and the impeccably varnished holly-and-teak floors though—all prime targets of a cat's claws—Dad vetoed this as well.

Then, fate took a hand. Our brand-new boat ran into more electrical engine problems during our second month in Grenada, and had to go back into the dock. Previously, we had been anchored in the remote outer harbor, tucked in behind the coral reefs. In general, we were always in favor of being in a gunkhole, usually a picturesque and peaceful spot away from the bustle of the dock. Here, we would be sheltered from the waves but get the full cooling breezes to power our wind generators, which were our main source of power on the boat for everything from evening lights to navigation equipment. Docks in the summer tend to be hot and windless, and a ship can also acquire all sorts of pests there, such as cockroaches and rats. While there are many ingenious tricks that attempt to keep the vermin off your boat, like using inverted funnels on all of your lines going to the dock cleats to keep the rats from being able to climb aboard, most of the vermin are also great swimmers. This raised the suggestion that we may not only want, but truly need, a ship's cat. The lobbying started in earnest.

Docks do have their upsides, including being able to run off at any time without a wet dinghy ride to shore. It certainly made provisioning with groceries an easier task, as opposed to loading and unloading huge canvas bags into the small rubber inflatable, and then driving out to the boat and trying to heave them onto the deck from the wobbly little craft. Docks are also quite good for boat-watching; beautiful boats of all vintages grace docks with their presence. Often wealthy people have exquisite ships and use them infrequently at sea, hence earning them the nickname "dock ornaments." Mt. Hartman Bay was no exception. There were gorgeous ships from all over the world: South Africa, Sweden, Guernsey, New Zealand, and a lovely pristine wooden ship, *Diva*, from our old sailing grounds in Newport. Living on a dock for a few weeks also puts you in close proximity to other crews. Most sailors are extremely amicable and always glad for a chat. One of the luxuries of being in port is to have the time to meet others. On the sea, there is no time for frivolities since you are constantly engaged as if your life depends on it—which of course it does.

On the dock, one lives within earshot of one's neighbors. As we were beginning our morning lessons one day, Lara, whose hearing is unusually proficient, said, "I hear something different ... a kitten, far away." We all knew she would be hopelessly distracted until she ferreted out the source, so we clambered up the companionway stairs to the cockpit and out onto the dock. She led our small band forward, cautiously tracking the intermittent and barely audible mewing. Much to our surprise, they led us to none other than the pristine *Diva*. Instantly, we found ourselves captivated by the gorgeous little kitten in the crew's arms. When we asked about her and the boat, they recounted the years of history of cats and ships and how she would be a lucky asset for them, and surely not mar the impossibly perfect finish of the woodwork. Moreover, it was their moral obligation to adopt her. They had just visited the Grenada Society for the Prevention of Cruelty to Animals; this organization had a surplus of pets, especially new kittens that they were trying to give away instead of putting down. On top of that, the *Diva*'s crew said, this wonderful group of volunteers worked in conjunction with the St. George's School of Veterinary Medicine; they would give you a pet of your choice with free vaccinations and spaying or neutering if a donation was made. When Lara found out what "putting down" meant, there was nothing short of hysteria aboard. The grand bowling ball of fate had just come down *Promise*'s alley, and we children were ecstatic. No amount of distraction or resistance would derail our crew from its moral obligation, lest a full scale mutiny erupt.

The following is from an article I wrote in September 2003; it was published in the June 2004 issue of *Caribbean Compass* when I was nine years old.

> At the GSPCA, Grenada Society for the Prevention of Cruelty to Animals, we adopted a five-week-old orphaned kitten. She was so tiny! She was brown and gray on top, and had a pure white tummy with polka-dots on it. That is the way a coconut is—white on the inside, brown on the outside—so we named her Coconut—emphasis on the *nut*!
>
> Once aboard Promise, she scampered about, and made mischief by scratching the leather cushions and hiding in cabinets. She had an infection and we had to give her medicine by a dropper for a week, which she hated. She blew bubbles of drool with it all over everything.
>
> She grew quickly and became extremely curious. In no time, she was climbing up the mast and running down the boom. She climbs the roller-furling jib and streaks down the teak rail.
>
> She is a great swimmer. My sister likes to insist that she taught Coconut how to swim, but it comes very naturally! We made a "cat ladder" so she can climb up the transom with no problem at all. Sometimes she even goes swimming with us on purpose. She falls overboard once in a while, when she is crazily chasing moths by the transom light.
>
> We keep her onboard all the time now, after a funny

adventure on the island of Mayreau in the Grenadines. We brought her ashore at Salt Whistle Bay, a beautiful beach. She wasted no time in scampering up a palm tree that my sister and I were trying to climb. We tried coaxing her down to no avail. Mom ended up shimmying up the tree, all the while saying, "Here, Coconut, come on, baby!" Other people on the beach, who had no idea that our kitten was up there, thought Mom was talking to the real coconuts! When she finally came down with our kitten in her arms, everyone had a good laugh.

Coconut is a delightful member of our crew, and will continue to provide us with more adventures, I'm sure.

We did eventually move on from Grenada. We headed first to the Grenadines, a string of small islands between Grenada and St. Vincent, most of which belonged to St. Vincent, all of them spectacularly beautiful.

Dad celebrating landfall in Annandale Falls, Grenada

Coconut joins the crew at an age of 5 weeks

Most local islanders, especially in the Windwards, love to sail

Lara conducting her own homeschooling session in the main salon

Chapter 4

THE GRENADINES

One charming and fairly common trend throughout the Caribbean is vending from local small boats. In the Grenadines, the islanders would often come out in their own small, vibrantly-colored wooden crafts, to sell fruit, vegetables, fresh fish, and occasionally local handicraft. This was a fantastic business for all parties involved: profitable for the sellers and convenient for the cruising consumers who were saved a trip to the grocery store. In Mayreau, which was our favorite of the lower Grenadines with its picture-perfect beach and thatched-roof bungalows, one vender was different. Joseph's boat was no less colorful than anyone else's, but it was half the normal size (maybe eight feet long) and had oarlocks instead of an outboard engine. One humid afternoon, my family encountered him for the first time. We bought some fish from him and started up a conversation, as he was quite gregarious. We found out that he was a pious man in his early thirties and single, not planning on marrying until he was fifty and, as he said, wiser. He offered to take me fishing on the local reefs. As we had towed a line from my high-tech fishing pole for thousands of miles and caught very little, I was quite enthusiastic about this event—a prospective angler ready for detailed local knowledge.

The following day, Joseph rowed up to *Promise* at about eight o'clock in the morning. I climbed aboard his boat covered in sunscreen, sporting one of Dad's caps on my head. In the bottom of his boat Joseph had two wooden hand reels, each with a hook on the end; a plastic bag full of chicken meat; and a cleaving knife. Muscles rippling beneath his bare skin, he rowed the two of us out beyond the point and out of sight of my parents. Almost half a mile from shore, he stopped and pulled the oars into the boat.

In his thick local accent, he said, "Ya ready to be fishing, boy?" I nodded enthusiastically, and he continued his quick lesson on using the hand reels. "So jus reel dat to da end of string, wait fo' a bit, and den pull it back. Got it?" This low-tech system was a far cry from my carbon-fiber pole purchased in New England.

I did as Joseph had instructed. I reached the end of the line and was pulling it back to the surface when it jerked back to the bottom.

"I got one! I got one!" I bellowed.

He smiled over his shoulder at me. "Man, you a lucky boy! Bring 'er up!"

I pulled zealously. Hoisting the fish into the boat, I saw it was a queen triggerfish. She was majestic and iridescent with a gradient from yellow to blue, which ran her length alongside striking turquoise streaks. With startling speed, the fish grew pallid, gaining a beige tinge similar to that of vomit. I frowned at its decaying beauty and asked, "Can you show me how to get the hook out?"

"Jus give a rip," came his response.

After that I had several null attempts, but Joseph had some luck. Hoping for some more progress, I pulled my hook back. About halfway to the surface, something bit. Arms over the side of the boat, I heaved away to bring it up. Progress was slow, but soon my catch came into view. I saw that it was a nurse shark that had taken the bait; it was thrashing around just underwater.

"Joseph! What do I do with sharks?"

The boat tipped further as he came to see. He looked impressed. "Let's jus let dat one go," he murmured, and cut the line.

The sun was at its zenith when we arrived back at *Promise*. Dad was in the cockpit reading. Waving as he stepped on the transom, he commented on the fish covering the bottom of the boat, "Well, sure looks like you two were productive." He bought the fish, which we later ate for dinner. The queen triggerfish did not taste very good—not after I had seen its exquisitely beautiful original form.

After a few days had passed in Salt Whistle Bay, we moved on in the nomadic fashion of cruisers. We travelled less than three miles; our destination was to the widely acclaimed Tobago Cays. This was a group of five islets all within about a square mile. Between the islands was the real treasure, though: reefs. Horseshoe Reef, the main one, arced over two-and-a-half miles through the shallows. We passed through the channel between the westernmost islands, Petit Rameau and Petit Bateau, vigilantly watching for coral heads. Once we rounded the point, we were in a lagoon of sorts, and a magnificent one at that. Since it was still officially hurricane season in the Caribbean, there were only about ten other boats. With a white sand bottom less than twenty feet below the surface, the water was an electric cerulean blue. The harbor was protected from waves by the barrier reef, but because this was underwater, it was open to the refreshing trade winds. As we dropped the anchor through the crystal-clear water, we watched it hit the bottom, stirring up a small cloud of sand, slow to settle.

That night my family and I lay on the deck looking upward. There was not a light for miles around, and the only land settlement about twenty miles away was relatively small and very solitary. Add in the fact that it was a new moon, and there was no light pollution whatsoever. Above us the sky was cloudless, and there seemed to be more of the stars than the black surrounding them. We found every constellation in that part of the sky, including Cygnus, the Big Dipper, Boötes, and more. I found a small arc of stars that looked too enticing to not be a constellation. Even Mom, who is highly proficient in celestial navigation, was unfamiliar with this star strand. I took our sextant and compass and took its bearing, the time, and the angle of inclination. Writing these details down, I proclaimed that they now formed "heaven's horseshoe." I guess I was hoping to submit it to some agency that would add it to the star charts. I never got around to that, and at some point later on I found it on some chart labeled as "Corona Borealis."

The following day we explored the lagoon in our dinghy, attempting to establish which island had the best beach. Baradol was pretty good; it was the northernmost island and rather windswept. The sand on its beach was a bit coarse, though. It was easy to be picky given the beauty of the islands and the plethora of choices. We went to the opposite end of the lagoon to Jamesby. The sand was silky and the shallow water contained some coral toward the western edge. The beach, perhaps a hundred yards long, was backed by a smooth rocky cliff with cacti growing from the various crevices. We proclaimed it "Ellison Island" and returned later for a beach fire and cookout. The only flaw I found was the quantity of burrs. We were often barefoot; we prided ourselves on our permanent "summer feet" and how tough they were. Apparently, however, they were not tough enough for the burrs. While my family cooked hotdogs, I went the length of the beach gathering burr plants. I put my fistfuls into the flames. The extermination was incomplete, but it sufficed for the moment.

Naturally we found the place to be utterly endearing, as, apparently, did many others. We were informed that our favorite uninhabited isle was none other than the one Capt. Jack Sparrow and Elizabeth Swan had been fortuitously marooned on in *Pirates of the Caribbean*. When we arrived, a new political controversy was also swirling about these spectacular gems. The tiny Grenadines were part of the British Commonwealth of Nations, but there was a hotel corporation named Elite Island Resorts that had developed an interest in the prospect of profitable management of the islands. This company already owned the magnificent Little Palm Island Resort a few miles to the south, a hotel that encompassed the entire cay. Although spectacular, the resort was out of reach financially for most of the local population (a room cost almost a thousand dollars a night) and was considered private. The lucrative management opportunity was widely opposed by the common people, but it would provide some much needed revenue for the government of St. Vincent. I was so incensed that I submitted an editorial, at the ripe age of nine, to the *Caribbean Compass*; the editor-in-chief, Sally Erdle, accepted and published my vehement opposition to this corporate abuse, along with the better crafted statements of erudite adults more familiar with the topic. There was much debate, but today these cays fortunately remain independent; they are considered the National Park of St. Vincent and the Grenadines, overseen by a non-profit group of locals with diverse talents and resources.

The Grenadines are so lovely, in part, due to their isolation and pristine state, but this makes soliciting help for various problems all the more difficult. Unfortunately, *Promise* suffered from debilitating electrical issues that we were unable to remedy easily. The boat, although still new and under her original warranty, had experienced myriad problems since the beginning of our voyage, probably as the result of modifications by the dealer's subcontractors. Our contact at Beneteau, the manufacturer of the vessel, was a patient, kind, and reasonable man. After countless local attempts to rewire our electrical system and rectify the situation had failed miserably, the company agreed to send in one of their chief engineers to perform the repairs on site. The lone technician wanted to work in isolation; hence, the company hosted us at the aforementioned immensely luxurious Little Palm Island for eight days. The only issue we had with removing ourselves from the boat was Coconut, our newly acquired kitten. Leaving her aboard for the duration of the repairs with the engineer was hardly a viable option, but the hotel strictly forbade pets (as well as children under sixteen years of age for a few months in the winter; fortunately, Lara and I were in season). At a loss for options, we smuggled the tiny animal ashore in a backpack, occasionally having to force her head back in as she tried to emerge through the zipper. We were able to keep her concealed in the bathroom for the entirety of our stay with minimal difficulty, and we just put her in the bag and took it with us when housekeeping came.

In addition to the perverse fun of concealing Coconut, and reveling in the exotic scenery of the island, we met someone very special. At one of the nightly formal beachside buffets, we met a waitress by the name of Chantel who is distinct in my memory for her situation. She resided on the larger Union Island a mile to the northwest, commuting daily by the hotel's ferry to work long hours. Forty miles to the north, and a veritable world away, was St. Vincent, the nidus of the nation and population. There, her son, five years old, lived with her mother, attending a private elementary school in her community. This provided him with an education rich in comparison to that which could be provided by the government school on Union Island, which was smaller and more provincial. However, the only job available that could provide sufficient funds for this privilege was the one at the resort, reachable with either a bank-draining plane ride or a costly day-long boat ride. The boy's father was also involved, but he, too, was working on Union Island; the parents only got to see their child once every four months. At the time we met her, Chantel struggled with indecision over whether to educate her son, or be with him; to do both seemed impossible. To my sister Lara and me, this state of existence was simply incomprehensible. We failed to understand her completely; it was simply beyond the range of our experience that we would not live with our parents. In my mind, there was nothing better than being with family. It was especially distressing to see Chantel in so much personal pain from the daily grief.

We all tried to console her by discussing our own state of existence. As a pediatrician, my mother elaborated on everything from theories of child development to concrete suggestions on how to make the difficult situation work; she even helped Chantel investigate the schools and child care on Union Island to determine the quality of their education. We explained how Lara and I had been taken from what was traditionally thought of as better education to spend more time with our parents. Granted, we were probably getting a better education from our parents, who were holders of advanced degrees and had both taught before. Regardless, we continued to offer our assistance so that Chantel could be reunited with her son. She was appreciative of the opportunity we gave her to be heard and for our genuine support, although after we left we did not see her again for several months.

We were reunited with Chantel when we returned to the Grenadines, this time to share the visit with my grandmother and great-uncle Joe, who were flying in from Connecticut. Flight times are not a reliable thing in the Caribbean, especially on the smaller islands. The connection was from Barbados, and we initially expected it to land at about three o'clock in the afternoon. Three o'clock came and went. Over the loudspeaker crackled a voice through the open air terminal, "Flight 203 from Barbados has been delayed and is expected to land at 4:30." We stayed at the airport waiting since there was no better place to go. A chicken scratched past and walked into the terminal.

As we waited we heard a voice call out, "Mary! Lee! Alex! Lara!" Chantel trotted over to us and embraced us all. For the first time we saw her out of her pale uniform. She was in a sunny, casual shirt with a faded pair of jeans.

Mom exclaimed, "It's so good to see you, dear! What are you doing at the airport?"

Chantel's smile widened. "My son! He's coming to live with me here now!" She hugged Mom again. She had befriended one of the teachers at the school who was going to provide after-school care on the days she worked, and she was able to reduce her work schedule to three days a week. She would be able to spend time with him, and tuck him in every night. The profundity of her joy over these simple activities, which we totally took for granted, amazed me. It was my first deep appreciation of how values shape one's choices. In addition, it was the first time I had seen how difficult some lives and some choices actually are.

As happy as we were to see her, we had to depart when our family arrived. I was ecstatic when they showed up. Their company was enjoyable, but their presence also brought some interesting disruptions of our daily flow.

Most immediately, we noticed the issue of space. *Promise* was equipped with three cabins. Alternatively, one could always sleep on the settees in the main salon with a protective lee cloth, a sturdy sheet of cloth tied to the ceiling from under the cushion to form the other half of a cocoon. With this you could not fall out of bed when the boat rolled with the waves. I was displaced from my berth by my grandmother; Great-Uncle Joe, a finicky sleeper, often slept on deck where it was cool enough for him. The greater disruption became apparent the following morning when we commenced the daily homeschooling. Even when Lara and I were relegated to the cockpit, our eyes and attention continuously drifted to our guests. Never was this more apparent than when I went to do math with Dad. Lara was down below with Mom; I was in the cockpit with Dad; where could our guests possibly go? After the first few days of their stay, we took an inevitable recess from school until our guests left.

Grandma and Joe were quite gracious and enthusiastic, ready to learn the ways of ship life. Despite the briefing we had given, Joe did not get the art of using the head (the nautical term for bathroom) on the first attempt. The system was plugged with excessive quantities of toilet tissue, and he had gone about flushing incorrectly as well. A ship's head accepts only sparing volumes of toilet paper and waste matter, which is flushed with a manual pump to induce the intake of salt water from the ocean. Joe missed both of those key rules of usage and required assistance from the crew—me. Our two guests also had to transition to our system of conservation of resources. Opening the tap all the way, they left it running as they applied a liberal amount of dish soap, which took extensive rinsing to remove. Almost a gallon was spent when sanitation could be performed with less than a cup of water. In a similar vein was the issue of showers.

"Where can we take showers here?" they asked.

"Both of the bathrooms have showers," Dad said. "Just take the sink head—it has a hose beneath—and put it over your head."

Grandma and Joe exchanged glances. Then Grandma said, "Could you show me? I don't want to do it wrong."

"I can show you, yes, but we don't have enough water for you to take more than one shower during your stay. You might want to save it for when you really need it," Dad replied, adding, "Unless, of course, it rains; then there'll be more."

It was a good thing Grandma did save her shower, since she got in the water with Lara and me almost every day, swimming off the transom or at the beach when we all went ashore. Joe was also an avid swimmer, especially at the beaches. If he was not swimming, he would be collecting shells, which I later helped him identify. I could do most of them from memory, but some I had to look up. Grandma and Joe quickly fell into the habit of surviving in a salty state, which was tolerable after one adjusted.

Grandma saved her shower for Saturday evening, in preparation for Sunday Mass. Saturday morning, while at the grocery store on Union Island, we chatted with the ex-cruiser Frenchman who found himself behind the cash register of a marvelous bakery.

"Do you know if we can get to the Catholic church from Dutchman's Bay, on the other side of the island?"

He smiled broadly. "But of course, madame! Zhere's a little path up the hill to a bus stop."

Just before the sunset, with Grandma in the shower, it occurred to Mom and me that we should go ashore and take a look at this path. We deployed the dinghy and zipped ashore. The place was totally deserted; a dilapidated beach shack bowed under its own weight, and above the coarse sand stood a row of scraggly brush and acacia. After walking the length of the beach we came across a vaguely possible candidate for the path, an overgrown chute full of boulders that wound up to and over the top of the steep, arid hill. At some point it may have been a goat path. Mom and I realized that it was *not* a good idea to try to get to the church that way.

Actually, it would have been a bad idea to show up in church anyway. Since we had already cleared customs and immigration out of St. Vincent and the Grenadines, we would have been illegal aliens there. So, we sailed for an hour and a half to Carriacou, the southernmost

Grenadine, which was part of the nation of Grenada. Grandma was convinced that Mass would probably start at nine o'clock, maybe eight, so we had to play it safe with the timing; Sunday morning we pulled up anchor at about 5:30 a.m., early even for us, and left the harbor and country. We arrived a bit before eight, and before we even anchored Mom took her mother in the dinghy to shore.

It was not long before they returned, certainly in less time than most services require. Mom started the tale. "The only church in town was on a group religious picnic to the beach."

As she sighed, Grandma continued their brief synopsis, "So, I just went in and prayed before the altar; I knew you did the best you could and I am very grateful." Her smile radiated kindness from behind her glasses.

Mom finished off with, "Yeah, and God will probably forgive you for missing one service. You tried pretty hard."

That was hardly the most trying event of our visitors' stay aboard, however. That came the following morning, when we sailed to Grenada. This was non-optional; their plane was leaving the next day. The sky was overcast, and the wind and waves carried more of a kick than normal. Friends of ours on another vessel, *Moonshadow II*, called over, saying we might want to delay the trip south, since we were in for a blow with winds at upward of thirty knots and rough seas. Given our guests' flight plans and hardiness, we decided to go for it. We chose to omit certain truths about this last leg of the journey, however, such as the fact that we would be sailing directly over Kick-'em-Jenny, a submerged and intermittently active volcano. The twenty-some miles of open sea between Carriacou and Grenada were much more turbulent than was typical: we were heeled over significantly, and we soared through the swells at about nine knots, close to our maximum speed. Grandma and Joe sat in the lower side of the cockpit for this period, quick to acclimate to the more boisterous waters. They simply carried conversation as usual, ignoring the topic of the weather until it was necessary—which it was not until we passed into the lee of Grenada. Normally, being in the lee of an island as mountainous as Grenada wind speeds would drop and moderate the conditions at hand. Indeed, the waves did decrease in magnitude and frequency; but to the east, our port side, the ridges of Grenada rose, and their valleys became deeper clefts. *Promise* continued to charge through the water, until we were perpendicular with one of these gorges. Suddenly, the wind spiked to gale force, almost twice what it had been before. Rigging groaning, we heeled over another fifteen degrees to starboard, and looking back at the helm, I saw Mom putting her whole body into keeping the wheel all the way to one side. The bimini whined ominously as it fluttered overhead; the wind generator, which had not been tied off, buzzed like a furious cicada. "Alex! Let out the main!" I wrapped the sheet around a winch to control the release, but just as I reached over to open the stopper, the bow shot into the wind. We lost all speed as we made an instantaneous ninety-degree turn. Grandma and Joe sat still, poised in case the boat made another sudden movement.

I started to furl the main, just to the first reef, a point where the sail is only partially out and therefore less susceptible to the whims of the wind. Joe got up and said, "I think I'm going to go below now."

I warned him, "You're more likely to feel sick if you go down below."

We had a few more such katabatic gusts, each successive one less of a surprise and better handled. Then, off Point Saline, when we were almost done, the clouds shattered and a world of water came down on top of us, in addition to the elevated wind speed. We pulled into the closest harbor, True Blue, and brought our valiant guests ashore for a night on land.

As we watched their plane take off from Grenada, I burst into tears. When we got back to the boat we put everything back in its place and and resumed our previous lifestyle routines. We sat alone at dinner, and at breakfast the next morning. School was definitely harder to resume. The week-long recess had been so effortless for Lara and me. Now we were back on our own, there to stay … at least until November, when hurricane season was officially over.

Looking for reefs as we venture into the Tobago Cays

Relaxation for the crew at sunset, Tobago Cays

Scaling a palm in Salt Whistle Bay, Mayreau

Alex fishing with Joseph

Chapter 5

THE WINDWARD ISLES

$\mathcal{N}ovember$ thirtieth was when we were freed from the constraints of the insurance company, a paranoia regarding hurricane season. We certainly did not hesitate to leave Grenada; although we had grown to call the place home after our few months there, we jumped the gun and departed early. We left on a cloudless day, the wind sweeping us northwards along the windward shore of the island. This was the more rugged coast, open to the fury of the trade winds and the Atlantic, and it was even more sparsely populated. Cays and reefs lay at sporadic intervals slightly offshore. The engine was completely unnecessary, for winds at twenty-five knots were enough to keep us moving at about eight knots—not our record, but nothing to complain about either.

We reached Carriacou around four o'clock. We stayed at Tyrell Bay, a popular cruising hub. It was a large harbor with multiple yacht clubs, one of which hosted the annual Carriacou regatta, a casual three days of racing in the summer that was widely attended. Many anchors were dropped beyond the mouth of the bay, farther than where they should be, for an opportunity to participate in low key racing and extensive partying.

My family has a custom of nightly predinner snacks, *hors d'oeuvres* as the French say (and as we like to call them). Taking out a cutting board, Mom sliced some cheese and put out a small branch of grapes whose presence was a small miracle. We almost always utilized only local produce, but Grenada with its large international university, St.

George's, had a population large enough to sustain imported goods and the higher prices they fetched. We had become quite proficient at preparing local tropical fruits such as mangos, papayas and coconuts, as well as venturing into the odder vegetables such as dashene and breadfruit. A local cookbook procured from a native chef in Grenada served as our template for epicurean adventures. Mom opened the microwave we had for the bread. The microwave would completely drain the house batteries after about thirty seconds of use hence it was never utilized, but since it was airtight, it was an ideal breadbox. Of course, it was not so great of a bread box when it was empty, like tonight. Mom called out, "Hey, Lee! Can you run ashore and get some bread? French bread would be best if they have any."

Before he could respond I said, "I'll go in and get it."

She responded, "Okay, you can go with Dad if you want."

That was not what I meant. "No, by myself."

Pausing, Mom and Dad looked at me. Then Dad said, "Well, he can drive the dinghy. He's old enough to do this."

Since I was the only weight, slight as I was, I knelt in the center of the dinghy as I drove so it would ride flatly across the water. I opened the throttle all the way. Shifting myself forward, I got the craft to plane. The steering was sensitive, so control seemed like a distant concept as I careened toward the Carriacou Yacht Club. I tied three bowlines with the painter, as an extra measure of caution. With the East Carribbean (EC) ten-dollar note crushed in my palm, I walked into the store in the basement of the building. There was a refrigerator full of drinks, a couple shelves of packaged foods, and a basket of baguettes at the counter.

"Two French breads, please," I squeaked, my voice small and reedy.

The matronly woman behind the counter smiled and said, "Sure, honey. That'll be seven EC." I passed her the bill and nervously walked away with my bread. She laughed and called, "Don't you want change?" I sheepishly took the three coins from her and scampered out. Usually I did seek out the Eastern Caribbean currency, which we all thought quite beautiful. The dollar coins had an embossed square rigger under sail on the back. Most of the currency was also embellished with the flora and fauna of the region, making it much more interesting than its American counterpart.

To minimize the bow spray on my return trip, I kept the speed pretty low. The baguettes were still a bit wet when I got back anyway. I did not really mind that they were a bit salty; I had taken the dinghy ashore, done something, and come back, independently. That was the first event in what would become a large part of my life aboard: being the errand boy. If anything was needed from shore, I would simply get in the dinghy and purchase it (and sometimes a bonus can of Sprite, too). Even if we were having company and my parents needed a bottle of wine, that was no problem for me to fetch in the Caribbean. A few years later, when we were back in the United States and I didn't have a driver's license, Mom still sometimes started to ask me to run in to town to get groceries or something; smiling sadly, I always reminded her that I couldn't.

After a few days, we pushed our boundaries of experience and sailed north to Bequia and Mustique, the northern end of the string of Grenadines, just south of St. Vincent. We spent about a week in Bequia, with its gorgeous beaches, quaint town and friendly people. One of our favorite places on the island was the far edge of town, where a few craftsmen congregated in a warehouse. There we discovered Mom's favorite jewelry in the Caribbean and, more to my and Dad's liking, ship models. These were famous throughout the region, and varied from a few inches to a few feet in size, some half hulls and some fully rigged miniatures.

After our week in Bequia we still were not quite ready to push northward, but we had one more Grenadine to go to: Mustique. Wrapping around the southern end of Bequia we passed between the sheer cliffs of two tall rocks. The wind funneled through at a peculiar angle, one that quickly thrust us toward one of the rocky edges. Taking the helm and firing up the ignition in one motion, Mom damaged her thumb as the boat spun about. Passing through those rocks slightly disgruntled, we continued to Mustique. Its one harbor is poorly sheltered, and the swells tossed the few boats in the harbor from one side to the other dramatically, several degrees to either side. We were quick to disembark and escape the sickening rhythm of the northern swells. Dad took extra care in tying the dinghy to the dock, given the waves. That would have been a bitter loss if the water swept our small but vital shuttle out to sea.

Immediately above the dock were two matching structures,

identical in gingerbread design, one purple, the other pink. In fact, they were glamorous boutiques, but their diminutive size and proximity to the beach invited visitors in to browse. Mom bought a bag and asked if there were any good places to eat around; this seemed unlikely, as the island appeared almost entirely uninhabited. The girl behind the counter was dainty, sunglasses perched on her brow. Pushing her hair back she said, "Well, the place on the hill, The Firefly, is pretty nice. I don't know if there's much else but that's a pretty good place." She seemed out of place for this Caribbean island—or, for any other Caribbean island. In this case, it kind of made sense; the British royal family had a vacation home on the other side of the island.

Walking up the grassy hill I tripped on a round lump I took to be a rock until it poked its head out and looked at me. Turtle! The hill was covered in similar painted turtles, just walking around, occasionally nibbling at the grass beneath them. There was a small aviary containing two glorious St. Vincent parrots, which to our amazement squawked out, "Morning!" when we walked past. After watching them for a moment we continued up the hill. I was thinking the restaurant would have been better named "The Mosquito," given that by the time we got up there, we were covered in bites. I groaned, "Did someone bring insect repellent?"

Looking out over the veranda, we saw the sun descending from behind some clouds: a fiery show tinged with purple. Since we were alone in the restaurant, Lara went off to the kitchen and talked at no end to the cooks, who were laughing genially with her. She often did this when she was in one of her more social moods, she would wander in and help shell fresh peas. A little while later, a couple walked in. She was gorgeous, a tall Italian girl with black hair curling about her shoulders and down her back, in a short dress of a shimmering dark green. He was a bit tall, scruffy, on the older side of the spectrum, and wearing a pink sarong. My parents looked at each other and something passed between them, but they managed to contrive some continuity to our conversation.

A few minutes later Lara skipped out of the kitchen, and went up to the couple, who were then sitting at a table for two by an open window. The guy had some electronic device, like a Gameboy, that he was focused on; the woman sipped from a champagne flute while staring across the water. Lara approached him and said, "Hey, Mister, you're missing the sunset!"

He smiled at her and, putting the device down, said, "You're right. You know, I came all the way from the other side of the island for it and here I am missing it. Thank you for reminding me."

Lara climbed over his chair to the window and said, "Let's watch it. And I really like your pink dress."

The man looked at Mom and Dad and shrugged. They nodded back.

Later that evening Mom was digging through the CDs for something. "What are you looking for, Mom?" I asked.

She cried, "The Rolling Stones, of course! After seeing Mick Jagger, I've just got to hear a song or two!" My parents were quite cool about the whole incident, valuing their own privacy and freedom so tremendously. They never mentioned it when we were in the Firefly, despite the fact that we were reading a book (while munching our snacks) that delineated how Mick Jagger, Pierce Brosnan, and other stars with homes on Mustique ran a children's education fund for locals, and shared their resources. My unique sister also had this uncanny ability to know who was approachable and intrinsically kind, and who was not. People must put out subliminal vibes, ones that hide under the more complex social signals which distract the rest of us. Later, on another isle, she would befriend Patch Adams and spend hours in his quirky, delightful and accepting company.

The next day we sailed past Bequia and up the coast of St. Vincent, dispelled by the untenable swells. The water frothed, and a pod of pilot whales emerged. They were dark gray and were more like dolphins, oversized and with a less pronounced snout. They were just visiting to breathe, and descended back to the depths. Grenada's shoreline was dramatic, but St. Vincent's was simply epic. It was a series of bays backed by vertical faces smothered in dense foliage. Higher up terrace farms grew, in sets of some twenty steps of earth. St. Vincent was barely developed as an island as well as a nation; it was one of the poorer islands, and thus suffered a higher rate of crime and drug use. We were going to spend just one night there, and the following day we would sail to St. Lucia, the next island in the archipelago.

As with many of the volcanic islands in the Caribbean, the largest peak was named after an acclaimed French admiral from the 1700s;

in this case, Soufriere. We anchored in a bay sitting right at the volcano's foot, the seabed plummeting to 200 feet, which is exceedingly deep, right up to the shore. When the anchor dropped, no noise was produced, at least not heard. There were a few old concrete buildings on shore, their paint peeling and roofs rusting. It was tremendously remote and wild. The air was still, *Promise,* the only boat in the harbor, hanging limply on the water's surface. I went up on deck, at the base of the mast, to change the courtesy flag. The courtesy flag is flown from a low halyard on the right side of the mast, just below the first pair of spreaders. Protocol dictated that this little flag, slightly smaller than a piece of paper, be that of the country in whose harbor you were staying. If you were at a country departing or checking in with immigration imminently, a yellow quarantine flag was to be raised—a relic from days past where a ship carrying active disease could bring an unwelcome pestilence ashore. I dropped the tricolor cloth to the deck and left the rope empty. Alone in the harbor, there was no one to observe the blank yellow flag.

No one official anyway. We had all settled in down below, it was too early for snacks or preparing dinner, when we heard a call from outside the boat. "Hallo sailboat! Any'un' aboard?"

Assuming the role of ambassador, I went up the companionway to see who had addressed us. A burly man in a rowboat leaned over his oars, " 'Ey, kid, your parents around?"

At that point Dad came above and waved. "Hi there. Can I help you?"

Gesticulating a bit, the rower called back, "Yessir, I'm Boyboy, and I was wondering if I could sell you some fruit here." He held a paltry bunch of bananas up for inspection from afar. Dad declined the offer. Boyboy pursued from his rowboat, some twenty feet from *Promise,* "Well, if you won't buy my bananas, then let's just talk." Talk they did, and at great length and with reluctance on Dad's part. Boyboy began to complain bitterly about how he got wet when it rained and ventured to ask us for a raincoat. I chimed in, "I have an old poncho you can have!" This was the first article in the pile of our belongings he accrued, which later included a flashlight and a bag of Tostitos.

After an hour he was still there, and that was when Dad grew dismissive. "Listen, Boyboy, it was nice meeting you, but we need to have dinner now, so if you'll excuse us we need to go."

Boyboy pleaded, "No, wait, I've got to tell you about one mo' thing." This was my first encounter with begging in the Caribbean, where I discovered that granting a request will often induce more.

As I was talking with Mom about it later this evening she said, "It's better not to give blindly what is asked; our guide book says, and there've been studies on it, that instead, you should offer to remunerate them appropriately for a task or job you need assistance with, or some item you need. It's a big problem in some poorer places." Even bearing that in mind, I hardly lamented the loss of the poncho.

Very early the next morning, the ignition beeping, the engine shook to life. That was the one thing I could not sleep through, so I grabbed my journal before heading onto the deck. The sun was just starting to rise, the sky and Soufriere illuminated in the hazy purple. The wind was still calm, obstructed by the peak. Sitting on the windward side of the cockpit, I put the journal in my lap and turned to a page devoid of my logs. Moving made it difficult to draw consistently, the other challenge being the profusion of coconut palms on the northern slopes. They were a struggle to capture even for Dad, who majored in art before medical school. I developed a technique involving drawing the stems of each frond, then making a zigzag across and down its length.

The swells rose dramatically as we passed the northern tip of St. Vincent. The waves were often more turbulent around northern and southern extremities of the islands, where the predominant trends of air and water broke sharply. St. Lucia was a distant haze, forty-some miles away.

The southeastern port of St. Lucia, Vieux Fort, took many hours to reach, as it was essentially a beat. We dropped anchor around three o'clock, and Dad dove to make sure it was soundly dug into the bottom. The boat had felt tentative as we backed down on the anchor, our way of ensuring we were secure. We engaged in the rites of official entry; I went back to the base of the mast and raised the courtesy flag of St. Lucia, deep blue with a depiction of a sharp peak in the center, as well as our yellow quarantine flag. Dad had the more grueling task of going to customs and immigration. He arrived back at the boat more than three hours later, dusty and sweaty. He recounted his adventure. He'd had to go all the way to the southern airport (St. Lucia was remarkable in that regard, having two separate airports). Hitchhiking was a fairly standard method of transportation. The ride he hitched, though, was even more bizarre than usual: in the bed of a large truck with a pig and its owner. Once at the airport, he logically followed the signs through the small terminal to immigration. It was a small, dark room, with a desk at the back, a guy passed out in his chair behind it. Two other local officials played cards in the corner. Walking up to them Dad asked, "Who do I talk to about immigration?"

They laughed and pointed at the guy sleeping in the chair. "Him."

"Should I wake him?"

Their smiles vanished. "I wouldn't do that," one said slowly. So Dad waited for the official to awaken and then proceeded with the formalities.

"But there's an upside to the long journey," Dad told us. "I found out there's an amazing beach on the windward side, around the corner from the dinghy dock, with some great windsurfing stuff. We should all go check it out." The next morning, a Saturday, we found ourselves looking out across a wide, golden beach to the rollicking surf. Several kids splashed in the shallows; families picnicked and played games; several groups rode by on horseback—not a canned tourist ride, but riders who were one with their horses, galloping at full pace down the disappearing stretch of beach. Several windsurfers planed over the waves in the distance, humming at high speed in the tempestuous wind, unbroken by land since Africa.

Dad pointed excitedly to the windsurfers, "Doesn't that look neat? Let's go check out that place down the beach." Taking the lead, he walked off toward the open shop, beach shack-like in design, with lively colors and coarse wood, but the size of a warehouse, large and open with boards and rigs hanging from the ceiling. Dad avidly tried various boards and rigs, and got me to try it out, too, even though I had no idea what I was doing. We bought a board and two rigs, one large and one small. Aside from their cumbersome storage on deck, and the rigs and sails (which were relegated to my bunk), it was a fabulous investment for the boys aboard *Promise*.

On the third day, we escaped the confines of the arid south and proceeded up the increasingly dramatic coast, passing sugar fields with the crumbling mills still looming over them. The climax of this coast, and maybe all coasts in the Caribbean, was our destination for the day: the Pitons. The Pitons are a pair of volcanic plugs about a mile apart, a secluded harbor and an old plantation on the beach between the two. Volcanic plugs are the atypical remnants of volcanoes, formed when the shaft inside solidifies, and the surrounding cone erodes away. Basically, we were anchored between two sheer cliffs with peaks high overhead— the sum of their heights exceeded the distance between them. This was another harbor frequented by vendors, and we bought some fruit. I made an illustration for the second day in a row, meticulously noting each crevice in the smaller, steeper plug to the north, Petit Piton.

Our time in St. Lucia was brief this trip, as we knew we'd be back in a month. Within a few days we had skimmed through the harbors on the leeward shore and were on to Martinique, the first of the French Antilles, to rendezvous with *Navigator*, a boat we had grown to know well while in Grenada. We arrived at the southern harbor, St. Anne, which was part of the larger Marin area, a vast harbor that was one of the best and most patronized cruising hubs in the Caribbean. Incidentally, our second evening there happened to be Thanksgiving back home. Although many of the cruisers we had encountered were somewhat rebellious, anti-establishment and certainly anti-Bush, no one was going to pass up the opportunity for merriment and good food. So, *Navigator* arranged an American Thanksgiving banquet to be held ashore in a pavilion on the beach. It was potluck, so we went ashore to go grocery shopping, in hopes of finding some ingredients and inspiration.

Once in town, it was clear we were no longer in the third world. The center of this small town was a boulevard, trees with little fences around them running its length and shiny new cars that stood in stark contrast to the beat up collection of miscellaneous vehicles that dominated the roads of Grenada and other independent islands. Speaking of roads, the ones here were perfect: asphalt, curbed, clean. This was all quite charming, but we were duly stunned by the grocery stores. The floors were immaculate, the produce fresh and clean, and everything was French. Near the back of the store, I looked into a glass covered refrigerator and asked, "Hey, Mom … do people really eat chicken feet? And quail eggs?"

She frowned at the meat and then laughed. "That would be very French."

We bought so much food that the dinghy rode low in the water. When we got back to the boat, we immediately began cooking. The main salon was covered in both plastic shopping bags and their extensive contents. We always brought our recyclable canvas bags to the store to bring food back in, but this time we exceeded the bags' capacity in our zeal. The galley was tight, but we managed to get an apple pie in the oven, stuffing on one burner, and mashed potatoes on another.

We showed up at the pavilion with our various foods. *Navigator's* crew was there, and those from a few other boats, as well, with whom we quickly became acquainted. This included the crew of *Moonglow*, a gregarious and generous couple, Ian and Maggie. He was American; she was originally from the Philippines. Also on this list was *Seatrek's* crew, an American family whose boat was a permanent resident of Martinique; their daughter, Micala, was enrolled in a local school. This was a new group of cruisers for us, expanding our contacts. After grabbing a turkey leg each, Dylan and I went down to the beach to build a sand castle. I taught him the technique of dribble castles: take wet sand between your thumb, index, and middle fingers, and let it slip down to consolidate on the increasing sand deposit. We took periodic breaks to grab more food, sand from our hands sprinkling the stuffing. We bolted before anyone noticed.

Festivities continued the following evening when we brought a tradition of ours to the Martinique cruising community: Pictionary. We had initially extended the invitation to host the event, but *Seatrek* was the superlative party vessel. It was an elegant old wooden schooner, with glass panes along the raised stern and multiple decks down below. Lara asked, "Hey, can we live on a boat like this?" However, since we were the only boat equipped for home schooling, we brought our huge white board and markers. Food was served from *Seatrek's* granite countertop, which would be heavy enough to keep *Promise* listing permanently to that side. Teams were made on the basis of gender, and we set about creating slips of paper with content to be drawn. The only criterion was that all content be nautical. The highlight of the game was probably Maggie from *Moonglow's* misfortune. Just working her way through the English vernacular, she got both "old ironsides" and "prairie schooner"; a great dispute ensued over the validity of the latter term. It did have the word "schooner" in it, but the term referred to Conestoga wagons, whose covered tops were said to look like sails as they crossed the plains of the Midwest, the sea of grass. The argument was made even more entertaining by the liberal quantities of French wine flowing amongst the grown ups.

Later in the week we experienced another French tradition, popularized especially in Martinique. The beach at St. Anne was fantastic, and kids were always swimming in the shallow water. However the greatest part of the beach was really just above the sand, in the dust beneath the towering tamarind trees: *boules.* The beach ran for several hundred yards, and so did the dirt expanse for boules. Every so many yards, a cluster of Frenchmen would have a drink in hand, and their raucous game a bit ahead. It is basically bocce: the winner of each round throws a small target ball, the *cochonnet* or *bellini*, and everyone throws their steel orbs as close to it as possible. I first played with folks from *Seatrek* and *Moonglow*, and caught on quickly. Most people threw their balls so they rolled toward the bellini, but after watching the intoxicated Frenchmen down the beach, I took up the habit of throwing it upward with a backward spin so it stayed where it landed. Picking up the next target ball, I looked for a good place to throw it. The intricate root system to the right seemed like a good pick. Everyone grumbled, but I had won the prior round, and I could put it wherever I wanted, and flaunt that. Looking back, I realize that my relative skill might have corresponded to the fact that I was the only one not drinking, but that hardly detracted from my victory.

Another thing that we all loved about Martinique was the wind. Somehow, despite having a large hill to the east, the source of the predominant trade winds, the breeze was always about twenty knots in St. Anne. Twenty continuous knots of breeze meant a wind generator that never ceased spinning, and our batteries were always fully charged. We never had to run the engine to charge the batteries, and we could leave the fridge on more often, so our food tasted better and kept longer. Additionally, we could run the inverter, a device that supplied electricity to the few power sockets we had aboard, so we could charge the laptop and watch movies a couple times a week. *Finding Nemo, Treasure Planet,* and *Monsters, Inc*: two months of movies in a single week.

The wind could be a double-edged sword, though, which became evident when we first took the dinghy into Marin. Marin is a humungous, intricately shaped harbor, but the main boating center and town was at the innermost point—an extensive dinghy trip, taking almost thirty minutes. The duration would not have been a tremendous issue had the bay not been swept into whitecaps. We had to go more slowly than usual, since if we did not, every wave we hit would have spilled into the boat. Our first trip in, we actually stopped about halfway at a boatyard with a restaurant, just for a respite from the spray. The four of us walked in totally soaked, shirts plastered to our skin and hair dripping. We picked a table in the sun with hopes of drying off. The waitress came over and spoke some rapid French, to which Mom responded with an order. The waitress scribbled it down and looked at me. I exhausted most of my French vocabulary by saying, "Je voudrais un croque-monsieur et un Orangina"—I would like a toasted ham and cheese sandwich and a carbonated orange juice.

This was what I had learned thus far from the new French addition to our curriculum aboard. The curriculum was dynamic in that way; it often changed to fit wherever we were. So, when in the French Antilles, you got to learn some French; when in an area with amazing ecology, science was the most prominent subject; in areas like the Tobago Cays, biology took a more detailed look at the functioning of a reef. St. Anne was the training ground for French, where we explored both the academic side, working with tapes and textbooks aboard, and the practical side, speaking (albeit in a limited manner) in the field. The academic side was not as gratifying, since it never resulted in a baguette or a "chausson aux pommes" (literally, an apple slipper, but fortunately it was really an apple turnover). However, it could be quite entertaining, with comical songs about stating basic feelings and emotions, such as hunger and happiness. Now, years later, Lara will still teasingly torture me by singing those same songs.

Since education was always in our parents' minds, they had asked permission for us to visit the primary school, or *l'école*, with Micala. In addition to their colorful classrooms and airy building, we were impressed with their schedule, which was very French as well. They were all dismissed at noon to go home and have lunch, and school restarted at 2:30 p.m., and then went until 4:30. They had half a day on Wednesday, which we envied, but then had to attend Saturday mornings as well. We decided our own schooling schedule was not that bad after all.

French became our first class of the day; since Lara and I both enjoyed it, this made it easier to get up and start school. As we started one of these classes, early in the morning, we were surprised when someone knocked on our hull and called out, "Hullo? Anyone aboard?" British—the accent gave that much away. Dad and I went topside to see who hailed us and found a cheerful chap saying, "Right, we heard you had children aboard." This intriguing opening line was followed by, "You see, we're desperately in need of a playdate."

Their story: they had just crossed the Atlantic, a two-week trip, and had arrived during the night. The kids, five-year-old George and six-year-old Tommy, were stir crazy and needed some mates. Apparently they had gone to several boats in the harbor looking for kids, preferably ones that spoke English. They had been referenced to us by *Moonglow*. This family's boat was *La Novia*, a custom built sixty-foot junk. It was really state of the art, all the latest racing equipment and navigation gear. This modern junk was extraordinary because of its rig. The "junk" part meant that the boom extended both to the stern as well as the bow, making the main and jib functionally into one massive sail. The expedition was all funded by the father, actually an English lord; and it was certainly necessary, given that their crew was really only two people—and they'd just crossed the Atlantic! A meeting was arranged with the crew of *La Novia* around four o'clock, "just in time for tea."

La Novia glowed. Down below, soft light came from indirect sources, behind panels or ledges. As Lara pined for *Seatrek*, I was excited by the fantasy of living on a boat like this one. Tommy and George shared a berth in the stern. The floor space was extensive, covered in various British plastic toys, and behind it one huge sleeping surface covered the king size floor. I walked up to a vase secured to shelf. "What are they?" I asked.

George came over and exclaimed, "Those are sea monkeys! They're our pets!" He proceeded to give a detailed profile of the species and how they got them.

I replied, "I guess they're cool. Why don't you have something bigger though? Like, we have a cat."

His eyes widened. "You do? That's so cool! Our parents wouldn't let us get anything big; you guys are lucky."

We spent almost a month in Martinique, and formed incredible friendships. As with so many places, language was always an optional part of communication. We became friends with French, Italian, Swedish, and Polish sailors of all ages, having boules matches and potluck dinners on the beach. One favorite evening, my sister was dying to teach our English and French friends how to make s'mores by a bonfire. Our vocabulary bloomed as it necessitated finding *chamallos*, or marshmallows, which Lara greatly preferred to *pamplemousse* or grapefruit. One French boat from Normandy brought their healthier version of fireside dessert: they roasted apples soaked in a mixture of cinnamon, brandy, and brown sugar on sticks. Not surprisingly, all the adults preferred the apples, and all the children, no matter their ethnicity, preferred the chocolate and marshmallow s'mores.

We did not go back south again until almost Christmas. *La Novia* and *Promise* both went to St. Lucia for the holiday. On Christmas day, Mom's sister and her family were going to fly down to spend vacation with us. As with all kids of the culture, the whole week leading up to Christmas was charged with anticipation for Lara and me. My grandmother had brought an American Girl Christmas tree for us, including beautiful working lights and tons of ornaments. When we had taken that last long passage from Martinique and were in the lee of St. Lucia, we were finally allowed to take it out and decorate it. Although it was only thirty inches high, it transformed our main salon with holiday magic. On Christmas Eve, Mom, Lara, and I went to the supermarket by Rodney Bay, a marina not quite as extensive as that at Marin. We managed to find the better part of the Christmas shopping selection, included a Butterball turkey. The turkey was the hardest to pick, since we had to compare dimensions to what we each thought the oven was, I was pretty sure we could do the twelve-pounder, but we got the ten-pounder to err on the side of caution.

Later that evening, we found that the smaller turkey barely fit. As with Thanksgiving a month before, the kitchen was at maximum productivity: stuffing, mashed potatoes, and multiple vegetables in various stages of preparation. As the food cooked, we took out the satellite phone. The satellite phone operated from satellite signals, and was therefore theoretically usable around the globe, though sometimes it proved quite frustrating, and cut out arbitrarily. But even in the most obscure locations, such as between the Pitons that Christmas Eve, the phone still gave us access to loved ones far away. We all crowded around the communicational brick in the cockpit and called Grandma, with whom we had not spoken since she visited us in the Grenadines. Her sweet voice said, "Hello?"

We all cried out in greeting. "Mom!" "Grandma!" "Helen!" "Grammy!"

She laughed and inquired about our wellbeing and location. We avidly described the Pitons, and that we were having a dinner not too different from what she was probably having that evening. The conversation was terminated prematurely, the satellite lost behind the towering Pitons. Pragmatically, this may not have been the worst of occurrences given that food was just about done.

Using all our napkins as trivets, we kept the food on the folding table in the cockpit. The bottles of wine and soda were on the floor, close at hand. The sun had set, and the night was dark, the few other boats glowing like fireflies, and from the hotel music dimly reached us. The centerpiece of our table was the kerosene lamp, giving an orange glow to the food and each others' faces. For the first time in our collective memory, Mom said, "I think we should say grace, guys." After a pause she dove into her proposition, "Thank you, very much … God … for such a wonderful family, for our amazing health and luck, and for the extraordinary opportunity we have to do such a rare thing and see so much. Amen." The rest of us all threw in our two cents of gratitude and we commenced our feast in the magical dark.

After dinner, Lara and I hung our stockings by our tiny tree. Actually, we hung foul weather boots, artifacts from the frigid New England sailing we once engaged in. We plugged in the Christmas tree, its multicolor lights illuminating that side of the main salon. Sitting by it, we all read from Christmas stories, including the famous the *Night Before Christmas*. I wore a Santa hat. Mom and Dad enforced an early bedtime, so Santa would arrive when we were asleep. There was a good deal of speculation revolving around where he would land his sleigh. We reached a consensus that he would land on the spreaders closest to the deck; that way he could drop down a halyard through the hatches in the main salon.

Christmas 2003! That's the heading I scrawled across the page of that day in my journal. Like any kid, I could barely control my excitement upon awakening, although I managed to retain some sense of consideration, not even peeking at anything but the clock until seven o'clock. At that point, I sprinted from my room and tackled Lara and then my parents. The morning was unmistakably Christmas, the rain boot stockings filled with candy and smaller gifts; beneath them, the larger presents. I have no idea what my sister was given, by I distinctly remember receiving an Apollo Mission Lego set, with which I was utterly enamored and which I assembled shortly after.

Over the course of Christmas, Mom's sister and her family flew in, arriving late in the night. The following day, Boxing Day, we heard a call from the near shore.

"Hey, Ellisons! Marybeth! You up yet?"

I clambered up the companionway and looked to shore and shouted, "Aunt Susie!"

She waved and asked if Mom was around, who shortly after came up and screamed, "Susie!"

The four of them came aboard late that morning, with a luxurious and perhaps excessive amount of baggage. We had had some challenges fitting two guests aboard earlier that year, so this proved to be quite a storage puzzle, in which my cousin Kyle and I were relegated to the main salon. After getting their belongings stowed away, the entire expanded crew went ashore. Eight was then the most we had held in the dinghy at any point, and the gunnels being low to the water was adamant proof of that. We walked into Soufriere, the waterside town by the Pitons, in search of a cab. That was an easy find; in the Caribbean, vibrantly colored passenger vans were commonplace, their drivers quick to call out to any potential customer. As we walked over to a cab, my uncle Gary was approached by a poor man, dirty, with clothes brutally worn down,

"G'morning, sir. Might I have some money?"

As Gary reached for his wallet, Mom stepped in, "We don't actually have any cash to spare, since we just have enough for the cab, but if we can find you later, there's something you can do for us and we'll gladly pay." Mom was very good about following the rules she studied.

As we climbed into the cab, our driver introduced himself. "Hello, everybody. My name is Jermaine; where would you all like to go?"

"The Rain Forest Botanical Gardens and Trails, please," announced my father.

With that we took off into the hills, the trees growing denser and darker as we went. We reached a graveled parking lot, and from there we took a wide path, trafficked by several people who were obviously tourists, wearing floral print clothes and each with their own camera. To either side, a selection of tropical plants had been groomed, including heleconia, anthuriums, and various variegated shrubs. Susie and her family, as well as all the other tourists, marveled at each plant, stopping to lightly prod the leaves. I acknowledged their beauty, but as I wrote in my journal at the time, "To me it was nothing too special." We continued down the path, farther than the majority of tourists got, and hiked a short trail into the actual forest, less colorful and denser. Then the rain fell—but it was odd. One minute, the rain was off; an instant later, it was a deluge. Moments later we were all soaked through, and we turned around to take the path back to the parking lot. The path went down farther than I remembered, but I kept pace with the exodus from the forest, which ended in a greenhouse isolated in the woods. Wrong turn. Pacing about under the glass rooftop, we laughed at our state. The rain was over in about five minutes, and the sky peeled back into its typical radiant form. We were just stepping out onto the path when a cab came careening down the path. We waved, and it ground to a stop. The driver grinned as he leaned out the window and asked, "Where you wanna go?"

He took us back toward town, and then brought us up the nearby Mt. Soufriere, ashy and covered in scree. No foliage dared to grow. We got out of the cab, paid, and thanked the driver. We stood a few hundred feet above the town of Soufriere. The eight of us walked up a road that split the slope in two. To either side, huge pits sunk into the earth, in the bottoms a viscous, grey fluid bubbled. The air smelled of rotten eggs. I picked up a small yellow stone: sulfur. These captured my attention more easily than the groomed jungle we had come from.

Kyle asked, "Can we go swimming in those pools?"

With a macabre chuckle I noted, "No, you'd boil instantly. But we can in the pools a bit further down the slope."

We walked down the rough road to one such pool. This pool was still bubbling, and the water was thick and grey as well. I grinned enthusiastically and teased, "So, who's going first?" Some ten or fifteen minutes later, we emerged from the water, flushed from the heat and grey from the mud. I commented, "There's no way any taxi will take us like this."

Single file, covered in light grey mud, we paraded down the slope, through town, and to the dinghy dock. We all dove into the bay to rid ourselves of the plastered mud on our skin. We then drained an entire tank on showers for all.

We fell into a different rhythm with guests this time. Before, we had tried to make our normal style of living continue, but this time we simply decided to go on vacation as well. So for the week they were there, school was suspended, and excursions were frequent—as were games of Uno. These became perverse events among my cousins Kirsty, Kyle, and me, during which we would pick up until we got a "Draw 4" card which we would then play, forcing the next person to pick up four more cards. The week passed quickly, full of easy laughter and many adventures.

We departed from St. Lucia the day after they flew out. We crossed the tempestuous twenty-four miles to Martinique in record time, with a heavy twenty-five knots roaring from the east. The swells were particularly large, too. Coconut came up to join us; she curled up on the coiled jib sheet in the cockpit, knowing it was better to be above deck in rough seas.

After a few days in St. Anne, we continued up the coast through picturesque harbors, past the metropolis Fort de France, and to the northern harbor and town of St. Pierre. This diminished town was located at the base of the largest volcano, Pelee, in the Windward Islands, a dramatic positioning. In the early 1900s, Pelee erupted, killing almost the entire population of the city, with the notable exception of a drunkard who had been put in jail and was liberated by the damage inflicted upon the jailhouse. Dramatic photos in the small museum gave testimony to the spectacle of St. Pierre's previous fortunes, which was once referred to as "the Paris of the Caribbean."

We went ashore to clear immigration, which was a simple matter of completing a duplicate form, and dropping one of the copies in a box. In addition to being free, clearing into and out of the French islands was an efficient, pleasurable experience, especially when juxtaposed to some of the island nations we visited. We stocked up on all our favorite French foods that were only obtainable in those islands. This stockpile needed to enrich our diet for the next week or two, before we got to the next French island in the archipelago, Guadeloupe. Before that, though, we were going to Dominica.

Alex capturing his first sighting of the Pitons, St. Lucia

The night before Christmas

Alex at the helm for the departure from the Pitons

Alex and Lara exploring the South of Martinique

Chapter 6

THE LEEWARD ISLANDS: A WORLD APART

𝒟𝑜𝑚𝑖𝑛𝑖𝑐𝑎 was a foreboding island, and one that impressed me quickly. It loomed in the distance beyond the clear waters of the Martinique passage as we set sail under tremendous Pelee's shadow. About half way across the channel, an apparition appeared. It arose so suddenly, it seemed an island was generated *de novo*. Without warning, the island spouted a humungous spray of water into the clear blue sky. Sperm whales, their silhouette and description made most famous in Melville's *Moby Dick*, are distinctive for their unreasonably proportioned brow. The rectangularity and sheer size of the head epitomized my child's view of the ultimate whale. The propinquity to our ship was so awe-inspiring, we did not even have to time to react or ponder fear. We were under sail, with a strong breeze off our starboard side, heeled over in a six- to eight-foot swell; our companion, barely 100 yards off our port side, glided effortlessly across the top of the sea. To our amazement, our new friend accompanied us for almost an hour, maintaining his distance, and remaining on the surface. As we gazed at him, his eye, which seemed to be several feet in width, watched us, equally transfixed. He seemed quite curious and even friendly, in our anthropomorphized view, and he escorted us more than half the distance to Dominica. This boded well for unparalleled adventure at our next destination.

Spellbound by Dominica's tremendous beauty and rugged terrain, I contributed another article to Sally Erdle at *The Caribbean Compass*.

This took the form of a travelogue in my enthusiastic nine-year-old voice:

Dominica was outrageous! Lush jungle erupted from every land form. It was so verdant and bursting with life. Even the animals were amazing there, such as agoutis and parrots. There were huge waterfalls—some were naturally cold, but some were hot, warmed by volcanic heat seeping through the crust. Hot springs cascaded over rocks and formed natural hot tubs in between the rocks. We had so much fun in them. When we were exploring the pools, we found out they had tunnels underground leading to other pools. To climb to the highest falls, which was several hundred feet, we had help from a local friend, "Batman"—appropriately named! Mom and I made it to the top and we swam under the thundering water. We were the only people there that day, which made it especially magical. The plants looked like something from a fairy tale. We also explored rivers and rainforests that had tunnels formed from the trees. It was so beautiful; we had art class there under my father's direction several times, drawing various specimens of plants and animals, and landscapes as well.

The people were also so friendly. We even had Sunday lunch with a local family with seven children—and Mom and I counted fourteen different dishes with ten types of vegetables! We met native Caribs who showed us how they grew and made foods on their farms. The grandmother even showed us how they made chocolate from the cocoa, and we had samples! They also showed us the amazing process of making their fishing boats from *gommier* trees. They cut the tree and carve the hull. They fill it with water and rocks, then burn a small fire under the boat for two weeks. The heat and water soften the wood, and the weight of the rocks pushes the sides out to increase the width of the boat. They then carve designs into the sides. They could travel far out to sea in these small boats once equipped with a sail. These crafts were very well balanced and sturdy.

The people were so generous with all they had, even though they had very little. They were some of the nicest people we have ever met. It was my favorite island so far and we spent quite some time there. It is a gem of an island and a great place to explore.

Happy adventuring!

I was duly impressed by the nature and topography of the isle, and we anchored in various harbors along the leeward shore. We enjoyed a few days in the northernmost harbor, Prince Rupert Bay, where both the lunch with the family and the tour of the river occurred. One of my sister's and my favorite features was the national flag: it was red, green and black, as were the flags of several other Caribbean nations, but this one had a Dominican parrot right in the middle. As in all countries, we had to fly the nation's flag when in port, and we were in no hurry to take this particular one with the parrot down. We glossed over the fact that the red symbolized blood, and the green, tropical plant life. Like most of the islands here, that verdant foliage hid a more sinister past.

The Caribs who inhabited the northeastern shore were descendents of tribes from South America who had migrated here in war canoes centuries before. An aggressive and fierce people (according to anthropologists), they overran the more peaceful and bucolic Arawaks, who were the original inhabitants of these islands, having landed here after leaving from the eastern Central American coast. Evidence of the Carib's past history of human sacrifice and cannibalism, as well as the planned enslavement and extermination of their enemy, was rampant. The modern word "barbecue", in fact, originated from this culture, and it does not refer to the roasting of cows. These Caribs, then, became the perceived indigenous peoples when the European powers arrived to exploit the islands' resources and claim them for their own. These ferocious warriors were legendary, especially on the more rugged islands such as Dominica and St. Vincent. The European powers, of which there were many, including: British, French, Dutch, Danish, Spanish and Portuguese, all viewed the indigenous people similarly. When the Europeans were not trying to wrest more colonial possessions from one another, they spent their time and resources trying to rid the islands of these local populations that were not immediately subservient. We read some sections of James Michener's *Caribbean* out loud as a family, until my mother finally vetoed it as a family affair due to the egregious, and unfortunately quite historically accurate, violence.

Promise continued to travel northward in the Leeward Isles, and we crossed the Dominica passage to Guadeloupe, about fifteen nautical miles to the north. However, we stopped first at a cluster of cays just to the south of our actual destination. As with many of the smaller islands, these cays, The Saints, had a relaxed feeling exaggerating the predominant sense of island time. The narrow streets of the town were deserted mostly that Saturday, the cool white buildings lining them sealed entirely. It was unmistakably French as well, with *boulangeries* dotting every corner and a very active sailing community. All the people absent from the streets were on the water in some craft or another.

Our time on the main island of Guadeloupe was brief, as we found it to be too urbane for our cruiser's taste; while there, however, we frequented our favorite French stores such as Champion (Lara's favorite) to stock up on Petits Ecoliers, Orangina, and other epicurean treasures. We also visited the local spice market, and were rewarded with bountiful herbs, fresh sugar cane, and pungent fresh spices. After replenishing our galley stores, we sailed southeast to a distant one of the Saints, Marie Galante. The other Saints may have seemed laid-back, but this place was a *century* back. In our rental car, we passed oxcarts full of crops weaving down narrow roads, cleaving the sugarcane fields apart. The island was almost entirely undeveloped, and the roads unlabeled; we found our way with a map and by comparing the shape of the turns we made with those on the drawing. In this way we navigated to a *gouffre*.

I asked, "Hey Mom, what's a gouffre?"

She replied, "It's a … I actually have no idea. But it's listed as a tourist destination, so we may as well check it out."

Tourist destination was a fairly broad term, and provided no help in visualizing the gouffre. At a height of 300 feet above sea level, we scrambled over the broken volcanic stone, grass clumps growing through it. We approached the edge of the gouffre: an abyss plummeting into the sea below. The stone encircled a lagoon, with an archway into the surrounding cliffs that served as a funnel for the thundering surf.

Behind us the blades of a stone sugar mill rotated slowly in the brisk trade winds; the moment could have been from any of the past four centuries.

Local people on these islands, unaccustomed to tourists, smiled and helped with translations whenever possible. Armed with years of continental French, my parents were fine in Paris, but less so with this unusual dialect half a world away. Even the illustrious French-to-English dictionaries we had were not as helpful as we might have hoped when it came to arcane or unusual marine words. Inscribed into one of the covers, we had our own lexicon of dozens of French marine words including essentials like *fond* (depth), *le brise-lames* (breakwater), and *s'echouer* (run aground). While driving one day during torrential rain, we came across a sign reading "Ague." My parents, being doctors, thought it was the quaint anachronistic word for fever. Looking it up, it said "pointed, sharp," and so they surmised it must be a lookout or turn ahead. Following the road as it got narrower and turned to tracks, we rounded a corner to see the road end in a riverbed about a hundred feet across and of questionable depth. We stopped, wary about proceeding. A smiling farmer came over and translated it more like "ford," as in, to cross a riverbed. He waved us on, assuring us it was a safe depth. My dad, who had been washed off a road in a Land Rover in Africa earlier in his life, remained unconvinced. The kind gentleman then proceeded to cross it himself to show his sincerity. We, too, traversed it without difficulty, thanked him profusely, and were on our way.

Sailing north the next day from Guadeloupe and the Saints, we crossed the windy stretch back to Antigua. This was tremendously exciting for me; as I wrote in my journal, it was like seeing an old friend again. It had been the first destination I sailed to, and was my first island where I was a cruiser, not a tourist (a distinction my kind fight hard to maintain). I was really looking forward to returning to English Harbor, mainly for the bakery and the fort. Instead, though, we went to Jolly Harbor, another massive cruising center with multiple boatyards and a supermarket right on the water, definitely catering to a specific demographic. We quickly provisioned up and sailed around the corner to Five Islands Bay to gunkhole for a few days, as well as to catch up on school work. Passage days were mostly oral lessons such as spelling bees, twenty questions, and other mind games that could be played in the cockpit in rolling seas while heeled over.

More exciting than our return to Antigua was Antigua's sister island Barbuda, a poorly charted spill of sand and coral. This incredibly low-set coral island had a high elevation of only thirty-one feet, making it difficult to see until you were upon it, and off-limits to approach during stormy weather. We set off from Jumby Bay, a small private isle on the north of Antigua and an exclusive resort—so exclusive that we were not welcomed ashore. It was clear midday when we set sail, but intermittent clouds blocked the sun, which was critical. We made the mistake of approaching when the light was flat, due to the unexpected cloud cover, and with no accurate charts aboard, or even in existence, we had to pick our way through harrowing and plentiful large patches of coral. When we got reasonably close, we dropped our sails, and I went up on the foredeck while Mom climbed the rigging wearing polarized lenses. We wound a serpentine path slowly through the labyrinth of coral mounds. The island was a sandy ring encircling a lagoon, with a colony of frigate birds and a small community of reclusive fishermen. Eleven continuous miles of sand to ourselves! It was the perfect location for a beach day. Several hours and most of a bottle of sunblock later, we had amassed an impressive assortment of shells collected from the steep pink sands.

Back on *Promise*, Mom and I emptied the contents of our canvas bag onto the cockpit's foldout table. With our shell books and an identification sheet, we sorted the lot into five categories, and learned each of their common as well as Latin names. Murexes, cowries, turkey wings, and scallops represented a mere sliver of what we hauled aboard that day.

We explored that island with zeal during this halcyon time, full of pink beaches by day and campfires at night. Places like this compelled Mom to spout British Romantic poetry, especially Lord Byron; she would recite by heart, "There is a pleasure in the pathless woods / a rapture on the lonely shore / a society where none intrudes by the deep sea / with music in its roar / I love not man the less / but nature more." In addition to teaching me the words, she, in fact, also taught me inadvertently to internalize the sentiments. Often when approaching a beach by dinghy with even a few people on it, my sister and I would say, "Let's go around the corner, and see if there's one that's deserted instead." On Barbuda, that was quite easy to do.

Changing destinations frequently, we continued westward over open waters to yet another of the French Antilles, St. Barts. Its main town and capital, Gustavia, is now known as the "Paris of the Caribbean," a title bestowed thanks to the prevalence of designer shops, gourmet restaurants, and mega-yachts galore. As it is not a volcanic isle, it is unlikely to lose the title as unfortunate St. Pierre did a century earlier. This was not a spot typical of cruisers, but it did become a favorite of ours. Lara felt especially at home among the luxury. She picked out a nice diamond tiara in Bulgari for mom's upcoming birthday; she could not understand why Dad declined her suggestion.

After a few days of basking in the classy radiance of Gustavia, we motored about two miles to Anse de Colombier, a national park and Rockefeller Trust. With the best reef in the northern Caribbean and a short walk to cliffs hanging over raging surf, this was every bit the opposite of the capital, yet every bit as elegant. It would become one of the most idyllic spots to restore our equilibrium over the next few years.

Our next destination was really somewhat less exotic: St. Martin. With *Promise* being prone to succumb to unusual mechanical issues, we found ourselves trapped inside the large lagoon characteristic of St. Martin's Dutch side. The island is split on an east-west line, the south side being a very developed area under the protection of the Netherlands, the more tranquil north being a protectorate of France. With little drainage and a huge quantity of boats and buildings in close proximity, the water was not healthy for swimming, or for use. There is actually a blotchy purple fungus that grows on the underside of boats that is believed to originate from this lagoon. It took over a week for our mechanical problem to be resolved, and it was with great haste that we fled the crowded, windless lagoon for the harbors along the outside of the island, from which we had a stunning view of high-rise hotels over small beaches. Still, it felt too much like Florida. We snuck across the tiny pass to Anguilla, another British protectorate with perfect beaches and a more relaxing tone.

Within days, we had hit the waves again and were crossing the largest open cut of water in the Leewards, the Anegada Passage to the British Virgin Islands, or BVIs. This collection of islets was a favorite of ours before we sailed away; we would often come for Presidents' Week vacation and charter a boat. Now on the cruiser side of the coin, it was apparent just how touristy of a place it was. More so than the rest of the

Caribbean, this area's economy relied on sailing tourism—in fact, there was no other industry, except some private business that also generally revolved around tourism to some extent.

We definitely had our inevitable brushes with tourism, and indeed did some of our own when we had three batches of visitors in about that same number of weeks. First came the Pengs, long-time family friends—our "chosen family," we called them. We augmented our music lessons with them and had a blast. After sharing our small maritime space with them so easily (nine people in all), we left for the US Virgin Islands to receive more family: Grandma was back, with her oldest daughter, our aunt Nancy. For our third set of guests, more acquired family, my friend Tazer and his mother, Karla, came, and we again sailed west to another set of Virgin Islands, the Spanish. Our constant travel was an attempt to add some diversity to the guest cycle for the crew's sake. Incidentally, we had also saved the best for last. The Spanish Virgin Islands were the least visited, without a substantial permanent population; the islands were remote, rugged, and exactly what we needed. Karla had actually been to one of the resorts there, and we sought to find the isles she had not seen, such as Luis Pena. The bioluminescence in the water around these cays was stunning; we were transfixed and could watch the show for hours. Lara insisted there were underwater fireflies, and Coconut fell in off the transom more than once chasing the elusive flickering lights.

Culabrita with its historic light house was entirely uninhabited, and was largely a nature preserve. We anchored under the stratus in the lee of a long, curved stretch of sand. Walking it later, we came to a towering maze of boulders and cliffs, remnants of a crumbling bluff. We picked our way through the tide pools, some refreshingly cool and others lukewarm from sun exposure earlier. Suddenly, the water washed out from beneath us, and after an irate hiss, it returned with all the terrifying force of the ocean, water streaming through an aperture in the stones about as wide as my narrow shoulders. Mom pressed a hand to my chest as the sea washed back out again. She shook her head, cautioning, "You know people die from riptides and waves like this every year, right? Never turn your back on the sea, Love."

After that whirlwind month of visitors, it was time to return to our routine. As much as I would miss the family and friends that had come to visit, it had been a long time since we had been simple cruisers.

March was careening to an end and our time in the Caribbean had been spent. We were due to keep going west and north, to Puerto Rico, the Bahamas, and finally back up the coast of America to New England, just in time for Mom and Dad to resume their careers and for me to join the loop of public school I had left so readily.

"So, guys," Dad addressed Lara and me, "we've had a great time out here, right? Made good friends, seen some cool places, and going home will be tough."

I chimed in, "I don't want to go back home!"

Dad nodded. "Right, and maybe we don't either. But as a family, we need to make a decision. Do we want to go back to Connecticut, or do we want to keep sailing?"

Many discussions ensued, pros and cons weighed, but the decision was unanimous. We charted our course to the southeast, across the Anegada Passage and back toward the heart of the Caribbean.

On the east side of the Anegada Pass, there are a couple of islands including a little bump known as Saba. We arrived as the sun was setting, and the orange light ignited the bare cliffs reaching into the sky and toward Saba's misty peak. It was not until the following morning that we realized just how steep the island was, when we took a cab to town. Normally, one says that they go "into town," but this was definitely going *up*. The town at the lower altitude, called simply "The Bottom," is at an elevation of about 1,000 feet, with the next town, Windward Side, another 500 feet up. All the homes were tiny (as befitted a tiny island), each with white walls and a red corrugated roof, gingerbread dangling from the gutters.

The small streets were only lightly trafficked, but not so quiet that they felt desolate as we navigated the paths through the grassy fields, their plane interrupted by sporadic peaks of a much darker green. Hiking to the pinnacle, we were completely enshrouded by cloud, the stunted trees of the rainforest all short and twisted, the volume of the moss draped over them probably greater than their own. Several hundred feet below, we were out of the cloud cover, and sat on the edge of a soaring cliff. We overlooked the valley in which Bottom sat, the road to Windward Side winding between two dark spires of stone. It was a dramatic place, a craggy alp misplaced in the Caribbean sea.

Also on that small grassy plain stood a medical school. We stayed on the island over Easter, and Mom and Dad toured the facility, spoke with the deans, and then were referred to some local real estate agents. With sheep at pasture in the adjacent lot, the little white cottage at the edge of the cliff seemed really quite charming. "We could have sheep next door!" became one of the major points we used to try to interest Dad, but in retrospect that was probably a huge deterrent. We did not actually settle on anything; although prospective job offers for our parents were enticing, nothing trumped the call of the sea, and we sailed on.

About forty nautical miles away lay the duo island country, St. Kitts and Nevis. We sailed past the closer St. Kitts for Nevis, allegedly the more scenic and appealing of the two. Nevis rose from the sea like a giant sombrero; from above, it was round, and its lone peak curved exponentially, asymptotic to the ocean. I wasted no time in grabbing my journal to generate sketches of its palm-smothered slopes.

The medical school on Saba had a sister school on Nevis, and as soon as we'd cleared customs, we rented a car to drive around the island to explore. The houses around were fairly standard for the Caribbean: brightly colored concrete walls, metal roof, tiled floors. The medical school was similar, except with the red-and-white color scheme more characteristic of Saba. Nevis was a much larger, and a much more Caribbean, island than Saba, which we often describe as a European peak cut off and placed in the Caribbean; Dutch language, little stone churches and all. Of course, that also means that in Saba there is no beach, just cliff. Well, to be fair, it did have a small stretch of large stones that came into season for a few months a year with the annual oceanic patterns. Nevis was looking more appealing than Saba, but still not as enticing as *Promise*.

We lingered in the area for almost a month, returning to St. Barts and the northern, French side of St. Martin. A nighttime passage past Montserrat reminded us all that this was an active volcanic archipelago, with some peaks dormant, but few extinct. On a moonlit journey to Guadeloupe, we passed the south side of Montserrat, its volcano spilling ash into the air and spewing cascading lava down the rocky slopes toward the sea. We had passed this isle earlier and noted the once-active town was reduced to flat, arid ash. At night, however, it was a spectacular display. The major eruption had occurred the previous year, and there was so much ash in the air that flights were cancelled for days in places as far away as Puerto Rico. Since Montserrat is a British protectorate, the islanders were relocated to Great Britain for their own safety after the eruption. That next summer, however, many of them returned, preferring the risk of incineration on their home island to the gray bleak winter landscape of England. We understood.

By mid-May, hurricane season was drawing near, and we needed a few weeks to get to an officially hurricane-safe area before the season began. Our return to Grenada was sealing off options; we would be trapped below the twelfth parallel for quite some time, but it was quite liberating, really. From here, the choice was easy. South America beckoned. Most importantly, it was adamant proof that we would not be going back to the US anytime soon, except maybe to visit.

Alex exploring the volcanic falls of Dominica

Alex investigating the construction of the Carib's canoes

A treacherous hike along Saba's rocky peak

Saba's idyllic village

Lara and Coconut on deck

Friends in Culebrita, Promise at anchor

Our first visit to Nevis

Coconut stowing away for a passage

Chapter 7

Paradise on Pause

The sailing and cruising community was extensive, and our interdependence on one another fostered familial level bonds. So, on August twenty-first, like the year before, we had my birthday party. Every kid from the Grenada boating community came and joined in celebration at the Moorings pool. One of my buddies cut himself on the side of the dock, and my father sutured his wound on our boat in a matter of minutes.

The following day, my parents had arranged for a local bus, an exotically painted van, to take us and our closest friends to the Mt. Carmel waterfalls, some of the most dramatic landscape on the island. I was ten years old that day, and I was definitely driving the dinghy ashore. Twisting my hand, I opened the throttle all the way. Water splashed the bottom of the dinghy in a mesmerizing rhythm. My parents and sister sat with me on the pontoons, staring toward the dock. My vision did not waver until we bumped into the dock, bouncing along the edge and skittering to a stop.

Striding from the wooden dock to the grass, I noticed the flamboyant van was parked in the shade of a mango tree, eclipsing the sun for a surprisingly large area. The hatchback trunk was up, like a metal hand raised in greeting. "Hop in the boot," said the driver, a huge Grenadian with a grin characteristic of the island.

"You mean the 'trunk,'" I teased good-naturedly; since this was a previous British colony, Grenadians used that vernacular.

Pippa, a girl my age from Britain, took offense at my bastardizing her language, and often told me so. Ironically, her family shared the same surname as our family—Ellison. Her dad, Roger, happily informed us that due to our illustrious name, we were free to graze our sheep and livestock on the village green in York, England, their home. Apparently, it had been written in the town charter from time immemorial, and should the need ever arise, we'd be accommodated. Of course, this heralded area in England was also the hailing port of a much more famous sailor, the renowned Captain Cook. They told us an illuminating and amusing tale of how the Board of Shipping had to approve every ship's name that had York listed as its hailing port. Every name they submitted, no matter how charming or erudite, was rejected. Finally, Pippa said, "Why don't we just write our name backward as a joke and see if they accept that?" Ironically, the name Ellison spelled in reverse is Nosille, and that wound up the name of their sailboat that was finally accepted, and carried this family across "the pond," as the Atlantic is fondly known to the Brits.

A pair of beaming faces peered from a back window. "Alex! Come on! Get in the van!"

I grinned and called, "Hey, Drew! Hi, Riley!" Then I sprinted across the dusty parking lot, the soles of my feet grinding the gravel against itself. I leapt into the van, landing on a vacant bank of seats.

Moments later, the face of Drew and Riley's dad, masked in stubble, leaned into the van. "Hey, Alex! How are you?"

"Good, thanks."

He smiled and then looked us over. "Okay, guys, you all need to scrunch in real close. There're a lot more people coming."

Lara was thrilled that she got to sit on Dad's lap without protest. Drew and Riley were the respective son and daughter of the family that lived aboard *Panacea*. There were another four boat families coming, from *Scud, Wanderer, Nosille,* and *Dreambird*. The family from *Wanderer* actually also hailed from Connecticut, and the skipper, gregarious Vito, had been one of my parents' classmates when they took their course in celestial navigation in Mystic. Several thousand miles later, we met up, neither of us having initially known that the other would be embarking on a comparable voyage. The van sank as it filled, one person at a time. A sticker from the manufacturer curled away from the wall: *Max. Capacity 10 Persons.* The door moaned as it slid shut. I attempted to figure out how many were in the van, I lost count around twenty. I slapped the cloth interior; a cloud of dust erupted from within. Our driver sagged into his seat and put his shoulder into turning the key. Amazingly, this was not the most crowded van in which we had ridden; that distinction went to a van in Carriacou that carried twenty-one people, a chicken, and a goat.

One of our favorite facets of the Caribbean mentality was just this: the relaxed disregard for the minutiae of the rules on all levels. The people did not really care if the car was overloaded; they realized they were not in any peril and it was more convenient anyway, and the police would not care as long as no one died. It just created an easier atmosphere for living. The characteristics of flexibility and resourcefulness amongst the people living in the boating community also spoke volumes about their values. That we were able to double the maximum quantity of people in a van for a forty-five-minute ride on a serpentine and poorly maintained road to the mountains is an adamant testimony to our comfort with each other, and our having become accustomed to tight living conditions.

We passed through the capital town of Grenada, St. Georges. It was set in a harbor with steep hills rising all around, giving it a secure feeling. Winding through the crowded streets, we made our way from the harbor up into the surrounding hills. Just a week before, the same crowd of cruisers with kids had been parading along with most of Grenada at five in the morning for Jouvert, a part of the Carnival festival. Trucks and vans had cruised down the main street at minimal speed, each rigged with elaborate makeshift speaker systems, blaring their favorite pieces of Caribbean music at full volume, the beats driving our erratic march. Several vans had their doors removed, and passengers with buckets of blue paint doused anyone who came near enough. We competed chromatically in our own small way, each of us having brought paint. With all the kids present, a paint fight was inevitable, and we all came home looking like the canvases of Jackson Pollock. We had walked several of the miles through town, but the cab to Mt. Carmel groaned up hills we had not previously climbed. From the apex above the town, I looked back. Green skirts of land folded in toward the shimmering harbor, speckled with houses partially on stilts since the land was so steep. Dropping down the other side of the range, the population density fell drastically. As the area became increasingly agricultural, houses grew sparse, with fruit-bearing trees growing up the sides and hanging over the roofs. The road quality declined with the bucolic surroundings—and it didn't start out very high.

Finally reaching a hamlet secluded in the side of a mountain, the van came to a stop. Five boat families stumbled out, relishing our newly returned capability of motion. Some scruffy chicks followed a hen down the empty street. Excepting our group and the chickens, there was no one to be seen. Paying the cab driver was not necessary, as he knew with certainty that we would need him to return in a few hours; moreover, there was a level of trust and openness within these societies. At home we were never allowed to pick up hitchhikers, let alone hitchhike ourselves. Here on Grenada, and throughout the Caribbean, it was absolutely routine. Offered a ride on a hot day on the way to town for provisions, my mother and I would gratefully hop in any vehicle that stopped for us, even if we were not requesting it. Lorry, compact, ramshackle van: all were welcome. Likewise, in those times when we would splurge and rent a car for a few days for sightseeing or larger errands, we would happily offer our spare seat to anyone in need. The driver pointed the way to a slight dent in the vegetation behind Cookie's Snackette, and we found the overgrown path leading into the jungle. Rising and falling with the terrain, we approached the waterfalls, towering over a shore of saturated boulders. The mist and spray made the border between sky and the top of the falls indistinguishable. It reminded us all of the stunning scenery from Jurassic Park, before the T. rex arrived, of course.

Although epic, these mammoth falls were not the actual destination. We followed the course of the river downstream. As we pushed the bushes back, the riverbed in front of us dropped away. The rock underwater had been carved into distinct chutes that sped down to a rocky landing; then, a smooth face, overrun with the water, dropped into a natural pool before the river picked up its course to the sea. Abandoning all but an old bathing suit, I shot myself feet first down both the upper and lower slides. I beamed up at everyone else from the pool and cried, "Let's go!"

Treading water, I looked around for the path leading back to the top of the chutes. In doing so I noticed the bamboo façade on the other side of the pool had been cleared since our previous visit. It had been replaced with a pasture crowded with cattle. One bowed by the water to drink. I ignored them and stepped out of the water—and pierced my foot on a stick. The mud between my toes picked up a pattern of red. Not telling anyone, I simply continued up the path and back down the chutes. A day of rapture ensued for all of us. Our imitation of otters sliding down the rocks, plunging great heights into the pools, was the stuff of magic. Everyone was rendered into an enthusiastic child, and it was a memorable day for teenagers, young children, and adults, all united in joy.

The following morning in the harbor I woke up to see my mom at the SSB radio, listening to a weather broadcast. The SSB (single side band) could be used for long-distance calling. You could contact someone on the other side of the globe with it, but you couldn't call your neighbor; it simply didn't work over the short range. My mom was getting her weather report from George, a meteorologist based out of St. Johns.

I asked, "Weather's okay, right?"

She put a finger up and leaned in to the radio to hear better. She turned up the volume. The tinny voice carried on, "Hurricane Ivan is category three at this point, getting worse and going to reach as far south as twelve degrees north…" Grenada was about twelve-point-one degrees north.

A tense twenty-four hours ensued for all of the vessels snuggled into southern Grenada, waiting out hurricane season at supposedly safe latitude. Our parents met regularly with the other captains and navigators, trying to analyze the incoming data and decide our tactic: tie ourselves to shallow mangroves or run the hundred or so miles south to South America or Trinidad. Although we all shared information and ideas willingly, the decision of every vessel rested with the captain and navigator—in our case, Dad and Mom. We children were not as terrified as we should have been, I suppose, but rather revved up by what we took to be another adventure or wild experience. It was about 6 p.m. when we cast off from our mooring. Several other boats, all of which had children aboard, were doing the same: *Dreambird, Nosille, Scud, Panacea,* and others. Hurricane Ivan, which was ratcheting up to a category four storm by now, was hurtling toward the west across the Atlantic and would arrive in about a day. We slipped through the reef behind a boat called *Jasp,* an acronym for the names of the family members aboard, and headed due south. Only one of the vessels in our group, *Scud*, with their intrepid crew (including my older teen buddies Adam and Warren) had made this journey toward South America before. They decided, however, to head southwest for Margarita, Venezuela, where they felt they'd be safer; so once at sea, we parted ways. The adrenaline was high aboard all of the vessels, and we all talked to each other frequently on the VHF, especially as the cover of darkness enveloped the ships. I decided to name our adventurous gang the "Friendship Armada," which dissipated some tension and made all the crews smile.

After a bit, a headache began to creep over my skull, so I said, "Hey Mom, I don't feel well. I'm going to go below for a bit."

She responded, "Could you put up the mainsail first?"

I undid the stoppers, mechanisms that prevented the ropes from changing position, and wrapped the sheet around a winch. A minute later, I was done and down below. My mom called, "Feel better, honey!"

Curling into a ball on my parents' bunk, I clutched my stomach. I needed sleep even as I lay awake.

The following morning when I awoke, I sensed that the vessel was flat but definitely moving. I poked my head above deck. On either side of us, jungle-draped cliffs rose a few hundred feet. "Welcome to the Boca del Dragon, Alex," my dad said.

"This is an interesting place," I said, gesturing toward the sharp cliffs.

He responded, "Yeah it sure is ... off our port side is Trinidad, and off our starboard, Venezuela."

This notoriously treacherous passage, where the Atlantic slammed into the northeast corner of a continent, was eerily serene this morning in first light—the literal calm before the storm.

"How are you feeling today, Ace?"

I shrugged. "Could be worse."

He nodded, "All right then. We're about to go around this point, so would you mind trimming the main?"

As I eased the sheet, the sail swung out. "We're good," I called.

As we rounded the point, a forest emerged. This was the first of its variety I had seen. A couple square miles in size, about fifty or seventy feet tall, it was a forest of masts. Countless boatyards cluttered the shoreline, each filled to maximum capacity with boats hiding for hurricane season. My parents, along with the other vessels in our armada, had called and arranged berths in Chaguramus; we all knew this would be valuable and much-desired turf in the near future as Ivan beared down.

For the first few hours we were there, I played in the marina pool with the other cruiser kids. Then my health declined. I started to take periodic breaks to lie down, and those quickly evolved into a constant state of existence. I lay stagnant. I clutched my head as it ripped apart and vomit streamed from my mouth. I barely was cognizant as Ivan the Terrible, with his winds markedly diminished by our distance from the eye of the storm, churned over us a day later.

The day after Ivan, my parents took me to Trinidad's new and not entirely finished hospital. I was on a cool bed in a large room while some young medical staff murmured between attempts to establish the source of my malady. This often involved drawing blood. That was fine in general, but I was dehydrated, and apparently that made it significantly more difficult. I did not mind that they had to try a couple times—until that exceeded fifteen attempts. I was furious with myself for having falling ill and into their incompetent hands. I was referred to the larger, better established, Mt. Hope hospital. By that time it was about five in the afternoon: happy hour. I breathed deeply in the back of an ambulance winding well above the speed limit through rush hour traffic, thinking, *Just get me there.* Looking out the back windows I saw a mosque pass by. That was a first for me, as none of the other islands in the Caribbean we'd seen had sizable Muslim communities; they were primarily insularly Christian.

Mt. Hope was an old hospital. It was open air, with large wards without windows or screens and nothing seemed clean. It had the island's best cardiologist, though, and the only CAT scan machine. The cardiologist walked in and smiled; he was a kind-looking man with a thick beard. He procured a needle and I screamed. Convulsing in a feeble attempt to escape, I was held down by my parents. He got the blood though; the twentieth time was the charm. When they performed the CAT scan, the tech called in the radiologist from home, an erudite woman who had trained in England. I do not remember much, other than a few words sprinkled about in my wavering consciousness: liver, blood, critical.

Looking back on that night now, it could not seem farther away.

And it is half a decade and a few thousand miles away; but certain aspects of the ordeal remain clear for me. During all the needles and scans and poking and prodding of various medical personnel, I had a warm parental hand to hold against my pale skin. I always had one parent with me. As the clock crept into the late, dark hours of the night, with most of the island asleep, whichever parent was not with me was on the phone—first with medical friends and family back in the US, then with insurance companies, hospitals, and more doctors.

The following morning, the product of their handiwork emerged. On the runway, a sleek red and white jet buzzed, ready for immediate takeoff. AirMed, a company of ambulance-jets, can get you out of anywhere they can land with a medical crew. Their policy is that the afflicted and one other person may come aboard to the closest American hospital, which was their intended destination. After a performance that I missed because of my state, but that my father assured me was worthy of an Oscar, my mother had convinced the crew to take the patient and the remaining three family members, not to Miami as was the original plan, but all the way home. A few hours later, my family and I were in Hartford, at Connecticut Children's Medical Center.

In Hartford I received a month of hospitalized treatment, a euphemism I like to use to describe myself in a bed, blinded by headaches and barely capable of motion. This was all caused by *Leptospirosis ictohemoragica,* a spirochete. This corkscrew shaped bacterium is carried by 160 species of mammals and livestock, including the cattle swimming with us at my birthday party in Grenada. From this, my whole body was drained of all strength, and my brain wrought with encephalitis and meningitis, leaving no part of my body unaffected and without agony. Some of the worst days were blotted out in a veil of sedation and sleep. According to my parents, I was critically ill. I was in DIC, disseminated intravascular coagulopathy, which I came to learn was a state where your body is so sick, it consumes its own platelets and clotting factors and internal bleeding ensues. Normally, one's platelets are a robust 300,000, but in Trinidad, mine had dropped to 6,000, a level at which there can be spontaneous brain hemorrhage. At CCMC, I had to go to the operating room twice to have cerebral spinal fluid drained, due to high intracranial pressure. I probably survived due to my parent's vigilance, along with the help of my medical team. My uncle, John Peng, was the physician at CCMC who facilitated my transfer, as did a brilliant and quirky pediatric neurologist, Ed Zalneraitis.

Finally released from the confines of the hospital after multiple admissions, I continued to bear the scars of the illness. Most noticeable of these was my strength. I could not walk very well, and hence Dr. Z sent me to physical therapy; I would attend for several months to relearn the art of walking, something I had previously totally taken for granted. The most painful difference for me, though, was the diminishment of my mental strength and capacity. According to the very kind Dr. Z, I was exempt from school officially for six months, since my brain was truly injured. The following may be one of the most poignant memories in my academic career. My mom and I were sitting at the counter in our house, and I really wanted to engage myself in my favorite subject, math. We were not going to commence school per se, but simply do some multiplication and division of numbers with a few digits. I stared at the paper. This was no problem, right? I had been doing these at lightning speed over the summer before my illness. However, I couldn't remember what to do. Not even how to start.

My mom was patient. "It's fine; do you want to try some addition and subtraction?"

I nodded. I would get this.

My mom wrote out an expression: 327-215 = _____.

I vaguely remembered how to do this. I knew to start with seven minus five. I sat cogitating on the answer to step one. Seven ... minus ... five ... equals. Nothing came to mind. Back five years. I lost all control and sat sobbing.

This particular incident fueled my proclivity to the notion that I was unfit to mingle with the world. I was ashamed, and I hid, reluctant to see anyone—or just about anyone. One of the select few I was willing to see was Don Treworgy, the professor who had taught my parents celestial navigation before we embarked. Patient by nature, he bolstered my education of the stars. This was a facet of my knowledge that had been resilient, safe from the wrath of leptospirosis, or lepto, as I grew to abbreviate it. Professor Treworgy ran shows at the Mystic Seaport Planetarium, and between shows, he gave me the run of the artificial sky, teaching me the art of manipulating what was displayed based on geographic position and the day of the year as well as time of night. I grew familiar with all the constellations and the astronomy behind them. After a few sessions, I grew facile enough to conduct a show. Mimicking Don's routine, I guided a small crowd of onlookers through the nighttime sky, which they probably rarely gazed at on their own. Don not only taught me the stars, but also much about Mystic Seaport, the museum of America and the sea. Through the underground passages connecting buildings, beyond Staff Only signs, and into the innards of the church steeple we went, every step accompanied by arcane historical facts and intriguing vignettes. Through these unobtrusive lessons, Don restored my intellectual curiosity and, most importantly, my hope.

As I opened myself up to the world again, we received guests who were good friends of ours from the Caribbean: the British family aboard the neo-junk *La Novia*. Having heard of my malady and wanting to explore America, they had sailed up to visit us. The plan had been for them to sail up the Connecticut River and moor in the harbor near our house in Essex; but the bridge spanning the river was a mere sixty-five feet high, and with their unique rig, it was impassable. So they resorted to a harbor down the coast and we collected them, since hitchhiking was not a valid option in Connecticut. With a profusion of hugs, their visit was more than welcome, and had the additional effect of enhancing my yearning for the sea, that lifestyle, and *Promise*.

As the year progressed, my recovery became more robust. My survival of this arduous period relates to Mark Twain's maxim: "Don't let school get in the way of your education." Although unable to attend school, I learned to intrinsically appreciate life, a subject absent from most schools curricula. Having learned that, I eventually went into a school system two months earlier than scheduled, albeit in a different country. I resumed the busy lifestyle every ten-year-old craves. My residual weakness, however, persisted for months, and I was cursed with horrendous headaches. According to my team, even though the bacteria had been killed, sometimes a nasty infection causes a sort of sludge to build up over the drainage system of cerebrospinal fluid in the brain. My body kept making fluid, but it could not drain and circulate as normal; hence, the pressure increased and headaches ensued. Dr. Z had a bag of tricks and medicines which helped for the most part, but they remain one of my souvenirs of this chapter in my life.

Alex in the rigging as *Promise* made its way southward

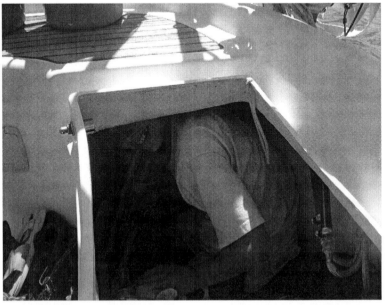

Alex always was the one to retrieve articles from the lockers

Lara at the helm

The fateful Mt. Carmel falls

Chapter 8

NEVIS, CARIBBEAN QUEEN

Christmas came and went, and so did our time in the States. Our autumn had not been an easy season; we all wanted that particular chapter of our lives to close. I had interrupted our circumnavigation, and I wanted to go and pick up right where we had left off in Trinidad and sail north of South America, through the Panama Canal, and onward to the Pacific. This was an idealistic dream, since all our companions who had sailed with us, the Friendship Armada, were by now thousands of miles ahead, and going without buddy boats was simply unsafe. The other factor preventing us from resuming sailing was the fact that I was still recovering from a life threatening illness, and was not well enough to endure that rigorous lifestyle—not to mention that if any complications arose while out there, I would likely not be as fortunate as I had been this time.

So, with an exodus in mind but sailing out of the question, a very strange possibility occurred to my parents—one that has completely shaped my life in almost every dimension imaginable. They had been offered positions at the medical school on Nevis, since they were both acclaimed physicians as well as educators. The dean had said, "Just give me a call and I'll be happy to discuss this more with you." So, a few phone calls and meetings later, my parents agreed to teach there beginning with the January term. Logistically the timing was perfect as we had just agreed to sell our house in Essex, and merely needed to go to Trinidad to pick up our floating home, *Promise*. I vastly preferred the prospect of returning to our sailboat—and continuing our journey in some way—to being land-bound during a New England winter.

Sailing *Promise* the several hundred miles from Trinidad to Nevis did not seem an unusually daunting task for us, except that I was still in a weakened state and neither as agile nor as fit as I used to be. When we first arrived onboard, we spent the day reacquainting ourselves with the ship. We held our breath on our way to the bookstore on the wharf to see Coconut, and to ascertain how she had weathered the transitions in her own life. The store owner petted her lovingly as she lay curled in a basket on the floor, looking much more corpulent than when we had last seen her. The owner said she loved Coconut, who had become a great mouser. A reluctant and poignant look passed between my parents and the woman; quietly, my parents said we would stop by later.

Coconut would not be making the journey with us northwards, despite tears and pleas, since she had a new home. By the time we cleared customs and set out, it was late afternoon, and we knew we needed to clear the Boca del Dragon by nightfall. This treacherous stretch of water often had surprises in store, as the waters of the Atlantic, unfettered since Europe and Africa met the eastern continental shelf of the Americas.

As the sun was setting over Venezuela and the stars were coming out under a clear sky, we fell back into a rhythm. Everyone above had their harnesses on and attached; I was down below in my bunk. The sea was a reasonable five to six feet, mostly off our starboard beam, as we headed north into the night. The winds blew at a steady twenty-five knots, a bit higher than normal but very characteristic of December (these winds were often known as the "Christmas winds"). As it was getting dark, we reefed the sails a bit, choosing to sail cautiously rather than be heeled over abruptly by a katabatic gust.

Without warning, I heard my mother shout, "Lee!" to my father at the helm. I never saw the wave break. According to her it was huge, rogue in that it was alone, and towered five or six times the height of its neighbors. A deafening crash of water filled the cockpit, cascaded down the companionway and enveloped the nav station as well as much of the main salon. The boat, which had been cruising along nicely at about eight knots, sluggishly wobbled forward under the ponderous weight. After the initial shock wore off, we bailed to augment the capacity of the automatic bilges which were working overtime. My sister and I slid around the cabin like we were surfing. Mom took the helm, and Dad and I tried to take inventory and salvage what we could. The nav station was hit, and the electronic GPS was down, but the radar was working. The VHF was out, although the SSB was working. Our computer, a new Mac, was drowned. We all dried with sponges, and then towels; nervous laughter, and sighs, and hugs followed. The sky was clear and we had our sextant; it would be light before we arrived at Grenada's south shore. The weather forecast was unchanged: clear. That wave had just been bad luck. We would continue on our way. Although it was an inauspicious start to our Nevisian journey, we all secretly hoped it was not a sign of things to come.

Nevis was a sombrero shaped island of about 20 square miles in the leeward islands of the Caribbean. Its dominant feature was a huge central volcano, the dormant Nevis Peak. It had a permanent rain forest and its apex was often shrouded in clouds. There were no defined bays or protected harbors on Nevis. Given this topography, the best option for Promise was a small mooring field in the lee of Nevis Peak, in between Nevis and her larger sister island St. Kitts. These moorings were on the eastern edge of a two-mile-wide channel between the two known as the narrows, and offered at least minimal protection against the brunt of the prevailing waves and trade winds. We had enjoyed the natural beauty when we had visited the previous spring, with no real intention of returning there to live.

Nevis had been a component of the British Empire for hundreds of years, serving as a naval base and agricultural center, specializing in sugar cane, which required droves of slaves. Alexander Hamilton had been born on Nevis and spent much of his childhood there. Nevis had been inhabited by Amerindians for 2,000 years, prior to European explorations. The history was marked with numerous incidents of violence between the British, French, Spanish, their African slaves, and the local Caribs. The latter group was effectively wiped out from the country by European weaponry. St. Kitts and Nevis became a sovereign country achieving independence from the UK in 1983. Since then, the people have striven to be as independent as possible, and by the time we arrived, the country was a far cry from where it started almost thirty years ago.

In some ways though, Nevis had not changed so drastically from Colonial times. The economy was almost entirely sustained by foreign enterprises, now mostly tourism. The majority of the island's land was still in the hands of foreigners and a small Nevisian Oligarchy, and the largest employers were foreigners. Many of the local islanders did not get running water until a decade ago; and the Peace Corps still had an active presence on the island. The redolent streets of the capital Charlestown had open drains of all kinds that emptied into the town's main harbor, and there were vast economic disparities between various groups on island. Much of the land remained bucolic, and the people were transitioning from agricultural to service industries. Their world which had been a more family and village centered society was becoming more modern and materialistic with recent introductions of cable television, Internet cafés, cell phones, and credit. That was the world we just dove into.

Upon our arrival Mom and Dad assumed their faculty positions, teaching courses in Physical Diagnosis and Anatomy, respectively. This meant a daily commute by dinghy to the dock of the Galley Pot, a waterfront restaurant that owned the mooring we used. Mom was always in a dress; Dad wore khakis and a shirt and tie. The dock was a series of square floats loosely linked together. This made for wet, salty entrances to work for Mom and Dad.

When they were not at work we had the other task of finding schools for Lara and me, and also the issue of finding a house, since this commuting daily by boat was not going to work for long. The owners of the Galley Pot had a son my age, Thomas. One afternoon, after an hour of discussion for the parents and an equivalent amount of time on the trampoline for Thomas and me, I had decided I needed to cling to whatever I had, my first and only companion.

The following day we took a look at the two private schools on island, only one of which was actually independent of the government. That school was Bellevue, a primary school that catered largely to expats, and consisted of a one-room school house in the middle of a grassy, goat-laden field. The other school was Charlestown Prep, a government-supported private school whose main clientele was wealthier local families. Comprised of several old buildings, it sat in a dusty lot sealed off by chain-link fencing. This was the school Thomas attended. I peered into the fifth-grade classroom. The room full of scowls was the one I would be joining should I choose that school, which I did.

The principal who had given us the tour handed us a book list and told us where we could get the appropriate school uniform. It took several small stationary stores to find all the books and materials I needed. That night was also the first we spent in a rented house. It was a lonely concrete edifice on a plot in the jungle that smelled of decaying perfume.

The following day was my first day there. At 7:30 I walked into the classroom I had seen the day before. The teacher's desk was in the corner. Her name was Ms. Flanders, and she did not acknowledge me as I came in. I was the first in the class and I asked, "Ms. Flanders? Where do I sit?"

She looked up dourly and pointed to one of the two-person desks, "You'a gwine sha'h wit Anthony."

I missed what she had said totally, but I saw where she pointed, and put my bag there and sat down. My classmates slowly filed in, each taking a moment to ask my name and then scattered their various ways. One boy, Carl, took a moment to converse with me.

At eight o'clock, a cowbell summoned the motley seventy-five or so kids to assembly. We stood in disorderly rows. Everyone took out a little blue Bible and recited some psalms. Where was I supposed to get one of those? At the end of the assembly, the principal called me to the front, and I was put on display as the new student. I glanced at the sea of faces. I saw Thomas and a girl who might have been his sister. The rest was a mixture of South American and black kids. At the time, the significance of my being in the ethnic minority did not even occur to me.

Day one, class one. My desk mate, Anthony, gave me a supercilious look as I sat down beside him. He scratched a line allocating me a small region of writing room, and sneered, "That's yours, whitey." I gave him a quizzical look; the jibe really made no sense.

Ms. Flanders stood at the board and said we would be starting science with food chains. Okay, that was easy. She droned on about the various tiers of predators and prey, and went on to explain how the "decomposers," fungi, returned nutrients like NPK to the soil. She continued, "NPK stand for t'ree elemen's: nitrogen, phosphorous, and kryptonite."

I looked at the periodic table in the back of my science book and addressed her the way all the other students did. "Teacher, I think *K* actually stands for potassium."

She laughed. "Boy, they's no *K* in *potassium*. I'm the teacher here."

I looked back in the book. Right under sodium sat potassium, atomic number nineteen and marked with a large *K*.

After another dull class, Ms. Flanders left the classroom for an hour until lunch. I asked, "Wait, so what are we supposed to do? Is it lunch?"

A girl named Brenda replied, "No, we can't eat, but she won't be coming back until after lunch." A few kids grabbed Gameboys from their bags; the others either congregated around the miniature monitors or, like me, made paper airplanes and threw them at the fan swirling overhead. Dust rained down every time a piece of paper collided with the blade, which happened about every ten seconds. Through the dust one of the more outgoing of my classmates asked, "Hey, new guy, you like Ice Cube?"

"I kinda do like ice cubes actually."

"Ice Cube, the rapper, not ice cubes."

"Who's that?"

The boy's face fell into a look of severe disapproval. "How 'bout Fitty Cent?"

"Dunno, who that is."

"Usher?"

They gave up on me around the tenth musician.

Finally, somewhere outside, the cow bell rang for lunch. The dynamic of the class hardly changed; some kids started eating, some left, and a few came in. We were free, and I went to the bathroom. To get to the bathroom you had to go down the thirty feet of hallway away from the school yard; after a few steps along the perimeter of the building, you were at the doors.

I found Carl and several other boys playing Pokémon on a pair of Gameboys. I asked, "Why are you all playing in here?" The pale closet was dusty, dark, and smelled horrendous.

"So teacher no'a gwine catch us!"

Gameboys turned out to be a major black market in school. They were prohibited on pain of confiscation, but games were still swapped frequently. I joined the spectators watching the battle between the two colorful sprites. The sound of heavy footsteps resounded on the ground outside, and there was a frantic burst of whispering as the game boys were hidden. The corpulent teacher stuck her head in just in time to see the plastic disappear into someone's pocket. Carl knelt in the shadow of the sink, and I stood there blankly.

Ms. Flanders shouted, "You'a all gwine come to da principal office now'u!"

All but Carl, still unnoticed, walked out with their heads down. I followed them. The teacher put her hand on my chest, "Nah you! You new; me a gwine give you a chance."

As she walked off Carl crept out and whispered, "They're all gonna get licks now."

"Licks? Is that like, what, hitting?" I asked incredulously. "Is that legal?"

I was informed that the principal, had a leather belt in her desk, named Big Henry after a particularly mischievous, expatriate boy who had seen more than his fair share of the cracked leather.

The dejected line of boys trooped out of the principal's office, rubbing their hands, some crying. They glared at me and shouted, "S'nah fair! You no get licks 'cause you white!" This was the start of a very long trend of racism against me that so often took a form similar to this. It followed the incorrect logic that I was invulnerable because of my race. Clearly Henry had not been exempt from such punishment because he was Caucasian. Henry and I both demonstrate that the opposite of this was actually true; we were more often ostracized for our race and differences than we were protected by them.

Later that day we had Physical Education with Mr. Ramsey. In Nevis, winter is the running season. I watched Anthony cross the crooked arc of chalk along the road. Mr. Ramsey passed him a twenty-dollar bill. Giselle stumbled in behind him and was graced with a ten-dollar bill. Behind them another half-dozen or so dripped over the line, none the richer. Another twenty-five kids, including me, sat around. Someone covertly played their Gameboy, taking the risk wantonly. In my boredom, I volunteered to run.

Eyebrows raised, Mr. Ramsey snickered.

A boy from the grade above me shouted, "You can't run! You white."

Unsure of the sudden denial, my head fell in resignation and I stared at my arms folded in my lap. My arms and legs and hands leapt out in my vision, as pale as a coral beach. I jolted my head up and swerved around with an epiphany. My skin tone was not paralleled in any of the thirty-plus people surrounding me. I asked myself if that could really be the point of differentiation. Yes, yes it could.

When Dad picked me up at the end of the day he said, "Hey, how'd your first day go?"

I sighed and responded, "Eh, it was fine."

"Did you make any friends?"

I answered with the closest thing to the truth that would not cause concern. "Yeah, this Guyanese dude named Carl."

We eventually purchased a house on the other side of the island, in a small development above the town of Jessups. Our house was perched on the edge of chasm, called the *ghaut*. Although our new house was much closer to the med school, Charlestown Prep, and the beaches than our original rental, it was high in the mountain rainforest and daunting to reach. The island is circled by the main road, and from this road we headed uphill through the village of Jessups over dirt roads, and then onto a road that went even higher up the mountain. This nameless path was worse than what I had seen in some videos of off-roading: the two parallel concrete strips collapsing and eroded, the ground beneath them a minefield of large stones. The road was one lane, and in the event of oncoming traffic, both vehicles had to pull into the bushes to scrape past each other. Near the apex of the hill, this tortuous path crossed over the stream that eroded and formed the "ghaut," or gorge, and then went down a paved hill, descending almost as far as we had just gone up. We lived at the bottom of that hill. On a calm day, the stream splashed softly beneath the tires of our four-wheel-drive Land Rover; on days following storms, it was so torrential it was not safe to cross, sometimes for days.

Our house was pink concrete, the only material you could expect to last in the tropics, especially in the rainforest where we lived. The yard was spacious but unnatural; the developer had cleared the lot and planted most of what was there, with the only original flora being a pair of huge mango trees and several coconut palms. There was an unparalleled view over the rainforest to the Caribbean Sea, and in fact, we could see *Promise* on her mooring with binoculars. The most exciting feature for my sister and me, though, was that we had a troupe of Vervet monkeys that lived in the adjacent ghaut. Much like the ones we had seen in Grenada, these also were not indigenous to the island, but rather had been transported inadvertently from Africa. Their antics never ceased to amaze us as they swung from tree to tree, or snuck onto the expanse of grass to snack on mangoes and other fruit in our garden. However, Lara's love affair with them ended when, with the help of our neighbor, Chris, she planted a spectacular garden. The oblong planting bed included cucumbers, peppers, lettuce, watermelon, and even corn from the left-over kernels in the popcorn bag. Despite our dismissive comments that it would never grow, she tended to it with great ritual and it flourished. Just as it was approaching harvest time, we came home one day to the ravages of the monkeys, plant debris scattered about the yard. Only the vestiges of her labors and ruined vegetables remained. From that day forward, we could not even get her interested in the baby monkeys, who clung adorably to their mothers' underbellies as they traversed the lawn. Our realtor, Suzanne, who checked in on us periodically just to ensure all was still well, mentioned that we were definitely making the transition to locals; tourists always loved the monkeys, but residents often had to clean up their mess, and sometimes in poorer sections, even retaliated and used them for bush meat.

Above our house, the historic Upper Round Road passed just over the crest through an old coconut plantation. Unlike the main road, which went around the rim of the island and had secondary roads trickling up the mountain, in the Upper Round Road's prime the secondary roads started at the shore and went up the peak where they were linked by this road at an altitude of almost 1,000 feet. A few days after being settled in the new house, Mom and I decided to go find this old plantation. We walked up our hill to where the path allegedly started. At the vertex of the road, where it crumbled away into the ghaut on one side and was paved behind us, there was a third route, a shady road into the jungle. It was totally covered; dense mango trees and other dark foliage covered the road beneath us.

We came to a gate of wire and smoothed tree branches. Lifting the latch, we walked from the jungle into the swaying fields. The road went from dirt clearing to two strips of concrete. Although a century old, they remained in almost mint condition, so rarely were they trafficked. Our walk followed the undulations of the grassy hills, interrupted every 100 feet or so by a coconut palm, swinging more slowly than the golden grass around us. The path peaked on a knoll and then descended into an indistinct goat trail. The knoll was graced with giant casuarinas, their ambiguous outline of needles whispering in the breeze. Beneath these huge trees, the formidable plantation buildings stood in various states of disrepair. They were low stone structures, their mortar faltering in some places, resulting in a small pile of stones at the base of the wall. The centerpiece of this complex was the mill which was still mostly intact, except for the side facing the sea. Standing in the cylinder and looking through the gap at the flamboyant sunset was almost too perfect.

Not as enthralled by the sunset as Mom, I leapt down from the crumbling façade onto the grass and started to wander. There was an old pool, presumably a vat for processing crops that was now a center for cultivating algae. Mom walked out of the mill to find me dangling sloth-style from one of the casuarina's lower limbs. She called, "Alex, let's go! It's getting dark." I let go and landed in a haphazard crouch.

Over the next few weeks, school became decreasingly inspirational, and it really had not been very much so to begin with. Every morning, I walked to the bathroom across the hall from my bedroom and, with most of my hand down my throat, hacked and gagged. However. I was never able to induce vomiting, the concrete evidence which would have proved sufficient to keep me home. Still, I tried. "Mom, I really don't feel well! I cannot go to school today!"

She replied, "Well, if you feel worse later we can come pick you up. In the meantime, just pack yourself a couple of pieces of white bread or saltines for lunch; we don't want to give you anything too challenging for your stomach." After a week of going to school with really bland lunches, I ceased my efforts to stay home.

Almost on a nightly basis Mom and I would retreat into our fields of golden glow. It was the most removed sanctuary, and was therapeutic for stress on many levels. Those walks became increasingly essential to our mental health as time elapsed. Our other escape hatch was more inclusive for the whole family and, frankly, tremendously more exciting. Mom's best friend on the faculty at the med school, Marcy, was always willing to take her Friday class, giving Mom a long weekend. Dad was a dean at that point, and was about as much on Caribbean time as one could expect at a graduate school, and Lara and I lost nothing in missing a day of classes, so we would go out to *Promise* before the sun rose and head over to St. Bart's for the weekend. The fifty-mile downwind run to St. Bart's always seemed to be over before it had begun. Our time in the modern "Paris of the Caribbean," always elapsed far too quickly, and then we would have to make the long sail into the wind back to Nevis.

I treasured those glimpses of the life I had wanted to continue living aboard ship, the life I should have had instead of that on Nevis. Of course, it made it so much harder the following Monday to put on my uniform, a sky-blue button-down and khaki shorts. As the running season in Nevis approached its climax, classes often were not held, and the athletes, including my desk mate Anthony, were always out running. This meant a large portion of my time was spent throwing paper planes at the fan, disassembling and reassembling my retractable pens, and walking in circles around the younger kids' section of the school. This area was quiet for me, despite the fact that kindergarteners ran around screaming their heads off. They usually ignored me, and in their infrequent interactions with me harbored no animosity. Their truly childlike innocence was admirable.

The last day of the term, like many others, had no formal activities, but this time it was a fully intentional decision by the administration. It was an all-day recess and the dress code had been waived. I stayed in my classroom with some other fifth-grade boys, where Jeremy, one of the larger boys, was demonstrating wrestling moves he had seen on television. I was feeling optimistic about school that day; I was as close to being a part of the pack as I had ever been, and I tackled Jeremy. After a few seconds of trying to knock the legs out from under him, he reached down, locked my head in the crook of his arm, and ran my skull into the wall.

He must have heard my groan since he let go and asked, "Y'ok?"

Dizzied, I held my head and walked to the nearest chair.

Carl called out to me somberly, "Hey, Twitchy, check out the floor."

Someone exclaimed "Oh me ahm! He a'be bleeding!" A couple of red blots covered the floor. I looked at the hand I had had on my head. It too, was red.

All the students in the classroom escorted me to the bathroom, taking care to avoid teachers, for an impromptu clinic. Half an hour of nursing from my classmates did little to stop the bleeding, so I walked out into the sunlight and called, "Teacher!" I wandered around the school yard with half the school following as spectators, until I found a member of the faculty. I held my blood-covered hand up in greeting and then pointed to my head.

She demanded, "Who did this to you?"

I looked at Jeremy. He looked at me with deliberate, lucid blankness; I knew I would see him next term, so I said, "I tripped and fell into the wall."

The cut required multiple sutures, and was more than enough to push my parents to withdraw me from Charlestown Prep. After receiving no education and a decent injury, it was time for me to join Lara at Bellevue. First, and more importantly, though, it was vacation.

We used our typical escape hatch, and sailed for St. Barts. With so much time on our hands, we also sailed to St. Martin. In a sudden twist of fate while on the French side of St. Martin we passed an animal shelter and walked in. Two kittens, about six weeks old, one orange the other grey (Buttercup and Smoky, respectively), and both terrifically fluffy, came home with us.

Upon returning to Nevis, we declared the kittens to Customs, and produced their certificates of health noting that they were vaccinated, dewormed, and from rabies-free St. Martin. The one veterinarian on island proclaimed that the French did not have enforceable policies, and that they needed to be deported immediately or incinerated the next day. We would also be fined $2500. We frantically searched for an expeditious solution, calling everyone we knew. It was the last hour for the kittens when we were contacted by Jillian, owner of the popular hilltop restaurant Bananas, who happened to be flying to St. Martin the following day. The coconut telegraph had worked efficiently and she had heard about our plight. Amazingly, the government was willing to let her take Smoky and Buttercup back to their country of origin. My father still refers to them as the $5,000 invisible cats, after donations made to the various animal shelters, shots, transport, and fines.

After our dramatic spring break, it was back to school, and this time it was an incredibly different experience. I joined Lara at the only truly private, primary school on island, Bellevue. Although only half a mile away from Charlestown Prep, it seemed to be a different island. The one-room building was under a grove of towering flame trees, with a field expanding behind it. The school was run by three teachers, one for each pair of grades. The fifth- and sixth-grade teacher (and principal)—my teacher—was Marcella Jones.

My emotional and personal memory regarding this woman has become slightly faded with the passage of time; however, about fifteen months after starting Bellevue, I wrote this on my boarding school applications:

> In my fifth- and sixth-grade years I had an outstanding teacher who meant a great deal to me. Mrs. Marcella Jones was an amazing person whom I really admired. Let me show you why.
>
> During fifth grade, I moved to the small Caribbean nation of St. Kitts and Nevis. It was a radically different culture and society from what I was used to. Mrs. Jones helped me acclimate to my new surroundings with endless kindnesses. There were so many different customs and subtleties of language here that I was totally unfamiliar with. She introduced me to the local greetings, which require always establishing a relationship with someone prior to directing business. That is, you have to meet someone, exchange "How are you?" greetings, listen for the responses, and respond appropriately, before even considering requesting help or direction! She handled, with gentle good humor, my interpretation of the local dialect and accent, and my pronunciation of Nevisian phrases.
>
> Nevisians, and especially Mrs. Jones, love music; it's a tremendously important part of their culture. We had to sing local folksongs for performances like the National Schools in Concert. The night of the performance, I was terrified. She stood where I could see her, flashed me her radiant smile, and gave me confidence as the only Caucasian on stage in the national stadium belting out the tunes.
>
> Mrs. Jones was a large person, a true presence; she was married to a preacher and we often commented that she

96

had similar qualities. Because all of the members of the community respected her, she had complete control over her class, and the school, as she was also the Principal. She led by positive example and love, not fear, and that positive energy spread throughout the school. I felt safe in her presence because no one would dare to tease the new kid if she might be just possibly around the corner.

While teaching me about the culture of Nevis and helping me to grow into it, she also was one of the best teachers I've ever had. She had a way of making normally obscure concepts crystal clear. She also kept an air of openness and warmth in the classroom, which meant you were always safe asking questions. Her enthusiastic and lively presentation of material kept everyone actively involved and focused on whatever lesson we were doing.

I admire her for all of the components she has that make a terrific teacher: wisdom, intelligence, kindness, and positive energy. She helped me tremendously during a difficult transition in my life. She has been a great influence on my life in a very positive way, and it has been my great privilege to know her.

Honestly, Mrs. Jones was the most charismatic woman I have ever come across. This was apparent that first day she showed me around. She had an ebullient personality, a booming voice, and upon meeting me was just short of hugging me instead of a shaking my hand.

Kids continued to trickle in as the start of the school day drew near. The student body was significantly more diverse than that at Charlestown Prep; there was an almost even distribution of black, South American, and Caucasian children, and they proved to be open and welcoming, including me in a preclass game of capture the flag. I had not run and laughed so genuinely in months, not since before my bout with leptospirosis.

As we ran about, a large golden Chevy Suburban pulled into the driveway, unloading two children and their mother. The two siblings bore more resemblance to each other than either would ever admit:

both had cherubic faces, although the older brother was blond and stocky while his younger sister was a dainty redhead.

"Alex! Come here and meet another new student!" Mrs. Jones called.

I trotted over and waved to the two and their mother behind them. The two new kids waved back.

"I'm Max," said the boy.

His sister added, "And I'm Kate."

Their mother extended a hand for me to shake. "Hi, I'm Millie." She had the distinct accent of the British upper class. Max and Kate followed me back to the game.

It turned out that they had just moved to the island, and specifically to Fern Hill Gardens, adjacent to where we lived. After school, I went home with Max, the both of us desperate to break our solitude. He had only been on Nevis for a week or two, and he missed his old life, too. I remember trying to dissuade him from that by introducing the notion that it really was not so bad here. I forced optimism upon myself—although I, too, was pretty happy to be in the presence of someone I could grace with the term "friend."

Max pulled out a boombox and started blasting some rock music; then he grabbed a couple of Airsoft guns, diminutive versions of BB guns that could be shot at other people, safely. I bombarded him with questions: "How do you load this thing? Oh, by the way, who is this singing? I've heard it before, I think …"

He smiled. "It's Green Day, man!"

I lied, "Oh, duh, of course."

"Here, you need this," he said, handing me a plastic face-mask. "Before we can use this stuff we need to see if you can take a shot." I stepped back a few paces and removed my shirt. He lazily brought his arm up and fired. The pinprick hit me in chest, leaving a small pink dot.

I shrugged and said, "Your turn," as I threw the mask back to him. He donned it and ran. Picking up the gun he had loaded and then dropped, I ran around his house the other way.

Max made Nevis bearable. I had a friend, and he lived very close. Just how close did not become apparent until we had known each other for a month or so. It was his turn to come over to my house, and when we got there he called to my mom, "We're going to be outside!" Then turning to me, he said, "I got something to show you. Come on!"

We walked down the driveway and he made a right, walking along the outside of the fence, toward the ghaut. We kept our hands out so we did not trip onto the barbed wire on top of our fence. Although intimidating, the fence was not there for the purpose of keeping out people. Indeed, Max and I grew quite proficient at getting over it, as did the myriad monkeys who lived in our forest and often sat on or swung from it. Rather, its purpose was to keep out goats and other foliage eaters who fancied the tropical shrubs.

We reached the corner of my yard, and a path extended downward before us. Totally overgrown, the dirt strip wound down the steep slope. We skidded down it on our heels, keeping one hand out to slow ourselves down on trees and the other in front of our faces to block the frequent spiderwebs. A few hundred vertical feet later, we were in the bottom of the ghaut, a dried streambed strewn with boulders. The irregular streambed wound away in both directions, closely followed by the jungle-covered cliffs we had just come down. The largest trees extended over the ghaut, leaving little direct sunlight to reach us. What did reach us, though, was far more intriguing: vines. These natural bundles of fiber easily held us, and standing on the tallest boulder, we swung out over the stony ground a good twenty feet up: a fatal fall if done wrong, amazing at all other times.

Just as we had come down from my side of the ghaut, there was a path leading up his side of the ghaut. It ended right in someone's yard, and that someone lived right in Fern Hill Gardens. With sticks and spiders in our hair, we walked proudly up the path to his house.

By that time, not only had my own social life expanded, but our family acquaintances had also. We established friendships with some of the other expatriate families whose children were enrolled in Bellevue. This included the Terry family and the Sinclair family. The Terrys had come to escape the first world (Great Britain), and had lived there for the better part of a decade. Sarah was a physician like my parents, and her husband John was a sailor-turned-financier who always preferred to be barefoot. The Sinclairs had been brought here on work. The husband, Martin, who was from New Zealand, was head manager at Nevis' Four Seasons Resort, a favorite of Princess Di; his wife Tori was an artist.

June and hurricane season came hand in hand, and Nevis was well outside the insurable zone for boats. So Dad pulled together an impromptu crew of John Terry, our neighbor Harry Hallstrom, and Max's dad, Jason, and they sailed *Promise* to safety in Trinidad. During the four days they were absent, the families of the intrepid crew organized mass sleepovers. The first night was hosted at our place: the four mothers and nine kids left on Nevis all came to spend the night. We watched movies from sleeping bags. Popcorn was abundant.

The second night was at the Terrys, and that was of a similar, euphoric nature.

The day before Dad came home, Mom picked us up from school late. As we walked to the car, she said, "All right, guys I have a friend in the backseat, and I want you to be nice, okay?" Looking through the windshield, I did not see anything, but when I opened the door her guest bleated. On a hand towel in the backseat was a black baby goat, umbilical cord and all.

I laughed, "Well, he's cute! We … we're not keeping him, are we?"

Mom shook her head, "Oh, God, no! He's too cute, but he was abandoned so I think we should bring him up to Dan and Marty's!"

Dan was another close friend, an MD and PhD who taught at the medical school. A little on the old-hippy side, he had long, thinning blond hair, a brilliant mind, and a maniacal laugh, and he ran several miles in the Nevisian heat daily. Marty was his upbeat bohemian wife, and together they ran an Animal Rescue Center, the ARC, in their backyard.

Dan and Marty's home and animal center was in the low, dry hills by the med school, a small wooden cottage with an extensive yard full of goats, sheep and chickens. There was also a donkey and a mammoth pig.

Marty called out in her Kentucky twang, "Well, who'd you bring over?" She smiled as she took him in her arms. "Well, thanks for bringing 'im in. Definitely the right place for 'im." She put him down on the ground and he wandered away. Looking back at us she asked, "Hey, are you guys interested in kittens abandoned by their momma?"

After the St. Martin cat incident, and with Dad not around to veto, our answer was an enthusiastic, "Yes!" The only trouble was digging up the well cover they were under, and then fishing out the ones that fell into the water as we reached for them. They were as feral as kittens could get and hissed and sputtered in a vain attempt to keep us at bay, and delay their first flea bath and deworming. They were pathetically ineffective, as they were malnourished and only about five weeks old. Lara aptly named them the ferocious felines. They acclimated quickly enough once saucers of milk and oodles of love were heaped upon them. When Dad returned, he only allowed us to keep two; one was given to a med student feeling lonely, the last and tiniest feline went to the Sinclairs. This particular kitten met an untimely demise as it was literally devoured in their yard by a semi-feral dog, unfortunately right in front of the children.

Summer was over before it started, and in the fall, most of the pupils and all the teachers at Bellevue had transferred to the new Lynn Jeffers Primary School. Lynn Jeffers had been a mediocre, very small, private secondary school on the island for some years, but after some issues arose in Bellevue, and some ensuing lobbying, Lynn Jeffers expanded to include students as young as first graders.

To accommodate the larger student body, the school also moved buildings, into a newly constructed, two-story yellow structure right next to the old Bellevue (which incidentally moved as well). The school budget was wan at best, and after the walls were raised and the floors were laid, construction ceased from lack of funds. So, throughout the preceding August, several parents of students had come in to work on a daily basis. Tori worked with some others on painting the building, and Max and I were always in there helping our parents, hauling trash, scraping cement spackle off windows, or clearing debris from the yard.

The result was quite a neat schoolhouse. In my third different uniform of the past eight months, school seemed basically to be the same as at Bellevue. It was mainly the same group of heterogeneous kids, and the faculty, with some additions since now each grade would have its own teacher. After a herculean effort by everyone before school officially started, on the first day we students all lined up by grade and marched in to the downstairs atrium, where assembly was held for the primary school. The secondary school students had their own assembly upstairs.

Father Francis, whose daughter was in Lara's class, conducted assembly. This involved the same little blue testaments they had had at Charlestown Prep. He selected passages and had us read aloud with him, and then he dove head-first into a self-righteous speech proclaiming that if we did not live by the words we had read, we would go to hell. A small Indian girl from the first grade raised her hand and asked, "Father Francis, why are we going to hell?" This was how we always started our day, and the questions of confusion came to a stop after it became apparent that they would just result in our damnation.

Mrs. Jones was still my teacher, since she had chosen to teach sixth grade again. We were a small class, four strong and all transferees from Bellevue. Although the curriculum could be mundane, Mrs. Jones brought it to life, often with her voice alone. During the more desperately dull days, she would take us outside and we would have class under the enormous mango trees in the school yard. The only class I did not have Mrs. Jones for was science, which had a volunteer teacher from the medical school: Mom. She taught the whole primary school science, clustering us into three groups, two grades each. This meant Max, who was a year younger, would have this one class with me. She had an attitude borrowed from Ms. Frizzle and the *Magic School Bus* that encouraged getting messy, making mistakes, and subsequently learning from them. Science was often the highlight of my academic day, both in and out of the classroom.

Generally, the primary and secondary divisions of the school kept their distance from each other, but not entirely. Two older expat students who were both children of faculty, Rachel and Patrick, frequently hung out with Max and me. They were not really expatriates; they had both spent their whole lives on Nevis. Rachel was an aspiring musician, and Patrick was an amateur physicist and mathematician. I was the only one who would play his arcane games of numbers and patterns against him with any success, and he taught me plenty of cosmology, quantum mechanics, and electrical circuitry. One day, at the lunch table, he opened his lunchbox and out fell a sandwich, some wires, a piece of foil, and a transformer from a car. We set it up so that when you tapped one wire on the foil quickly, it would send a high voltage current through the other two electrodes. We wanted to see who could endure the current through their hands the longest: Max or me. That was practical science at its best.

Mom had more organized, and perhaps more civilized, opportunities to test our scientific competence practically. Toward the end of the year, a science fair was organized by the science teachers (Mom, Patrick's mother, and Ms. Joshi, the secondary-school physics and math instructor). About half the student body did a presentation, including everyone in Mom's fifth- and sixth-grade class. Max made a wing based on Bernoulli's principle, and I made a wind generator from coat hangers and components from Radio Shack that my Grandma had brought down on her last visit. Our projects both required wind power, and we were put at a demonstration table together with the one fan in the school. In my naïveté I actually proposed putting up large-scale versions of my model on the windward side of the island, to harness the constant twenty-plus knot trade winds for free energy. Similar facilities existed in the French islands we had visited and were quite successful. This seemed especially pertinent since Nevlec, the island power company, was dysfunctional, so almost every home had a generator, and electric clocks were never counted on in Nevis given they reset with each power outage.

Sixth grade was a very happy time for me: academics were easy but inspirational, and my social world underwent a total renovation. My breadth of experience expanded outside of school sessions as well. Some of my favorite events were the school music-festival fundraisers. Held at a downtown courtyard café, these evening activities always drew a crowd. Students with any musical capabilities were put under the spotlight early on—I performed the Eagles' "Hotel California"—and then the more skilled parents, friends, and medical students brought out their instruments.

The medical students, an eclectic and diverse group of people, came at the drop of a hat when my mom said, "There's a fundraiser for kids if you want to play some music ..." They responded with generosity for any of a number of causes, be it the local school or the Special Olympics. Max and I joined half a dozen future doctors from around the world in performing Coldplay, and their enthusiasm was infectious. Part of their zeal was from their passion for music, but the event also inspired them. They knew the invaluable nature of education, many having grown up in desperate situations and having made an escape through education alone. The med students on Nevis were all bright and extremely dedicated, driven by real motives, and only missed admission to the American schools a tier above because they did not have the formal background of their more privileged competitors. For example, there was a girl who had grown up in Botswana and had been given all the wealth of her village to fund her education so she could return someday and maintain the health of her kin and neighbors.

Another remarkable encounter I had with people of the medical school that year was with Peter Schnabel. He had a PhD in pharmacology, and was pursuing his MD at the med school; and, he was an Olympic-level fencer. Peter may have been an outstanding scientist, but he lived and breathed fencing. The tall German had scars on his face from duels, and he looked every inch the nineteenth-century German cavalier. Together, he and Dad organized a fencing club, and after New Year's, several trunks of fencing gear arrived. Multiple families from Lynn Jeffers expressed an avid interest in joining.

Every Saturday at ten o'clock, fencing met at Lynn Jeffers. Peter taught us in the way of his maestro: nothing but drills for the first month. Standing in our thick canvas jackets and tight masks in the middle of the schoolyard, we moved as he directed: "Advance, retreat, double advance, lunge." As terrific fun as it was, it never really trained us for what to do in the event someone actually pulled a blade on us.

One Saturday had been an especially long session, as we had a ranked tournament, and Peter, Dad, and I were the last ones to leave. As Peter drove off, Dad and I loaded our gear into the trunk. Once I had sat down in the passenger seat Dad put the keys in the ignition and turned them, the engine cranking. That was when someone tapped his window.

Tall and skinny, he was about twenty years old, and had a bandana wrapped around his head. Dad opened the door and said, "Hey, can I help you?"

The guy pulled the door further open and slurred, "Hey, man. Listen, some guys beat up me uncle downtown. An' I really love dis uncle; he pay for my school and my phone … and dese guys jus' beat him up. I really got to get to town, but I can't get a bus since me got no money. Can you'a spare me some cash?"

He was clearly intoxicated; we were right in the heart of town. Dad tried to deny him, saying we had to go. The man frowned and yanked the keys from the ignition.

Dad remained calm and tried to placate him. "Hey, buddy, I need those; I'll give you some cash for a bus, okay?" He opened his wallet and took a twenty EC bill out.

The man said, "So, where do you live? I want to be able to come by and pay you back."

Dad held his palm up in refusal, saying, "No, this is an important thing for you and I'm happy to help."

The guy nodded, the bandana flopping as he did so. He then added, "Hey, did I tell you I was a magician?" In one smooth motion he procured a machete, reached over Dad, and held it to my throat. The blade, an inch from my skin, smelled strongly of rust, a similar odor to blood. "Gimme the rest of the cash."

No longer in a position to negotiate, Dad grabbed the wad of bills, about the value of $100 US, and handed it to him. The guy smiled as he pushed the machete closer to my neck, "Let me get a good look at your son, just in case you go to the police." He drew the blade back slowly, keeping it level with my neck. Taking a few paces back, he tossed Dad the keys and waved in farewell.

That began the downfall of my love for Nevis. It was also the start of a disturbing trend that contaminated our view of the island: precipitously increasing crime. As terrifying as the machete held to my throat was, it was not the most dramatic event that month. Our best friends from Connecticut came to visit us for the Christmas holidays. They stayed with us the first week; then, as a favor to our friend Marcy, decided to house sit for her as she was going off island and rented a house from none other than a sitting Supreme Court Justice of the United States. My friend Tazer had a gun put to him in his bedroom in the Justice's house, while his parents sat on the living room sofa. Although considered only a robbery (as no one was hurt), it was traumatic for everyone. Nevis was not supposed to have guns; they were banned. Their presence was insidiously increasing, though, along with gangs, drugs, and murder. While we were there, these problems were not quite significant enough to drive us away, however; there were other factors that accomplished that feat.

Alex at the helm for the passage northward to Nevis

Alex in uniform from Bellevue

Lara hiking up to the sugar mill with Alex after school

A surprising stowaway iguana warms himself on our dinghy

Chapter 9

PACIFIC BOUND

My third year in Nevis was marked by the transition from primary school. In the States, I would have gone to junior high or middle school. In Nevis, I went into high school. The British and consequently Nevisian system of secondary school uses the term "form" to define secondary grade levels, so I went into first form, and theoretically would graduate in sixth form. This was a complex transition, because it not only brought about a change in the dynamic of my education, but also that of the entire school.

That was the year Mom became the chairman of the school board. The secondary education system was horrendously outdated, and really quite provincial. Bringing the full weight of her academic and educational prowess down on Lynn Jeffers, she implemented an independent evaluation system in quantitative and linguistic proficiency; added well-trained new members to the faculty; and established a new, integrated curriculum for the secondary division that would incorporate aspects from each subject and all parts of the world. She envisioned the staff teaching to international standards, while navigating the tricky waters of local pride and the suboptimal existing curriculum called CXC, Caribbean Examinations Council. This meant that, when we went to visit family in Connecticut that summer, our bags came back significantly heavier; they contained several dozen textbooks for geography and world history, as well as a dozen copies each of several literary classics like *Lord of the Flies*, *The Tempest*, and *The Odyssey*. She was committed to bolstering not only my formal education, but also that of my peers. She had befriended the children through her efforts to teach them the scientific method and true inquiry, rather than the previous method of rote memorization. She recognized in the students the potential to learn more, to be more, than what was expected of them. However, that was really only a portion of her motivation.

One of the factors that pushed her so strongly to reinvent the school system, especially with specialized testing for children with learning disabilities, was because of Lara's teacher, Mrs. Anderson. Mrs. Anderson had three children, all enrolled in a public primary school. This included her severely autistic daughter, Sonia. The teachers had not known what to do with Sonia, who would wander and was non-verbal, so at times they simply tied her to a chair and liberally used their right of corporeal punishment, something uniquely banned at Lynn Jeffers. Mrs. Anderson's predicament was worsened by her husband, a pastor, who claimed Sonia was punishment from God because Mrs. Anderson had "done something wicked." He had moved to Antigua to distance himself from her, and had attempted to take the two other kids with him. Mom became a personal source of condolence and support for Mrs. Anderson, and was always greatly impressed by her strength and fortitude.

Under my mother's direction, the school expanded, as many new students and families were attracted to the school. Mom was on local television and met with the Premier of Nevis several times, as well as with his secretary of education, to try to facilitate better treatment for disabled students and better training programs for teachers throughout the island. She had learned that Nevisians had a strong national pride combined with xenophobia after years of abuse as a colonial jurisdiction. Although the Nevisians believed strongly in education, it was largely a system based on rote memorization and limited scope. She offered free special programs for teacher training on many subjects, from reading recovery to level teaching to differentiated lesson plans, and recruited talented, capable educators to help implement programs and donate materials. The combined student body of this improved private school more than doubled through her efforts. After the new enrollment campaign, assembly was now a conjoined event that took place outside, since there was no room of adequate volume for us all. We were lined up in rows by grade, and this put in me in line with the same three classmates from the previous year, as well as with a dozen other new students who had joined from other primary schools. I was the only expat in the class, as my classmates were all indigenous Nevisians, and I was leaving Max behind in the primary school, but still I felt cautiously optimistic as the year began. Our new volunteer principal, another member of the faculty from the medical school, strode in front of us and said, "Good morning, students."

"Good morning, principal," we chorused back.

He launched in to a speech about the new school year, how we were going to work together and excel. He also gestured to all the members of the faculty and introduced them: "… And we have some new faculty as well. Ms. Jesgar will be teaching history and literature to the high schoolers, and will be homeroom teacher for first form. Mr. Mengi, who will teach information technology, will be upstairs as well. And last but certainly not least, Miss Reynolds, who belongs to the Peace Corps group here on Nevis, and is to teach economics. Please give them all a warm welcome!" We clapped diligently.

We all filed upstairs, my classmates and I especially quiet, most of us strangers to each other. We all sat down in our homeroom, a well-lit corner room on the second floor. Ms. Jesgar, or Ms. J as she was more often called, walked in. She was the fiancée of a medical student, and had gotten her degrees in teaching a few years prior to coming to Nevis. After her US training, she had gone on to teach at a school for the deaf; she herself was reliant upon hearing aids after a bad bout of meningitis as a child. Her genuine smile was close to constant as she orchestrated introductions in her southern accent and reviewed what we would be studying the upcoming year. Fifty minutes later, first form was looking about as good as sixth grade; the work would be more inspiring as we started studying ancient civilizations and reading works such as *Animal Farm*.

"I'll be back after midmorning break and we can take a look at history then, okay?" she finished. "And Mrs. Wood should be here for math in a moment." In fact, Mrs. Wood was standing there. Ms. J smiled at her and slipped past.

Mrs. Wood took a step into the room and stood there, staring us down. She opened her mouth and said, invoking decades of Nevisian dogma, "Don't you know that you should stand when a teacher enters the room?" We jumped to our feet as she let the words drip from her tongue. Sitting at the teacher's desk she said, "Sit down and open your books to page one."

The Caribbean text had a cartoon depicting the construction of the pyramids, a scholar with a thought bubble performing the arithmetic of when they would finish, and a thought bubble over the slaves hauling stones with the text, "Instead of calculating, why doesn't he come help us?" She smiled at the image and said, "None of you are laughing. Isn't that funny?" No one could muster a chuckle.

We picked up where I had left off in fourth grade, and she paced about the room, stopping to comment on my work. "What are you doing? You missed a step, and why are the problems so close?" She yanked the notebook from my hands and, taking someone else's ruler, drew lines separating each problem. Handing it back to me, she said, "Like that. Now start over." I looked at the boy next to me, Kari. He had done what I did originally, so I asked, "Like Kari, Mrs. Wood?" She looked over his work and proclaimed it was satisfactory.

Mrs. Wood also taught geography, and gave me the lowest grade in the class (and of my academic career), a D minus. It seemed I simply could not put together a proper flow diagram for "how a school uniform is made," in geography class. Whenever I inquired for further detail or politely challenged a statement of hers, the response was always along the lines of, "You think you can do whatever you want because you're white and your mother is the chairman?"

This statement reflects her issues not just with me, but with Mom. For her geography class, Mrs. Wood used the 1980s edition of local national book, which outlined a year-long geography course dedicated exclusively to all 101 square miles of the country. In addition to excessive redundancy and inanity, this was also directly in conflict with the world geography mandated to complete the integrated curriculum—for example, studying the geography of the Mediterranean when concomitantly learning about ancient Greece in World History and reading Homer's *Odyssey* in World Literature. To be fair, the narrow focus was reactive to the previous British curriculum utilized before nationalism that had students just as inanely memorizing the names of boroughs in London. Passing by the faculty lounge's door after school one day, I heard a teacher say that she did not feel that it was right that the Board was now "making kids study Egypt, Marco Polo and other American heroes." Balance seemed elusive.

The teachers I had in first form were split about evenly, with half inspiring and half infuriating, but the selective animosity toward me tipped the scale, and school degenerated for me. Even in classes such as Information Technology, History, and Literature, where the teachers were as bright and animated as you can encounter, the antipathy of my peers was depressing.

Although of a different nature, Lara had her fair share of troubles. She was not concerned by the academics or lack thereof; her troubles revolved around her mild autism and the impact of that on her social world. In Lynn Jeffers, that was a very small social world. Ostracized, she only reluctantly would eat lunch with her peers, and during recess she would find a quiet, distant corner of the school yard to sit quietly alone and read. "What's wrong with your sister, Alex?" was a question I received frequently, and loathed more and more with each instance. I always defended her from the leering questions by saying, "Nothing; she's fine." I was becoming aware that this really was not the case, but the formal diagnosis was nebulous and abstruse, and I could come up with no better alternative.

One day, after having an all-school photo taken on the front steps, a girl from my class was as much in Lara's face as possible, literally nose to nose while prodding her verbally. I grabbed the girl's shoulder and snarled, "Don't we have to get back to class?"

She stood up and looked down her nose at me saying, "Your sister's weird."

I smiled at Lara and asked, "You okay, Acorn?" She nodded and walked back inside.

Ms. J pulled me aside, and said, "Alex, I know this may not make you feel much better, but I get what you two are going through."

I looked back at her and she continued with wet eyes, "Well, you know I'm pretty deaf, and people made so much fun of me in school, and my brother too, because I was his sister. I know this is a bit different, but I do get it."

I smiled sadly, "Thanks, Ms. J."

There was other support for me as well, including on the academic side, which was what I craved desperately. A large force in this was a brilliant Canadian who had recently moved to the island with his family, Poku Forson. Poku was an entrepreneur extraordinaire, a business manager and software developer whose overall focus and passion lay in education. This was a saving grace for me but a death trap for him as he got thrown into the Lynn Jeffers maelstrom. My mother and her education committee worked with Poku to try to get an International Baccalaureate (IB) program implemented. She cajoled him into running for a position on the board, and they were able to get the resolution for IB passed easily. They then set about the task of familiarizing the existing staff with the program. Predictably, the old and new faculty fell into their two camps, and it became clear that the ideological battle would continue for some time. After conducting midyear evaluations on the math and science faculty, Poku insisted that I escape Mrs. Wood's incompetence and be handed over to the math teacher of the upper forms (ninth to eleventh grades), Mrs. Joshi.

As Mrs. Wood stepped into the room for math, I stood with the rest of the class and then left alone, my back burning from glares. Knocking on the door to the faculty lounge, I met Mrs. Joshi at the large desk in the center of the bright, cluttered room. Mrs. Joshi was a petite Indian woman with short hair coiled on top of her head and with small rectangular glasses. I borrowed the text book from a friend two years older, and we tackled problems of geometry and algebra. My first encounter with algebra was a problem involving water at different temperatures, and what the temperature would be if mixed in varying proportions. I spent about twenty minutes on it for homework, and came in with the solution. She looked at it and seemed perplexed, then laughed, "Alex, you did get the right answer, but, you didn't use any algebra—that was the whole point!"

I pointed at the figures, saying, "But there's such an obvious connection there, you can just see what it is!" I also developed a tendency to over-solve problems, devising absurdly intricate solutions, which was a constant source of amusement for Mrs. Joshi. My one-on-one sessions for math were just before lunch, and this daily respite from the world often extended into my time to eat as we ignored the clock.

I was lifted entirely from the wrath of Wood when I came back from spring break to find a new teacher for geography, one who did not blatantly ignore the integrated curriculum mandated by the school: Mom. Finally using the dense textbooks we had brought on the flight from home, Mom taught us all about Africa, often pulling from her own experiences of conducting research in Ghana. This course was eventually handed over to someone even more experienced with Africa,

Mr. Mengi, who had grown up in Congo before escaping the slaughter euphemized as the "national revolution."

Mr. Mengi ignited the course with his passion, and creatively interfaced it with a series of world UNESCO days. In conjunction with our Peace Corps teacher, and other upper school faculty, we participated in this larger world event, which served to draw us more vigorously into global participation. Workshops were presented by some of the older students on the various sites where UNESCO fought to elevate the residents. My segment was on Jamaica, and on child abuse there. I had read multiple indignant articles on the treatment of children there but it was not until the middle of talking about this, while on the subject of corporeal punishment, that I realized that this was nearly identical to what happened on Nevis. I had gotten so involved with my research and taken on the persona of UNESCO spokespeople that I had completely forgotten my own experiences at Charlestown Prep. I was telling many of the students present that what they considered a normal childhood was actually abuse by some standards.

That realization was one that changed how I saw my own perception of Nevis. I had lived there for almost three years and had been educated in local schools; I thought I had gotten to know the place. But really I was only just beginning to understand the island and subsequently my hardships there. Given all that was said to me, race was clearly a factor in perpetuating such strife. This genuinely surprised me at the time, as all of my family and friends were of heterogeneous ethnicities and color blind. Xenophobia and nationalistic pride were a component; after having lived in a colony, Nevisians needed to prove their capacity for independence of international forces, which is why some of the local teachers were so intent on teaching their way, not the IB way, even though it was a private school. Social class could not have been a major part though, since there were many local families of distinctly greater wealth than us, and they partook in harassing us as much as anyone on the island. Those families all had congregated to Lynn Jeffers too, often complicating my education as they interfered with the school's inner workings.

Our Canadian educator, Poku, and his wife, Nicole—who was also deeply involved with education—became close friends of our family, outside of the battleground over Lynn Jeffers and the local education system. When people all greatly concerned about education are all put in the same room together, something is bound to happen, and in this case, it led to my reinvention. Sitting down in the Forsons' living room, I was presented a comprehensive list of top boarding schools in Canada and New England, their specialties, available clubs, and a handful of statistics. About a week later, I sat down to take the SSAT, the standardized test for boarding school admissions. Having not been in formal schooling with first-world standardized tests since grade three, my percentiles were weak, but would improve. After that, I was thrust into a second education, an all-round training from Poku. We trained in math, speed-reading techniques, vocabulary (and how to work with words I did not actually know), writing, and exam techniques. This was a couple times a week after school, although the schedule was sporadic; Poku traveled a lot. Regardless of these frequent absences, I still logged a tremendous number of hours under his focus.

A later phase of the self-revolution was the interview process, an integral part of applying to boarding schools. My options for boarding in second form (eighth grade) were few, since most US schools start a year later. My favorite option was actually Poku's alma mater, the prestigious Upper Canada College (UCC). One of their interview officers flew down to Nevis, and interviewed me in Poku's home. I was petrified as I walked in and shook the tall brunette's hand, but quickly discovered that the admissions director was an exceedingly amicable woman, who had a son my age at UCC and offered to unofficially adopt me for my time in Canada, so I would have a person whose house I could go to over long weekends and breaks. At that point, UCC really seemed like the way to go, and I was set on going there. Since my school was paralyzed with a divided faculty and overt tension, and Nevis was in the middle of an overall death spiral for me, I was fairly intent on leaving. I was done with my peers' hatred of my academic success and race. I was done with teachers without a sense of fairness. I knew I would be leaving much, though: inspiring faculty like Mrs. Joshi, Mr. Mengi, and Ms. J., and a cluster of friends with whom I had walked the burning path. Still, the presence of these amazing people simply did not outweigh the suffocating atmosphere. With a week to go before a final response was made, my vacillations had finished, and I held only the slightest hesitation about accepting my position at UCC.

I was lying in bed reading when Mom walked in with a spiral notebook. She sat down alongside me, and showed me the leaf of paper with the heading, "*The Mommy Plan: Two*," a scheme that tipped my world upside down, again. *The Mommy Plan: One* had sent us sailing away in June of 2003. In abstract, this second plan explained how we would leave Nevis in under a year, and we would have Ken, who sailed with us down the Atlantic from the Bermuda Race, sail *Promise* to Tahiti, where we would pick her up, then sail her across the Pacific to Australia to sell, and then fly back to Connecticut and pick up our lives there. I could apply to other boarding schools, as well as UCC again, for ninth grade. I looked from the paper to Mom and back at her writing. I had never wanted to come to Nevis; I had wanted to keep sailing. This would be a whole three years late, and we would not be performing a full circumnavigation, but it was close, and as good as we could get. It meant another term at Lynn Jeffers though. A dream resurrected, and a nightmare prolonged: it was worth it, and I declined the opportunity in Canada offered to me.

My portal to freedom closed, and my face was ground back into Lynn Jeffers. We were losing our second principal of the year, Mr. Arnold Kasey Abraham, to a short, austere woman with jet-black hair and eyes that contrasted with her papery skin named Ms. Mulberry. Mr. Abraham had been enigmatic: an imposing figure, a tall Nevisian who had made a break from the island to train and teach at an English school, and stayed in Britain afterward, until being accused of sexual abuse and misconduct with a student. He fled England before trial, and lived under his alias on Nevis, which cleverly had the initials, AKA. The members of the board responsible for performing a background check, the Whitmans, had clearly done a suboptimal job. It was just another form of abuse on island, one more severe than the physical abuse I discussed on UNESCO day, but one that was actually almost as common. The situation highlighted more than the disturbing issue of sexual abuse; it also told the tale of omnipresent corruption. The Whitmans were siblings-in-law, and prominent figures in a Caucasian family who presence on the island started several generations ago. This dynasty was wealthy from owning large tracts and from being unofficially inside the government. They were also significant in social circles on island, so it had been in their best interest to keep the same cluster of dogmatic faculty, and prevent the school from aspiring to international standards that could jeopardize their positions. Later, to ensure their school's monopoly, they would effectively prevent a new international Canadian based private school from even opening its doors on island. This convoluted system was one I was happy to flee, and I concentrated on the light at the end of the tunnel.

My applications to boarding schools became a more laborious process since I was now applying to eight schools, most of which wanted their own unique essays, some of which had really quite provocative prompts that made me delve for a deeper part of me. One of the prompts was, "If you could look out your window and change something you see, what would that be?" The essay I released from my soul was about another type of abuse on the island that was again tragically common.

> When I look out my window I notice the beauty of the lush peaks of Nevis and the neighboring island of St. Kitts, the peaceful ocean, and the blanket of exotic tropical plants covering the island. Yet amidst this beauty, I also detect a flaw in the scenery. In a small village I see and hear the abuse and neglect of animals. The lack of care and cruelty to animals in the nearby village of Barnes Ghaut is something I would change. The barks and moans of the dogs often filter up through the night air to our home in the rainforest.
>
> On the island of Nevis, animals are commonly neglected. They are not fed or given a place to live, and even mother animals and their offspring are not cared for. Dogs and cats are the most abused and are treated with a lack of respect. Livestock, like sheep and goats, fare equally poorly. Allowed to roam onto roads and personal property, they are disregarded by owners and sometimes ruthlessly slaughtered. Often sheep will have dogs intentionally set upon them to kill them. These vicious dogs, usually pit bull-Doberman mixes, are intentionally placed inside the enclosed sheep pens at night. The herders will then retaliate by poisoning all of the dogs in the area indiscriminately, resulting in a continuous battle between the dog owners and the shepherds, with animals as the only casualties.

Some of the more atrocious acts include direct abuse like a kick or a throw, but the most inhumane and cruel practice is dog fighting. Two dogs will be set against one another for entertainment; often people place wagers on which will triumph. The organizers usually set a weak and frail animal against a stronger, fiercer one. The dogs are frequently starved prior to the fight to enrage or weaken them. The squeals of pain and anguish during these brutal fights can be clearly heard from a distance; the fights are always to the death.

Although the predominant feelings toward animals here are neglect, disregard, and sometimes even hatred, some in the community care and try to enlighten the citizens and help the abused animals. The ARC, or Animal Rescue Cooperative, which my family belongs to, is trying desperately to prevent animals from suffering. ARC often hosts fundraisers to provide veterinarian services; these funds go both to injured animals and to a spaying and neutering program that is trying to reduce the feral animal population here on island.

At my school, Lynn Jeffers, we have a Young Leaders Group, which this year won second prize in the nation for promoting awareness and sensible choices. If our group of motivated students can help the animals or join forces with ARC, I am sure that we will raise awareness and money, and increase the number of volunteers for animal rescue and rehabilitation. Through donations and school fundraisers we could make an animal adoption system and get visiting veterinarians to help. One of the quotes on our school calendar this year was from Gandhi: "Be the change you want to see." My family and I wanted to see a change in animal treatment and that is why we help the ARC. If we can get through to the minds of the people who are abusive, we will show them that the beauty of the island deserves that its animals be treated beautifully, and with the respect they deserve.

As the above essay mentions, I had become actively involved in working at the Animal Rescue Center, the more ornate title of Dan and Marty's farm. Although the most severe animal issues revolved around dogs, the facility did not have the support for them, and instead my volunteer efforts mainly involved their sheep and goat herds, a large and motley collection of animals. I worked with a quiet Nevisian guy my age, and together we kept track of the animals as we took them to graze in the scraggly brush around the farm, dipping into small ghauts to allow them to drink a couple times. Despite the fact that the majority of problems were regarding canines, this facility for protecting sheep was invaluable, since it limited the damage that could be inflicted by the dogs.

My third and last summer in Nevis focused on the future. Several times a week, I went down to Poku's house in Fern Hill Gardens. We continued to train for the SSAT, and at home I worked on the essays for my applications. On Saturdays I went to Dan and Marty's to help with the animals. One week, for the sake of education and recreation, I took a scuba certification course. The lessons served to remind me yet again of all the incredible beauty in the world, juxtaposed with the anathema ashore. As all this happened, our sailing buddy Ken sailed *Promise* to Tahiti, where she would wait for us until the new year. The summer peaked with a brief return to New England to tour the schools and interview with the admissions offices. A kid from Bermuda was on the same schedule of tours as I was—someone else escaping the confines of an island.

Second form started with an even bleaker reality than what I had forecast at the end of first form. I held tightly to my hopes for the future; I had scored 800s on my SSATs. With our pending departure, I simply put my head down and moved forward. Mom had promised us that she would not run again for chairman, but hoped to pass the mantle to another woman who hopefully would carry her and Poku's academic visions forward. Unfortunately, the new leader of the school was ignorant of educational paradigms and data, and more interested in local political harmony than actual academic progress. The infusion of ineffective ex-pat leaders, mixed with the xenophobic bureaucrats of Nevis, had returned the school to the small minded; the visions of International Baccalaureate and an integrated world focused curriculum began to slip away. Old faculty returned, and our time as students darkened beneath the black eyes of Ms. Mulberry. To alienate me from my peers just a step further, I was formally taking math with Ms. Joshi's fourth form, two years ahead, and I was still the most proficient in the class. Our small group was an interesting mix: a sarcastic Norwegian, a former principal's jovial son, and a gregarious Nevisian girl who had missed out the generous dose of racism shown by many of her peers. She laughed at my success in math lightly rather than resentfully, and attributed it to fish hiding in my hair, which was longer than the school dress code allowed. Those three students were the ones I truly considered my classmates, and with Mrs. Joshi leading our troupe, it was a happy hour.

However, time outside of that class was wearing, even on faculty. Expatriate teachers such as Mr. Mengi and Ms. J. were exhausted by the apathy of their pupils and the discrimination from the populace. This was a particular issue for Mr. Mengi, because Nevisians seemed to harbor a special prejudice for black people actually from Africa. I gulped air deeply in other classes, and held it until Mr. Mengi or Ms. J. came through my day, trying not to breathe the acrid fumes of Mrs. Wood and her archaic cohorts.

My last day at Lynn Jeffers was one of euphoria. I felt some pity for the peers I was leaving behind; I fervently hoped academics would improve for them. Hugging my few allies for the last time was momentarily sad; my family and I had forged several lifelong friendships that would transcend place and time. In spite of all that happened, we had made some fond and quixotic memories together. That nostalgia was brief though, overridden by an enthusiasm to emigrate. After three years, I still had not figured out where my proverbial place was on Nevis. If you had asked a random Nevisian they probably would have answered "out." Nevis was ready to let go of us, too. Why though? Race, patriotism, and xenophobia were the most obvious reasons. Perhaps some of the more esoteric reasons will never be apparent. Regardless, I was done. I was jumping ship, ready to leap back aboard *Promise*.

Opening day of Lynn Jeffers, September 2006

Alex and a friend, optimistic on Day 1 at Lynn Jeffers

Bucolic Nevis

Monkeys on our back deck, a frequent occurrence

Chapter 10

FRENCH POLYNESIA

$\mathcal{J}t$ had been a tremendous amount of air time—about seventeen hours. Several time zones later, we were in the other hemisphere, which was a first for me. Mom and I plastered our faces against the plastic window overlooking the sea. I exclaimed, "Is that it?" indicating a geologic cathedral, an island whose stark topography comprised needle-like spires and blade ridges.

Mom had spent the past few weeks perusing regional guidebooks, and was well-versed in the geography, biology and culture of the islands. She replied, "No, that's Moorea, which is right next door."

The plane took a dive and banked. Another verdant mass appeared in the window, higher, larger, and much more developed. That was Tahiti.

French Polynesia is comprised of 118 islands, in five archipelagos, strewn throughout 5.5 million square kilometers of the magnificent South Pacific. These varied islands, some mountainous volcanoes and others flat, arid atolls, are about equidistant between South America and Australia. According to historians, this vast area was colonized from Samoa in the first millennium AD. Although Tahiti is the largest island in the Society archipelago, Raiatea, the second largest, is known as ancient Havai'I, or "the sacred isle," from which all of eastern Polynesia was colonized.

We landed in the metropolis of Papeete, surprised to see significant development over the city outskirts. When we finally reached the customs and immigration booth, we stated that we were transitioning back to our ship and outfitting it for an ocean crossing, so we would be there longer than the one-month tourist limit. Knitted brows on the official's face did not bring us reassurance. Mom babbled a constant stream of French and pseudo-French, trying to bridge the cavernous language gap. Fifteen minutes of holding up the pasty tourists behind us later, we were referred to the head of immigration. His office was a windowless addition in the corner of the room, sealed with a steel door. Although we were in a respectable first world nation, France, this hardly boded well.

The four of us meekly knocked and entered. The room had potted plants and the desk was decorated with pictures of smiling children at the beach, surely his own. The tall man wore most of a suit, missing only the jacket, and stood to greet us in accented English, "Ah, hello. You are ze family with the boat, *non?*" He did all the linguistic bridging necessary, and gave us the opportunity to rectify the situation. It seems that a plethora of would-be island stowaways try to sneak into the Polynesian nation on a regular basis, only to disappear into the fabric of the islands and vanish into another life. We reiterated that we had cleared it with the airlines as well as our boatyard in Raiatea where *Promise* awaited us, with both of those business establishments reassuring us that no additional protocol was necessary. Although we seemed an unlikely group of thugs and villains, the man in charge asserted that we would have to reboard the plane if we could not produce a bond of 6,000 Euros. Fortunately, though, there was a Banc Populaire next door and we could arrange for a transfer of funds, most of which would be returned to us if we kept the proper receipts upon leaving the country. A tense hour later, hoping in earnest that our adventure was not over before it had really begun, we received clearance.

Now legally in the country, we were each burdened with several bags containing our world for the next six months. Not that we were expecting an arranged greeting party, but there were numerous taxi vans parked, ready to take on passengers at any moment. Mom simply raised an arm in a wave and a van pulled up to the curb. "Le Meridian?"

The driver nodded vigorously, "*Oui, madame.* Eh, four people?"

As with the French Antilles of the Caribbean, Tahiti was graced with a full infrastructure; the roads were well manicured, often passing under bridges spanning several lanes (although, disappointingly, there was prolific graffiti under all such bridges and along the concrete embankments on either side of the road). Foliage was sparse for the first twenty minutes in the van, until we exhausted the expanse of the urban area. The road started to pass through increasingly rural areas, but the population density remained dense near the coast.

Our hotel was located at the least developed point we had seen thus far, where houses had become less frequent and fishing shacks more common. The hotel had all the splendor of the wealthy tourism industry, with a soaring, open-air main building, constructed of bare wood and roofed in coconut thatching. Our room was at the far end of a long white wing, on the second floor. Tropical plants of all varieties encroached on the outside walkway, leaving a smooth white wall to one side and an ornate, primarily green wall to the other.

After three days of living the tourist life we had tried so hard to dissociate ourselves from previously, we had recovered from our flight from the other side of the world and returned to the airport. This second flight was brief, aboard a buzzing tin can of a plane. Thirty minutes later, crossing some of the most stunning scenery on Earth, we were approaching Raiatea and its sister island, Taha'a. These two islands were a fair bit older. Tahiti had been mostly bare to the oceans around it, whereas these two islands were fully encircled by a barrier reef, leaving a tranquil lagoon between the land and Pacific. All the islands in this archipelago were sinking, albeit very slowly; and, in another few million years even these islands would be reduced to flat atolls. After a rough landing on a beaten airstrip, we all entered the one-room terminal, its single atrium built from a wood naturally so dark it was nearly black.

We claimed our baggage from one large cart they had been brought over on. Bags in hand, we walked toward the road on the other side of the terminal. I asked, "Wait, what about paper work? Security? Any of that?"

Without looking back, Mom said, "It's a domestic flight in Polynesia. It's all safe."

Dad commented on the side, "It seems a bit weird, but I'm just happy not to have to do *douanes* [customs] again."

Like most mountainous islands, Raiatea was ringed in a single main road, and that made for an easy finding of the boatyard, or the careenage as it became known to us as. To sailors, especially us, boatyards are fun to wander through, despite their rough nature. Parking our chartreuse rental car and stepping out, it became apparent that this was an exceptionally gritty specimen. Although fully functional, with several boats placidly on the hard, two corpse boats lay on their side on the asphalt, saplings growing out of the fiberglass. A few mangy dogs scuffled past, one stopping to lick Lara and another snarling as it backed away. Leaving the bags in the car, we sought out the head of the boatyard, a tall Polynesian named Dante.

Most Polynesians are extremely affable and we were greeted with a wide smile and the universal, "*Ia ora na*!" which translated literally to "Let there be life," and implies a good one. Dante took us out back to one of many boat lots, and pointed. "I believe that's your *Promise*, non?"

We all grinned. There, suspended in the air, was our home.

"So, when can we have her in the water?" asked Dad.

Dante replied, "She's scheduled to go in very soon; you can go aboard now if you want to." Dad and I scaled the ladder up against the transom, and climbed into the cockpit, followed enthusiastically by Lara and Mom. Fundamentally this was not too different from bobbing in a harbor fifteen feet deep; it just meant no jumping off the transom once we climbed aboard.

A repetitive beep sounded and Dante called up, "The lift is coming! You don't have to get off though. You can go in with the boat." The lift was a huge vehicle that resembled a cube frame from which two horizontal edges had been removed on the same side. Within the cube dangled a pair of canvas slings; they were adjustable, and after sliding them under the boat, they would be raised to lift the boat for transportation. The driver, in a little cab welded to one of the edges, gave us a wave as he guided the slings under *Promise*. The beeping resumed; *Promise* shook a little, and started to rise.

Twenty feet above the gravel and on a boat in the air and beyond control is unnerving the first time. Actually, there really was not supposed to be a first time, I found out as I read the orange safety sticker on the lift: "Do not operate while persons are on board." I shrugged, as by that time we were in the middle of a slow but sharp turn around a row of hauled boats.

The lift's trajectory became slightly downhill as we approached the slip. To inject some humor into the macabre, I asked Dad, "So, what happens if the brakes fail now?"

Each set of wheels of the lift found their way to a ribbon of concrete on either side of a rectangular pool, the slip. Dad shrugged. "Hope this guy's good at steering."

The beeping resumed, and *Promise* commenced a slow descent. With our keel submerged, the lift released one side of the slings, then raised the other side, pulling the canvas belts out from one side of the hull.

The spirit of *manava*, or Polynesian hospitality, abounded here. The local *kane*, or men, helped us get our bags aboard and dock lines secured, and we were home. *Promise's* smell was overwhelming, musty and of fuel and salt, but although atypically pungent, it smelled like home. After opening the hatches to release the stale, redolent air, we set up a bucket brigade for bags. Dad passed the bags from the dock to me on deck, and I slung them down the companionway to Mom. Once we had a heap of bags forming a blockade in the main salon, we set about sorting through their contents, which did turn out to be slightly deficient. Somewhere in the transition from the States to *Promise*, we had lost a bag, which contained mostly minor things such as a few school books and a set of nail clippers. It also had the slightly less trivial defibrillator, which hopefully would not be a necessity.

Although some of the more important things had been neglected, it was with great foresight that Mom had brought along about twenty-four hours of food for us. After all we had done that day, grocery shopping held little appeal. I ventured, "Hey, can we have dinner yet?"

Mom looked at the brass clock on the bulkhead. "Well, it is … wait, there's no way it's that time. The time zone must be wrong." Squinting her eyes, she proceeded to figure out our actual time, from the clock, which was probably still on Caribbean time. "It's only three o'clock. Sorry, not happening. And I can't imagine cooking down here tonight; it's so hot in this marina."

Forestalling dinner, Mom and Dad went ashore to speak with Dante again, since *Promise* had seen no end of issues, the most notable being the shaft for the rudder, which had sustained some damage and was the reason she was out of the water upon our arrival. It turned out we had several other issues of varying scale, and the prospective remedy was Fred, a mechanic who commuted daily from Taha'a, on the other side of the lagoon. Fred was a short, trim Frenchman whose life in the sun had garnered him a permanent tan and a weathered appearance only enhanced by his rugged attire so typical of the marine world. Meeting Fred was a reassuring experience; the amicable mechanic was fluent in English, and had a warm aura, which was an added bonus since he would be aboard daily, often in my berth accessing the engine. He gave a wry smile as he admitted, "Your boat, she's got a few issues."

By noon of the following day, we had exhausted the three meals' grace Mom had brought. We piled into the chartreuse mini-car and headed in to town on a drive that starkly contrasted with the comparable trip we made in Tahiti. The old coastal road often passed through nothing more than large tracts of jungle, which gradually gave way to concrete or thatch homes every half-mile or so, and then converted into a manicured boulevard with houses set far back on either side. The transition in the official confines of Uturoa was sudden; the buildings that were so far apart before were now too close for a cat to squeeze between. Even in the capital, the buildings remained low and modest, and they covered only two streets stretching away from the wharf. Litter piled up in the gutters and a greasy aroma permeated throughout the air. We parked at the periphery of town in view of the harbor.

The first store in the tight configuration of the downtown area was an optics store, and Lara gasped melodramatically that she had to go in because she "absolutely, positively need a pair of glasses!" Regardless of need, the immaculate, air-conditioned store was a gift to enter. Lara moved toward a pair of pink frames with white polka dots, exclaiming, "These are the ones! I can see now!" The specs had a heavy prescription, however, and Lara, who had perfect vision, could barely walk with them on. The clerk looked on, amused, as Mom went through the lengthy process of dissuading Lara. He did not speak a word of English, but the tones were universal. He finally stepped forward with a pair with a very weak correction, explaining in French that these might work. Mom shook her head and ushered us out of the store.

Lara's despair over her perfect vision, and consequential inability to wear glasses, was quickly overcome as we walked into one of the grocery stores. It was small and had a portion of what we needed. Upon checkout, we inquired if there were any other stores in town that might have some of the provisions on the long list of what we needed. It turns out that there were two more, and Mom and I (since I was always with her to schlep heavy things around) eventually developed an acute knowledge of which of the three stores specialized in which products, and the comparative prices between these. We next went to the store we grew to call "the dairy store," stocked up on a myriad of cheeses, and then went on to Champion, the French supermarket with which we had become well acquainted in the French Antilles.

A surprise to all of us was the extent of the Polynesians' genuine warmth and hospitality. There was a palpable joie de vivre and an exuberance for life expressed in a countless simple ways; one of our favorites was that the cashiers in the stores had full tiaras of freshly picked and fragrant gardenias and colorful local flowers. When my sister complemented one woman on it, she casually remarked that creating it was just a part of her morning routine, no more complicated than brushing her teeth. She had an easy grace and assented when we asked if we could take her picture.

In the local produce market, we came to appreciate the beauty of the island's offerings. Fresh flowers engulfed a full quarter of the huge central market square; there were pre-done arrangements, single flowers, and bunches of unique varieties. One elderly woman with an exceptionally warm smile told us about all of her flowers, and the tale of the elusive *Tiare apetahi*. This unique and sacred flower grows nowhere else on earth except the high slopes of Mt. Temehani on Raiatea, and no one is allowed to pick it. The flower has five petals like a hand, which represents a myth about a young maiden and her forbidden love with a chief's son. It also pops open so loudly at dawn that it is audible. Ironically, we had actually heard of this unique flower from Dr. Ishmael in Nevis, who once visited Raiatea as an avid botanist to see this lovely bloom, and had shared his adventure with us. Small world.

A few days after settling in and reestablishing *Promise* as our home, we set off with our tiny French rental car to tour Raiatea. As with all of our initial island tours, we jumped in, maps in hand; if we got lost, we'd certainly be able to find our way back later. Dad kept on driving and when Mom found some interesting site in her guidebook nearby, she would call it out and we would detour to see it. Two scenic outlooks into the mist-wreathed mountains of Raiatea later, Mom took the wheel; she knew where the most exotic attraction waited for us.

With Mom, the faster driver, piloting us, we plummeted from

the verdant peaks we had admired. The fog hung over us faintly, and masked a turn that sent us flying into a pothole. We all groaned in unison and then Mom exclaimed, "Wheee!"

Dad looked at her and said, "Does anyone else feel that vibrating?" Not waiting for an answer he said, "I think we have a flat." We did. Dad and I changed it.

Finally down on the shoreline, Mom started to sputter, "Here it is! Here it is!"

"What is?" I asked.

She replied, "The most sacred site in Polynesia! Raiatea was the center of the religious structure for all of Polynesia, and this is their most sacred *marae*, where they had meetings and sacrifices!"

"Human?"

"Yeah, human sacrifices and fire dancing. This is Marae Taputapuatea."

This was starting to sound really awesome, and I tried to visualize what the temple would look like. We pulled off the road and our zealous tour guide said, "We're here!" I leapt from the car and peered around—no temple.

I asked, "Do we have to hike to it or something?"

"No, it's right there," said Mom. "See those stones? That's it!"

I frowned at the large stones that tiled the ground and led up to a row of rough, upright boulders. Our historian took out her guidebooks and read that the platform, or *ahu*, was forty-seven meters long and was aligned with Te Ava Moa Pass through the barrier reef directly opposite the site. In ancient times, fires located there were beacons to ancient navigators. More recently in the 1990s, Polynesian voyaging canoes travelled here from as far away as Hawai'i and Easter Island to rededicate the marae and lift an ancient curse.

Even in the car, Mom was still hyper from her sacred site; I stared out the window, more impressed with the small, private, and collapsing dock we passed. Again, we all grunted as the car lurched. Mom said, "Sorry, didn't see that one." The car started jittering and sagging. We had another flat, and the spare had been exhausted. There were no houses or villages for miles, and a tropical deluge engulfed us once again. Driving on the flat for several miles was a slow process since Dad had taken over and he did not want to cause any further damage. We finally stopped next to a high school, which conveniently had just gotten out. The long, low concrete building was built on top of a small hill above the road, and behind it soared jungle-draped cliffs, water cascading a thousand feet down them. On the road in front of the school, open, tourist-style buses had parked, the pupils boarding them for the ride home. Walking up to the driver's window, Dad requested the use of the driver's cell phone, which took a lot of convincing, to call the rental dealer so we could be rescued.

Half an hour later, a replacement vehicle was driven in, with a tow truck close behind. The rim of the wheel had been damaged beyond by repair by our driving with the flat, and the repair cost exceeded 500 Euros. From this incident our family immortalized the maxim, "The 'whee' is de-wicked"—after the two flats resulting from fast driving, which often results in Mom going, "Whee!" and more, we were done with rentals.

That helped put an end to our touristy explorations, and kept us in the life of a cruiser. After being returned to the water, *Promise* had not been moved from the slip, because the list of her problems only seemed to grow. We fell into the rhythm of having mechanics aboard seemingly at all times and not leaving the hot, grimy dock space we inhabited. Homeschooling also resumed in earnest. Every day after breakfast, Mom and I started classes. Since Lara was still asleep, we used this time to work through the subjects that had no overlap with Lara's curriculum, such as advanced biology or European history. Age and experience had pushed my sister's and my academic levels farther apart, and there were few classes we could still take together. In fact, there were not any classes in which we studied the same material, but we did do our respective English work concomitantly. As we had done previously in the Caribbean, we also studied the local culture, history, and geography together to prep for our excursions.

English also involved an intriguing booklist, which Mom and I often read together. This is not because I was incapable of doing the work on my own, which I did do just as often, but because we both enjoyed doing the activity together, and the resulting discourse. This worked especially well for titles such as *Twelfth Night*, for which we would each claim a different selection of roles every time we picked up the play.

When our water tanks were empty, I resumed my role as the filler of water tanks aboard. I went ashore, grabbed a hose, and turned it on. The pressure was disappointingly low; this was going to take a while. Mom and I sat low on the deck, in the shade of the dodger. We each held a side of the No-Fear-Shakespeare paperback, and I had jammed the hose between my toes, keeping it above the fill port. We generally read from the page with the original text—well, Mom always did, although I occasionally stooped to read the modern language translation. I read my line from the translated side, and Mom chastised me, "No! No! No! That's the most famous line of the play! You can't skip that! Read the original!"

I laughed and read, "Love sought is good, but giv'n unsought is better."

Two acts later, the hose still poured into the tank. I commented, "There's no way this isn't full yet." We lifted the floorboards of the main salon, from where we could access the tank in question. It was leaking. So, about an hour later, Hiro showed up. Hiro was a brawny young boat worker who specialized in fiberglass. We all had to vacate the interior of the boat while he laid a new layer of fiberglass over the tank, toxic fumes swirling. I took a last look down before moving onto the foredeck; Hiro was perfectly protected from the materials he worked with by wearing goggles, a gas mask, and a white flower bud behind his ear. Everyone in Polynesia wore flowers behind their ear. The protocol dictated that closed buds were for men, open flowers for women, left ear for single, right for taken, and both for swingers (it is not a polygamist society). The most common flowers used were frangipani, small white flowers that grew on a tree, and whose sap is extremely toxic to ingest. It was probably as dangerous as unfinished fiberglass.

Promise was finally in sound enough condition to bob freely and go across the lagoon to Taha'a. Cutting through the flat water, we raised the main, letting it heel us over and give the illusion of speed. The first five minutes were phenomenal; we were free. By the time we were north of Raiatea and in the channel between the two islands, we had the barrier reef off to our port and a large flower of coral in the middle of the channel. Mom frantically consulted the charts below, and we all weighed in on exactly where we were in proximity to the intricate reefs. I was relegated to the foredeck as spotter, and I started to panic. The water was supposed to be tremendously deep between the reefs, but I was sure that I was missing something that would later end up puncturing the hull. It turned out that there was nothing to worry about; the clarity of water simply made the coral heads seem much closer than they were.

We went to the southernmost harbor on the coast of Taha'a. When viewed from above, Taha'a appears to be shaped like a hibiscus, a few deep bays between lobes of land that gave a vaguely round outline. The folding peaks were sharp and, despite being completely smothered in jungle, their stark contours stood out, later meriting an entry in my seldom-used sketchbook. All up and down the hills and across the length of the bay, there was almost no sign of human presence, the exceptions being about five houses on the water, and the Taravana Yacht Club.

The yacht club was a large, open building on the point forming a corner of the bay. We moored *Promise* securely, and then tied our dinghy up to their dock alongside a mutant catamaran. It was clear that the unusual craft was homemade: the thirty-five-foot cat had a tuna tower built onto the back, its owners clearly fishermen.

The owner of the cat was also the owner of Taravana, and was the first person we met on Taha'a. Richard had the weathered, salty look of a man who had spent his life at sea, because he had. At the age of seventeen he left Hawaii where he had grown up, and sailed down to French Polynesia alone, finding his way solely with celestial navigation. He had raised his family here, including his son Maui, whom we met shortly after. Maui closely resembled Ken in appearance and manner. He was tall and lanky, with a boyish face and a dark crew cut. In his mid-twenties, his liquid eyes shone with a quality seen in many cruisers, a total paucity of jadedness.

We were the only customers there, and even though we did order dinner, it felt more like visiting friends, with Richard letting us use his Internet connection and staying to converse. The harbor was black when we commenced our departure. We had not left the anchor light on, but we had brought a flashlight to find our way home. As we waved to Richard and Maui, the deluge came. In a glorious tropical way, the clouds had shattered in an instant and the downpour arrived with no transition. Mom laughed, "Well, guess we can stay for a bit then." Almost twenty minutes later, the rain had shown no signs of letting up, and this sort of tropical rain was not going to leave as suddenly as it came. We proclaimed a final farewell, and stepped into the rain.

Dad said, "This really won't be good for my shirt." It was his turquoise linen shirt from St. Bart's.

Richard called over, "You may as well take it off if you don't want it wet! Not gonna bother us!" Dad took the invitation, and packed his shorts in too, leaving him with nothing on but his flip flops and blue boxers. Dad was laughing so hard at the absurdity of the situation that he was actually snorting as he waved back to our hosts.

The dinghy was full of water when we entered, and only sank lower as frigid rain fell in. I opened the throttle all the way toward where I remembered the boat being. Mom turned on the light, but through the rain it shone only a few feet, the lights of Taravana had disappeared, too. We were alone in the dark, and the rain continued to bear down on us, freezing. A windswept wave broke over the bow, the warm saline flooding us further. The thermal comfort it brought was short-lived as we returned our attention to the fact that we had a visibility less than my height, had no idea where land or boat was, and the severity of wind and waves only seemed to be escalating. Lara screamed as a bolt of lightning cracked across the sky and illuminated *Promise* momentarily. It was a quick glimpse, but it was long enough for us to get to the ship, and get dry.

The next day, Sunday, we had no plans other than to lay low. The time in the breezy, scenic harbor elapsed all too quickly as we exhausted all our games and good portions of our respective books. In the middle of the afternoon we were joined by another boat, *Contigo*.

Extending hospitality, so common amongst cruisers, we had invited the crew over for the evening. It was yet another cruiser couple, Maggie and Chris, from Florida, who floated up in their dinghy, loaves of warm banana bread in hand. In the best of ways, they had led lifestyles about as atypical as you can find. In Florida they ran a program for troubled teens that involved taking them sailing for extended periods of time as crew. Apparently they had amazing results, too, which is not hard to imagine given how demanding and dynamic the maritime lifestyle can be. They were on their way to Thailand, where they would meet up with a friend who knew the area well. Another crew had been inducted into the Raiatean cruising club.

The Taravana Yacht Club became a favorite close destination of ours. It was one of only a handful of establishments on the quiet, verdant isle. Most of the local people live in small villages that ring the sea. Customs of Polynesian dance, including fire dancing, had been experiencing a revival here as in other places throughout Polynesia. After the Europeans, especially the missionaries, arrived in the early 1800s, many local customs and traditions were banned as indecent. In 1819 the Pomare code and religious interdictions prevented such indigenous traditions as tattoos and dancing, and the people adopted more European styles of dress as Christianity spread through the region. Tattoos at least were well documented by drawings from various visitors; even the word for the process of tapping the dyes into the skin comes from the Tahitian word, *tatua*. Dancing, however, was not described in enough detail for people to recreate some of the subtle movements and the nuances behind the traditions. Nonetheless, a resurgence of indigenous pride in the culture had ushered in an era of veneration for the old traditions.

Several types of dance had now found a revival, including the *Aparima*, or the dance where the hands tell a story, often performed by women. The *Otea* was originally a warlike dance for men; now it is one of the most famous types of dance and can be performed by men, women, or both together. On the small island of Taha'a, fire dancing, as well as these other dances, was being practiced in the village near Taravana. The traditional accompaniment usually involves percussion and stringed instruments. The friendly villagers were more than happy to discuss their craft with us through a mixture of French, English, and body language, with Maui translating in the gaps.

Maui made opening comments, and then they began to perform. The girls' basic motion was a hip swaying at high cadences in a motion impossible to recreate; it was a skill acquired while young, and even the youngest girls, some only five or six, had the technique down perfectly. The men's basic movement involved fixing the ankles together and bowing their knees in and out, and shuffling along with this motion. Each act had its own set of minimalist costumes. The last act was fire dancing, a display put on by two boys and their father who had trained them. A young boy, Ari, age eight, was a most impressive and energetic character. He had learned fire dancing from his father and older brother, and now was doing well enough to perform with them. With an infectious smile, he twirled the flames about his head and between his legs. Mom cringed in concern for him, but he did not drop the flaming rod, and received thunderous applause. Afterward, Ari said his favorite part is when he gets to stand up on his brother's back, twirling his baton of fire: "I like to remind him of that part whenever he tries to be mean to me."

A feast also accompanied the performance. Despite not seeing the undoubtedly enormous preparation work behind the scenes, we vastly appreciated the skill of the traditional cooks. As the Polynesians are people of the sea, fish and seafood play an abundant role in their diet. French Polynesia has the added bonus of having a traditional culture infused with French overtones for a uniquely delicious cuisine. Polynesian raw fish is usually done with red tuna, but there are more than 300 species of edible fish in the surrounding waters. The special with citrus and coconut was amazing. Meats are often done over several hours in the *a'hima'a*, or traditional oven usually dug in the sand, lined with hot stones and covered with banana leaves. Staples such as taro, which is a purple root vegetable and often made into a soft poi, sweet potatoes, and *uru* (breadfruit), are made more delicious with local herbs and fruits. One cannot mention breadfruit without considered the fate of Captain Bligh and his crew from the *Bounty*, whose goal of securing breadfruit to bring to the Caribbean and other British colonies made this staple the most infamous. Having grown to love breadfruit after living in the Caribbean, I for one was glad it found its way off these shores to a wider world stage.

By the end of the week, we were planning another escape from Raiatea, this time to Bora Bora, some twenty miles to the west. It would be our first sail outside the lagoon. Since our main GPS had lost all functionality and was soon to be replaced, I sat up against the mast with the portable GPS trying to reconfigure it. In my focus I ignored the increasingly loud whine of an outboard motor, and the voices that ensued.

"Hello, *Promise?*"

Mom and Dad responded from the cockpit, "Yes, can we help you?"

And that was how we met Mike and Barb, a Californian couple who were circumnavigating on their boat *Traveler*. They had just come over to introduce themselves, and simultaneously invited us to a cookout that would be happening the following day on the other side of the marina. They mentioned that we should bring a favorite dish, too.

Finally drawn from our shell of the slip, we met the rest of the cruisers in the area. Aboard *Cosmos* lived an older Californian couple, Sunni and Charlie, who had been in Polynesia for almost two decades. *Alana Rose* housed an Australian couple, John and Nancy, bringing their boat back home, and *Blessed Bee* carried a trio of Australians headed by the boat's owner, Bruce. Like *Alana Rose*, they were bringing their boat back to Australia. Several rounds of barbecue and a game of boules later, we were in the Raiatean cruisers' circle.

This was a different cruising community than what we had found in the Caribbean. The group was generally older, and much more serious. The Pacific was vast, rough, and severe. To sail it you had to be very skilled, or you would be swallowed. Also, most of us were not on a joy ride; *Alana Rose*, *Blessed Bee* and we were all in the act of performing a boat transaction, either shipping a boat just bought or one for sale. Another significant difference among these sailors and the ones we had found elsewhere was the fact that none of them had kids aboard. That was all right with me this time; since they did not have kids to befriend, I befriended them, and was always an ardent tagalong, staying around for adult discourse during and after meals. This generally was not onerous, since the discussion was always pertinent to the world I shared with them. The saving grace was that there was always playfulness in port, and games of all kinds abounded. We often played boules on the dusty top of the quay, and sometimes would have a massive game of dominoes, especially Mexican Train. Our cockpit was the largest, and the only one suitable for so many people to congregate around a plastic domino train station, which Sunni adored for the little train sounds that it played when you pushed the little red button.

A few days later, Mom and I packed up the Mexican Train and walked over to *Cosmos* to return it. Sunni was reading in the cockpit when we arrived, and welcomed us aboard. *Cosmos* had a strange layout, with its cockpit in the middle and two companionways, one descending toward the bow and the other to the stern. Mom and I followed her down below, and I exclaimed, "Sunni! You have a gecko on board!"

She put the game away and said, "Oh, he must be new, I haven't seen that one before."

Mom asked, "Wait; do you normally have geckos aboard?"

"Of course! I've got dozens. They're great little pets, no maintenance whatsoever, they eat bugs and are cute to have."

It was my turn to ask, "Where did you get them all?"

Sunni pondered for a moment. "I guess a few came aboard in some bags, and then they just multiplied. You want one?"

Our vigorous response was simultaneous: "Of course!"

Sunni then looked around one of the top shelves muttering, "I thought I saw one up here a few days ago. Oh, here it is!" She held a white orb between her thumb and forefinger. "Here's an egg. It should hatch in a day or two, I think."

Spike hatched later that day; actually, during the one minute I was not watching his egg (I say "his" with absolutely no knowledge of the lizard's gender). I returned to my bunk to find his shell in pieces, and him up on the bulkhead. I reached for him, and he disappeared into the crevices of the boat. After that he would show up every few days somewhere aboard: in a cabinet, on the ceiling, in the rigging, or in a locker. Sunni had been right; he was totally self-sufficient.

Our boat was not that clean but it was hard to imagine what he found to eat. With our newly acquired crew member, and about as close to a functional boat as we could muster, we set off for Bora Bora.

Polynesian children greeting us in Raiatea

Alex playing guitar at sunset

Dad diving on the anchor in southern Raiatea

Young brothers fire dancing in Taha'a

Chapter 11

Beyond the Barrier

The day of our first venture beyond the barrier reef beckoned a passage to be made; the wind was a brisk twenty-five knots and the sky was cloudless. After weeks without travel, we were restive, and we headed for the pass in the reef. There were two slits that would grant us access to the open Pacific; one was right by the careenage, but was a death trap of reefs, and the other was half way up the coast of Taha'a. At about a quarter of a mile wide, finding our way through proved effortless, although the humungous breaking surf to either side of us served as an acute reminder to remain vigilant.

The swells were commendably large outside of the lagoon, fifteen feet from crest to trough. Our first real experience in giant South Pacific swells was exhilarating rather than intimidating; *Promise* struck out under a cloudless sky with twenty knots of wind and rolling swells off our beam. In the trough of the waves, one could not see in either direction over the glassy mountain of water; at the crest, we could see islands in every direction. With the main and jib billowing on a beam reach, there was no need for the engine, and we cruised over the waves toward Bora Bora, or simply "Bora" as we grew to call her.

Bora looked like a sombrero floating on waves in the distance, its singular monolithic peak in the center of the lagoon getting steeper as we approached. A pod of spinner dolphins accompanied us off our starboard bow. We were amazed to see that they truly spun sideways in the air before landing again in the sea; they looked as if they were having a fabulous time as we all zipped along at eight knots.

Entering the channel into Bora's lagoon, I fell in love with that monolith. It was green for the first two thirds of the way up, but after that the soaring cliffs were too sinister for even the most tenacious of tropical foliage to grow. The central island and the surrounding reef were both round, and we slowly turned through the dark lagoon. The barrier reef here was a string of *motu* beads; between each low spit of sand was a clear view of the ocean, but the true eye-catcher was in front of the motus. In front of the palm-studded sandbars the water was a perfect turquoise, so vibrant it seemed charged with energy. This tier of shallow water crossed the better portion of the lagoon before falling from a sharp drop to the lagoon's deep water. The boundary was perfect, one side light and the other dark.

As we continued circling through the lagoon, the motus became origins for massive docks of bungalows above the water, hotels all identical from a distance. I held the camera, every few minutes stopping to take a dozen shots of the new and slightly different view of the peak we had found. By the pass, it had appeared to be a large slanted slab of cliff, but now looking at it from a new angle, it was apparent that it was really a thin and extremely tall slice of basalt.

We moored outside of one of the bungalow colonies in an ideal fifteen feet of water that summoned us all as soon as the boat had come to a stop. Lara was the first one overboard, and she called back up, "Hey! Can someone get me something to dive for?" She loved casting an object into the water and retrieving it shortly after. I grabbed a dead battery off the nav station desk and tossed it off the back. A few cycles of playing fetch with herself later, she put the battery on deck and asked if I was coming in. A minute later I flung myself from the cockpit, flying over her head and into the best water I had ever seen.

While we were in the water, two young Frenchmen came up to our boat in a Boston Whaler, in matching polos and khakis. They were from an environmental group. They took our trash for a small fee and then briefed the four of us on lagoon protocol. They concluded their message with, "Just remember, please don't stay in any one anchorage for more than a few nights, and do not throw anything in the water, especially batteries, since rays can eat them and die." Bora hosted a species of manta ray found nowhere else in the world, and we had given

Lara a battery to trivially play with. I grabbed the battery and tossed it into the cockpit. She scowled at me and I put a finger to my lips.

We did not leave the boat that evening, with a world of entertainment in the water alone. For me, though, the most wonder lay in the peak to our stern. During dinner, the sun set between the main slice of rock and its smaller partner to the south. The fiery colors shot through, golden rays charging the air with a hazy quality. The light-colored igneous cliffs appeared black from the strength of the contrast. This momentary magic was short lived, because my zeal for capturing this mountain with the camera failed, the auto-contrasting technology robbing the scene of its natural radiance.

Admiring the surreal backdrop, we noticed a fast-moving craft heading across the harbor. Muscular Polynesians paddled their outrigger with aplomb, practicing for an upcoming race, chanting and rowing in unison. In the sinking light, it seemed straight out of a movie.

A few days of hopping from gorgeous anchorage to gorgeous anchorage later, we brought *Promise* to the main harbor, where the center of the populace was located. We took a mooring, since the water was almost a hundred feet deep and we did not have enough chain to provide adequate scope. The mooring belonged to Bloody Mary's, a renowned restaurant that we visited for lunch. Outside the doors stood two table-sized placards, covered in rows of the names of celebrities who had visited: Johnny Depp, Cameron Diaz, Rod Stuart, Jimmy Buffett.

I said, "Well, if they liked it, it must have good food."

I was right, but the most exotic facet of the restaurant was the setting and layout. The ceiling was a high construction of coconut fronds. The chairs were polished and varnished palm stumps, and the floor was the smooth sand from the motus' beaches. Halfway through the meal Dad returned from the bathroom and said, "Alex, go use the bathroom." He responded to my quizzical expression with, "Seriously, it's really awesome."

I was skeptical since, in my experience of bathrooms, the awesomeness was a function of necessity, and that would put this one toward the bottom of the list—or so I thought until I opened the door. The floor was still sand; the far wall nonexistent, just the brush growing outside; the stalls were a dark wood with reliefs carved into them; and the sink a running waterfall. It certainly had character, attested to by the wooden penis that served as the flush lever for the urinal. Upon my return I admitted, "All right, that was unique."

That afternoon, the wind was negligible, and we needed to charge the batteries, so we had no choice but to run the engine. Bessie revved to life, but about twenty amp-hours later, she just stopped running. That was our cue. Dad and I tore apart my bunk and then had our access to the engine. Hot air swirled about our heads and I said, "Let's let it cool down a bit first." I opened all my hatches.

An hour of futile trial and error later, Dad said, "Hey, Richard, that guy from Taravana …he lives over here, right?"

I told him, "Yeah, I think he said he kept his boat around the point from Bloody Mary's—oh wait. That's convenient!"

We took the dinghy around the point to another harbor, where Richard allegedly kept his catamaran. With the unmistakable tuna tower off the back, it was easy to find. He himself was harder to find; his boat, also named *Taravana*, was locked up tightly.

That evening Dad and I were still peering at the engine, tweaking. I was usually Dad's assistant, holding, twisting, and fetching, since he was the one with a comprehensive understanding of the engine. After all my time helping him though, I had a cursory knowledge, and said, "Hey, do you think it could be the circuit breaker?"

He shrugged. "Sure; we haven't checked it yet. We might as well."

The circuit breaker was a small white button just about in the middle of the volume of metal, but it could be reached by sticking your hand into the crevice. It was popped out, so I pressed it back in and cried, "Mom! Try the engine again!"

The sound of the engine cranking was deafening at that proximity without the muffling, but it was better than no sound at all. That was the highlight of my mechanic's career, my first time figuring out an engine problem.

Back on Raiatea, we had a replacement GPS unit installed in the cockpit, one independent of our old system. That GPS had been fried, but the radar component was still fully functional, and utilized the old monitor down at the nav station. *Promise* was then fully operational, at least for a while, and with our recent taste of freedom, we were not about to be contained in the lagoon any longer than was necessary. We set out in the opposite direction of last time, and this time headed east, into the wind, to Huahine. This island, of all those in the archipelago, was called the "Wild One." Huahine had the most challenging navigation we had yet seen, and apparently was too challenging for some: a few wrecks lay strewn across the reefs.

Unlike Bora Bora, Huahine was not as well known for its waters as it was for its land mass. Huahine had a certain rugged quality apparent upon sight. A bit off the beaten path and of denser foliage and jungle, it came across as very remote. During the 1800s, Huahine had been used almost exclusively as a prison island. Criminals from the surrounding islands were all cast from their native shores there; as such, it still bears the reputation of an island full of troublemakers and their coarse descendants. Once ashore, it was clear that it may well have been the poorest of the Society Islands, the main strip of town consisting of some well-maintained homes and businesses, but just as many decaying homes, their yards centers for refuse. Looking at major trends of what showed up in these trash yards, it seemed that foosball had been tremendously popular about a decade prior, as several tables lay in various states of rot.

Much of the impoverished look of Huahine was in part due to the fact that it was not a major tourist destination. All of Polynesia has some tourism, but really only one of the town's shops catered to tourists. Interestingly, the most colorful building in town was certainly the local *gendarmerie* and prison: a bright, turquoise building on the shore with a spectacular view over the harbor, and the clearly printed word JAIL on the lagoon-side façade. Predictably, the town also had a rental car dealership, and we took off for a do-it-yourself island tour.

The soil of Huahine is incredibly fertile because the volcanic component is still relatively fresh. We passed through several fields of various crops. This was the other side of Huahine's reputation—it is a major center for local crops, supplying fresh produce to the Society Islands. Dad was behind the wheel and Mom had her guidebooks out as always. She said, "Hey, let's stop by this bridge, there's something cool we can see." The bridge we stopped by spanned a shallow stream that flowed into the lagoon, and at its highest point had a smiling crowd of local kids, all peering over the edge, their eyes on a dangling fish hook below.

As we got out of the car Mom said, "Well, that's ironic. Kids fishing here … anyway, see that thing in the water? That's an old fish trap, several hundred years old." This was significantly better than the Raiatean center of worship. It was a gutter formed with two neat walls of stacked, flat stones. At the end these two walls bent around and finally joined each other to form a neat mushroom shaped pool: a fish trap. From above, the kids were dangling their lines into the mushroom of stone. Apparently some hundred years later it was still functional, though traditionally, fish had been harvested from these traps by hand.

An archeological stop here and there later, we found ourselves in a random village at the base of the lush mountains. Mom had told us the entire island history as she read it, and I asked, "Is this the place with the sacred eels?" She nodded vigorously. We pulled off the road partially and got out next to a stream whose banks had been reinforced with concrete. This was an important site; I peered into the shallow water and looked for the eels. I really did not want another religious let down. I started voicing some disappointment but ended up shouting, "Oh! Those eels!"

The six-foot, pearl grey eels lay almost static, just under the surface of the water where the embankment had been undermined by the brackish stream. They seemed to study us coldly with their eerie bright blue eyes. I was staring back at them when a local guy a bit older than me came up and said with a heavy accent, "Watch this!" He waded into the stream, the water only coming to his mid-shins. He then snapped his arms down and lifted a writhing eel over his head, water dripping from its mottled skin onto him. Even with his arms spread, the eel had extra length to either side. Mom shrieked in what she considered vicarious alarm. Beaming, he lowered the eel back to the water; it flicked its tail and swam away up stream.

The eels, with their unusual blue eyes, are an important part of the island's traditional history. Huahine is actually two islands, Huahine *Iti* (Little Huahine) and Huahine *Nui* (Big Huahine), which are separated by a ribbon of lagoon. Legend has it that a giant eel severed the two with a flick of his mighty tail. The animals had looked to have strong tails, so a little hyperbole easily brought them to the level of geologic forces.

Our day on the road certainly provided for animated conversation that evening. After our stay in the main harbor, we sailed down the coast to a rare sight in Polynesia: a white sand beach on the main island, not a motu. We reveled in celebrating life on a beach, and spent close to a week there. Although drawn by the sand, we spent most of the time enjoying the abundance of sea life on the outer reef, including our first views of clownfish living in anemones, and seahorses, which were mesmerizing.

We eventually made our way back toward Raiatea, and mid-passage were pummeled with the most ferocious squall we had yet encountered in the Pacific. Lara and I huddled down below during the early morning hours as our parents dealt with strong gale-force winds of fifty-five knots or more, with blinding rain and lightning. There was not much to do besides wait it out; approaching the barrier reef in such weather was madness, as it would be easy to get off course and be dashed against the reef. After slipping through the reef cut on the east side, we gratefully picked up a mooring alongside *Traveler* in Uturoa. Barb hailed us over the VHF, and extended an invitation to a benefit the next day for schools in the Tuamotus hosted by the Rotary Club; even before learning the details, we accepted.

After a good night's sleep and a few hours of laughing at ourselves for the situation we had found ourselves in, we took the dinghy ashore to the Bingo Benefit. Dad could not keep a lid on his laughter, "I can't believe it; here we are, in the South Pacific, playing Bingo!" I had to admit, it did come across as somewhat bizarre.

We entered the waterfront auditorium where the event was held. The couple thousand square feet of floor were covered in folding tables, most of which were already occupied. The table we took was right by a cut in the concrete façade, a mammoth window. Dad sat down next to me saying, "Oh! They provided snacks!" as he reached into the bowl of dried seeds on the table. He popped a handful in his mouth and bit down, the crunch audible, but it was the crunch of teeth scratching against the uncooked chits. Groaning, he spat them into his hand and tossed the damaged beans out the window.

Barb came in and gave a wave before sitting down and reaching into the bowl of chits. We all started to speak, but her eyes bulged in surprise before we could start our sentences. I reassured her, "Yeah, you're not alone, Dad just threw them out the window."

"Hey guys!" Mike called out. He grabbed a handful too.

"Sorry about that, Mike. At least you're not alone." Sailors are always happy to grab available food; sometimes it's a misguided habit.

The announcer's voice droned the Bingo grid positions in French. I either remembered the language from years ago or was able to compare it to my more extensive Spanish vocabulary, because I understood. Several rounds in, Mom called out in her French accent, "Bingo!" at the same time as another woman. They both went to the front to claim their prize: eighty kilograms of goat meat. They were to divide it evenly, but Mom rather gracefully declined her share on grounds that we did not have a refrigerator of sufficient size aboard. Her co-winner was quite enthusiastic, however.

When they declared the victor of the final round, I stretched and stepped out. I was done, and so was everyone else. We confirmed plans with *Traveler*, and after casting away our moorings, the two of us headed down the windward coast of Raiatea. The small burst of human development around Uturoa was brief, and we were soon following the pristine contours of the island, with a settlement every few miles. It had not been until this leg that I gained an appreciation for the size of the island; it took a good two or three hours to reach our destination, a motu off the southern tip, an islet renowned for its reefs and scenery. It also had an old airstrip built there, long since defunct.

We found a few small sloops there when we arrived. They had anchored on a large, shallow sand shelf forming a wedge between the motu and the reefs. We joined them in the anchorage and made for the snorkel spots in great haste. The sunny waters were alive with fish, and the shallow waters made swimming a warm, relaxing act.

Traveler only stayed to appreciate the beauty for a night. We lingered another day, and lived to regret it. The next morning was overcast and we were ready to motor out of there—well, ready in every way except for the fact that the engine would not start. On the way down, the only navigable water was often a tiny channel, weaving through a maze of marks; to chance it sailing in light wind without an engine was ill-advised.

Dad and I eventually took the dinghy across the choppy lagoon after exhausting an array of possible solutions. A deep bay extended into the body of Raiatea, with about ten buildings located halfway down the bay. We found a dock, a "No Trespassing" sign hanging on the other side of the fence blockading it. Who knew when the last person had trod over the old wood? We leapt the waist-high chain-link fence onto the road. The hills rose sharply on the opposite side of the road, completely uninhabited. The road wrapped around a head of land, and we followed it inland. The cracking asphalt seemed to lead nowhere as we walked in silence under the mute sky. There were no cars, no birds, no goats; nothing moved but our feet beneath us. Even the trees were still without wind.

Finally I was able to break the silence by crying, "Payphone!" The battered booth was next to a dilapidated basketball court. The colors had faded from the signs inside, and the instructions were faint. A dead lizard lay mostly decayed on top of the phone box. I sighed, "Are you kidding? We need a card! Where do we get one of those?"

"You mean one of these?" In a moment of magic, Dad opened his wallet and procured a plastic card, a square of copper circuitry exposed. He picked up the receiver and after a moment swore and said, "Out of order."

We looked up the hill, beyond the decrepit ball courts, and started walking toward the school. It was not in session, and our footsteps echoed through its old halls.

"T'or ana?" a faint feminine voice called. Thank goodness; it was the secretary.

Dad managed to explain our unlikely scenario, and she dialed her phone to the careenage. Even after all my international calls, never had a call seemed to contact someone so far away. Dad reached for the phone but was shooed away by the old Polynesian, who mandated that she act as the relay. She asked us who we were, told the careenage, and finally managed to convey that *Promise* was in deep trouble and our location.

Power was rationed that evening as there was no wind; we could either use our small lights or the fan, but definitely not both. We saved our power for the VHF, which we left on for the following morning. Fred's voice came through at about ten: "*Promise*, this is Fred. You there?" We all heaved a collective sigh of relief.

We were hooked to his speedboat, his friend towing while he went below to see if he could fix our boat before we reached the careenage. He decided he was incapable without a certain part; Dad had replaced the solenoid, but we now needed a new ignition switch. Fred came up to the cockpit just to talk and hangout. We didn't mind; we considered him a total miracle man by now.

A week of confinement in the slip later, we were ready to leave and did so promptly. We went up the leeward side as though going for the channel to Bora Bora, but we passed it, continuing to the northernmost region of the lagoon. We dropped our anchor in the shallows preceding the barrier reef, in the lee of three close motus, the largest of which was called Taha'a Iti, or Little Taha'a.

The dinghy ride was long, choppy, and wet. Lara was nestled into the bow of the dinghy, trying to mitigate her chances of getting wet, though her going swimming was inevitable. We slipped in between the second and third motus and beached the dinghy on the latter. After tying the painter around a coconut palm, Lara opted to stay and swim in the shallows, while Mom, Dad, and I walked through the scraggly woods toward the ocean-side end of the islet. We stopped on a rocky beach, the shard-like stones straining even my tough feet. We put on snorkel gear, and looked at the water we were about to enter. The water rushed through at over five knots. By comparison, an Olympic swimmer maxes out a bit over four. We did have the advantage of flippers, but going upstream would be slow and exhausting at best. This was a go-with-the-flow moment, and we dove in. The water was shallow, about five feet deep, and the sandy bottom was studded with boat-sized coral clusters, with a few navigable feet between them. Sticking to these paths, we shot down the length of the channel.

The coral was perfect: reds, blues, greens, yellows, and oranges if you count sponges, and without blemish since the current swept harmful sediment away before it could touch the polyps. Fish of a hundred species poured in and out of the coral, ranging from tangs to leg-sized parrot fish to eels to golden butterfly fish. These were my favorite, for when I swam upstream, which resulted in a net movement of zero, and extended my palm toward them, they would approach and gnaw at the skin with their impotent little jaws. Their snack would always be short lived since the current would sweep me away backward before long.

Snorkeling is usually a highly social activity where you share the experience with the people you came with, wondering at the beauties before you both, sort of like a movie. Here we were so engrossed with the environment that we ignored each other and were quickly cast apart by the current pushing us through the coral matrix. About fifteen minutes later we all washed up by the dinghy and without hesitation got out of the water and back to the wooded path for another round. I left my flippers on for the path; although horrendously awkward, they protected my feet. The reef was just as amazing the second, third, and even sixth times we went.

Little Taha'a was a charming small island itself, with lush gardens and swaying coconut palms framing a distant view of Bora's distinctive peak. Back onboard for the afternoon, Lara, who I was sure would sprout gills, was back in the water diving off the transom. Over picture-perfect white sand, I did not think she would see much, but several amazing and varied rays swam by, and they even posed for pictures. The relative silence was broken by a loud "Ia orana." which was a surprise. We were hailed by a weathered, friendly Polynesian in a woven-grass hat. As he approached in his brightly colored wooden dory, we took note of the floor covered with produce: bananas, coconuts, papayas, and garden vegetables as well. He pulled alongside and we welcomed him. It turns out that Poolu lived and farmed on the motu and wondered if our ship's stocks needed replenishing, which we gratefully accepted.

The following day on *Promise*, we lifted anchor and headed back down the shoreline to Taravana. After picking up a mooring, I took the dinghy in with twenty euros, enough to pay Maui for the mooring and a Wi-Fi card. We needed the latter the following morning; it was March tenth, admission or rejection day for all the schools I applied to.

That morning, I ignored breakfast and grabbed the laptop. I opened the browser, and entered the Wi-Fi code. Mom and Dad had sat down on either side of me, looking at the monitor. Mom had a folder with all the schools' login pages and our passwords. She said, "Let's start with NMH; you felt like you had a really good interview there."

I typed nmh.edu. I logged in and clicked the button saying "Admission Status." A second tab opened, the text saying "You're in!"

I roared, "Yes! Oh my god, yes!" A video ensued of artsy students speed painting "You're in!"; geeks going to the white board with an equation and coming up with the string "You're in!"; and the jock dunking a ball shouting, "You're in!" I was in, and laughing with glee.

Eight schools later, I had been accepted everywhere. I started singing, "I'm walkin' on sunshine, whoa-oh!" That was my theme song for the day. We took out the satellite phone and called Poku. I could not curb my euphoria and when he said, "Hello?" I shouted, "Poku! I got in everywhere! Everywhere!"

He started laughing and lost his standard calm demeanor; he was as excited as I was. "Master Ellison, you've done it! I always knew you would do it!"

Over the next few days, I kept sharing my thoughts and kept an ear open for what people had to say. Maui and I had a huge discussion about prep schools. Maui had gone to a boarding school in Hawaii at the Hawaiian Pacific Academy, and had a wealth of wisdom to share about choosing a school and reasons for doing so. After perusing each school's catalog and website, I felt fairly set on going to Phillips Andover, which had awarded me half tuition and a pretty certificate saying so. The next evening, *Contigo*, who had been well aware of my academic aspirations, had us over for a congratulatory dinner. With a history in academics, they had plenty of insight to offer, including a fifth champagne glass for me. Cheers, friends.

I had until April tenth to respond to each school to confirm whether or not I had enrolled. Maui and I continued to talk, and after I had memorized the catalogs, I had my verdict: Exeter. "Big Red," three hours from where we would live in the States, and king of sciences, was perfect for me. I believed it at the time, but had no idea how right I was until years of immersion later.

I could not have asked for a better conclusion to our time in Polynesia. Shortly after I enrolled in Exeter, we cleared out of the country and headed for Bora, the last stepping stone before we left this idyllic group of islands. Hurricane season was officially over, and most of our friends were moving on with us. We had a feast at Bloody Mary's that evening, a raucous dinner with *Cosmos*, *Alana Rose,* and *Contigo*; we sang Beach Boys songs on the dock to cap off the evening. We were all going to scatter our various ways tomorrow, but they were all generally the same direction: west.

Promise at anchor in Bora

Practicing the unofficial national sport of French Polynesia

Ancient fish traps in Huahine

Alex on the boom at anchor, Huahine

Chapter 12

MOPELIA

Polynesia had been nirvana, but we were ready to move on. It was eight o'clock, and the sun was high and bright, hardly obscured by the minute cumulous clouds so typical of Polynesian weather patterns. Having stowed everything that could possibly be dislodged by swells, we dropped our mooring outside Bloody Mary's.

The day cheered us on. At this early hour, boats already frequented the lagoon, zipping from one motu to another. Other cruisers started to stir; some, like us, were heading toward the cut in the channel. The maritime zeal of the place was infectious—not that we needed any further encouragement.

The cut in the reef was wide, and proved no challenge whatsoever to pass through at a breadth of almost half a mile. As we pounced on the open Pacific, I took a last look back, and noticed that some catamaran had tried to go inside a mark, and had ceased all motion; they were probably tourists chartering. The reefs to either side of us quickly dissipated, and the swells gradually escalated, breathing charisma into our castoff. We set our course for Raratonga, the capital of the Cook Islands, a bearing of 300 degrees west-southwest. That was going with the trade winds, downwind, and having spent little time on the waves that season I was feeling ill. I craved the sailing within a barrier reef we had mainly done over the past few months. That was what I liked to call flat-water cruising, as opposed to the blue-water cruising we were just starting. Downwind sailing is usually the worst for stomachs, the rhythm of going with the waves irregular and nauseating. The boat often feels vulnerable as well, with its disorganized wobble; its sails often luffing or collapsing, only to snap back loudly when the wind catches them once again.

Staring at the horizon to dissipate my seasickness, Promise made for Raratonga. After several repetitive hours of dodging the sun and boredom, the sun finally set beyond the horizon and the explosive sky, each of the small clouds above a fiery crystal in an atmospheric chandelier. Mom brought up an abbreviated galley product, pasta with red sauce. Her lovely, more elaborate cooking style was simply not feasible at sea, even though the stove was gimbaled. I had my noodles sans sauce, not wanting to run the risk of exacerbating my already jeopardized stomach. Life at sea is stripped of the luxuries of relaxation and idle time. After the dishes had been cleaned, Dad took the first of the night shifts and Lara and I went to our respective bunks and Mom to hers, after she turned on the SSB and contacted our radio network, our informal lifeline should the worst happen. This network was a collection of people we had met in the Pacific, including *Contigo*, *Alana Rose* and *Cosmos*. We all gave our bearing and heading, and contributed what weather knowledge we had of the upcoming days. I liked to listen in to these conversations normally, but I was too tired to do so tonight.

After a few hours of sleep, I got up at three o'clock in the morning to share the last shift of the night with Dad. It was our first overnight passage in years, and for the first time I was old enough to take a shift. Regardless, it was my first time, and with something as vital as our home and lives, it was probably a wise choice to wean me onto the responsibility. My stomach still hurt, and although I had wanted to help Dad who had been up and was surely exhausted, I simply could not push myself to take the helm. I settled for babysitting the autopilot and trying to appear engaged, and inquired, "Hey Dad, what's our course?"

He replied, "I'm keeping it between 330 and 340; whatever keeps the sails full."

After a moment of thought I realized the disparity between that and our original course. It occurred to me that it might be a tack, but that would be unnecessary, since we could have sailed on a broad reach most of the way. So I asked why, and listed my trend of logic.

His response was, "Oh, I forgot to tell you, we're going to Mopelia. Mom's net check at seven informed her that there's going to be pretty bad weather around Raratonga, so we're avoiding that and going to ride it out in harbor." Mopelia was an atoll I had lobbied lightly for going to; it was out of the way, a wild little nub of coral with cluster of pearl farmers, some fifteen strong. Once we were inside the barrier reef, we would be well protected, since its lagoon would be totally impregnable to waves, and the wind on its own was a manageable force. This contrasted strongly with the situation provided by Raratonga, which was a geologically young rock, with a slight indentation for a harbor, the only protection provided by an artificial breakwater: an inferior hurricane hole, and one that was guaranteed to be hit by bad weather soon. I was also happy to have a harbor sooner, since I was still feeling ill, and idly crouched in the cockpit, waiting for the darkness and shift to end. An hour later, at about four, Dad gratuitously gave me the option of returning below to sleep. I gladly accepted. As I would later discover, night shifts are one of the most mystical facets of cruising. Not that night though, not for me.

It was almost seven o'clock when I emerged from my berth. The main salon was brightly lit, the rising sun shining down the companionway. Mom was asleep on the port couch in the main salon, held there by the lee cloth. She was sleeping in her lifejacket. Squinting as I rose into the cockpit, I heard, "Hey, look who's up! How you doing, Boot?"

I replied and completed the courtesies before asking, "So, where are we relative to our destination now?"

Dad hit the autopilot button as he answered, "The GPS says we're about thirty miles away, so we'll be there in a few hours."

A few hours took us to about noon, when we sailed around to the northwest side—the location of the single channel into the lagoon. Mopelia was my first atoll, but I could tell it was fairly standard as far as atolls go: a low ring of sand on top of where the barrier reef once stood, and the inner island sunken beneath the lagoon. The only difference was that the ring of sand was incomplete, most of the leeward part still a submerged, albeit shallow, reef. Another geologic tidbit I did not notice until some years later when I looked at a satellite image of the island was a shallow reef right in the center of the lagoon—remnants of the old volcanic peak, clinging to the surface with the assistance of coral growing toward the sun.

As we drew around the northern horn of reef, we scanned for the pass-through. We knew generally where it was, but our paper chart was regional, making a speck out of Mopelia, and our GPS chart, like all others, could not be relied on too heavily. "Hey, is that another boat?" The odds of it happening had not been high, but there was another boat leaving the channel as we approached, and it was leaving quickly. They waved in salute to one of the other few crews intrepid, or insane, enough to venture here. Standing up to wave back, I noticed that they were losing speed very quickly, returning to six or seven knots, the speed range appropriate for a small sail boat.

The water outside the channel was distinctly turbulent, eddies twisting over the surface, other parts frothing, and some as smooth as glass. We circled through these eclectic waters, finding the line down the ribbon through the reef. Dad was trying to use the GPS to line us up, and in the middle of one of his circles he observed, "Hey, check out the chart; it says we're in the middle of the barrier reef!" I panicked momentarily, but I realized there was no way that was correct. I took a look at it too. The GPS chart was off by some 100 yards. We were done using that instrument for a while. Mom reverted to her favorite hand bearing compass, which had an optic trench you looked down to get very accurate readings. Using that, we found our target and, sails down, motored down that line.

I went to the bow wearing polarized sun glasses. The lenses exaggerated the difference in colors and the subsequent difference between safety and sinking. Dad, in a moment of total seriousness and pragmatism, told me, "Alex, make sure you hold on tightly at all times. I don't want you falling overboard if we hit." Right. Thanks for the reassurance. I did not respond.

Clinging to the babystay, I was the first to be within the coral jaws. These jaws were about six inches underwater, every tooth of their serrated edge visible, a four knot current spewing from the lagoon through the 100 feet of width it had. That was twice our length, and sailboats cannot spin on a dime—not even close, and certainly not with a four-knot current. Turning around would not be an option, so when I was the first person from *Promise* in the channel, I knew the rest of the crew was in fast pursuit, and none of us would be stopping anytime soon. That was the plan, anyway, which was subject to change at the whim of the coral.

We slugged along at about three knots at maximum throttle, over half the speed robbed by the current. The trip through the channel took forever, time slowed further by what lay ahead in my view. The channel widened, cleft by a wedge of coral: a fork in the road with no road map. We had to turn one way or the other. To starboard, it looked shallow, and I saw a few coral heads. To port, it looked deep, a night sky blue. Loosely wrapping my hand around the babystay, I screamed back to the cockpit, "Go to port up ahead!" Dad stood on his toes to see what he could from behind the helm. He approved of what he saw, steering us gradually to port. Locked between the wedge of coral and the blade of the barrier reef, we headed into the lagoon.

The next thing I saw still makes the soles of my feet tingle in angst. Letting go of the boat despite all logic, I sprinted with my back low toward the cockpit, my voice shrill as I yelled, "Turn around! Turn around! Dead end!"

Mom poked her head out from under the bimini, and bringing her glasses down her nose barked, "Lee! Turn around!"

The next minute was my time in one of the finest moments in the history of boat maneuvering. Spinning the wheel hard, we banked toward the main reef, suddenly drawing away from it as the engine strained to tug us in reverse. Turning the wheel the other way, Dad completed the one-eighty and, crushing the ball of the throttle in his fist, thrust it into forward several thousand RPMs higher than was typical. When you live on a boat, you learn every sound it can produce, especially from the engine. The whine from the shaft was high, and something was buffeting the air in the engine room. Strained, the engine sounded like it was going to explode, and the wind whipped the acrid smell of burnt diesel exhaust into my face.

I stood up and ran back to my position on the foredeck, my palms burning from how tightly I held the lifelines as I ran along the deck. We pulled another sharp turn to port and swung in to the starboard option. The other boat had left through this channel, so we had to be able to get through. It seemed to be the only possibility, and fortune would not favor another miracle spin if something went awry. The water beneath was clear as crystal and a shocking blue, light and ostensibly shallow. I now had both arms and a leg around the babystay. "Port!" I called out, ensuring we dodged the coral head in our path. Almost immediately afterward I shouted, "Starboard!" Two coral heads really close together. "Port … more port … now starboard!" It turned out that it was not just two in rapid succession; it was the entire northern third of the five-mile lagoon. I was now standing at the bow, clinging to the furled jib; further forward meant better visibility. With the polarized glasses, coral stood out almost in a holographic way. That's more than I can say for everything in the lagoon. About a foot across and a foot beneath the surface, dull in color, even when I stood at the bow, I did not see it until it was only feet away. "Neutral! Put it in neutral!" It was a pearl buoy, a floating basket full of oysters tethered to the bottom with rope designed so it was just beneath the surface.

The floating buoys belonged to a few of the several hundred family pearl operations in French Polynesia. These waters represented only a fraction of the largest national export of French Polynesia (almost twenty times the combined value of all other exports) and are second only to tourism as an industry. Black pearls are created only in the black-lipped oyster, *Pinctada margaritafera*, which thrives in these Pacific waters of shallow atoll lagoons. Most pearl farms are concentrated on very remote atolls, since any sewage, fertilizer, runoff, or contaminants make it impossible to grow the pearls. The industry is actually drawing Polynesians back to the more remote atolls. The oysters nurture the pearls over three years, and most are recipients of a graft. A tiny graft can be placed in various spots of the iridescent mantle—hence the variations in color of the pearls from black to blue, from green to aubergine. Adding yet another tier of complexity to the process is the oysters' sensitivity to water temperature; they need to be monitored frequently and have their depth modified to keep them at optimal temperature. This was why this particular pearl basket was submerged: to keep them in cooler water.

Regardless of the sensitivity and exceeding value of the goods we were about to run over, we had insufficient time to turn away from it, so the best option was to stop the propeller. If the rope from one of those pearl buoys got twisted up in that rotating blade we'd be immobilized, and we would have no way to move the boat. Drifting freely in this minefield was suboptimal at best. Dealing with an irate pearl farmer who had just lost several years of pearl growth, however, would not be an enjoyable task either.

Dropping the anchor and hundred feet of chain that day was about the most relieving activity of my travels. Now firmly in place, and out of the way of any submerged hazards, it was possible to take a look around. The blue lagoon, with the dense palm matrix off our bow and from our stern a view of infinity over the barrier reef, was truly stunning. I was brimming with gratitude for the fact our boat was intact, and as I noted in my journals at great length that night, I marveled at how Mopelia had not been in our planned sequence of islands.

With the exception of late-sleeping Lara, the crew was fully recovered from the day before and was ready for a shore exploration. In our matching white swim shirts, Dad and I went on deck to breathe life into the dinghy, with the assistance of a foot pump. Twenty minutes of stomping on the pump later, we hooked a halyard to the painter at one end and the other to the power winch.

Dad nodded and said, "Bring her up!" He guided the dinghy into the air away from the rigging, and I managed the power for the winch. The little machine was hardly bigger than my fist, yet it managed to whir to life and lift the dinghy off the deck.

"Okay, ease her into the water, now!" I carefully let the halyard slip, bringing it into the water. As we fixed the outboard motor on I heard a faint, "Yoo-hoo!" from below decks. That was Lara's announcement of consciousness. Mom hugged her and informed her of our plan.

"Do you want to stay on the boat?" Lara nodded and Mom continued, "You know how to use the VHF, right? We'll have the portable one and be on channel nine, okay? Here's a page of spelling you need to do before we get back. Love you, and see you in a bit."

It took her a moment to process all that, but Lara then cried, "Wait! I want to come to shore with you!"

I waited for everyone to settle in and get balanced before yanking the ripcord, revving the outboard engine twice, and then flipped the throttle out of neutral. The dinghy was full, and with four passengers and a bag of snorkel gear and a dinghy anchor, we were not going to plane but made for shore pretty quickly. The water was shallow some hundred feet away from the sandy shore, so we tossed the anchor in there, and eagerly leapt from the inflatable. We orbited the dinghy in the pristine brine, a comfortable four feet deep.

After twenty minutes of floating and snorkeling close to the beach, I was ready for a more adventurous expedition. Dad and I waded in to shore, each of us equipped with a pair of footies, tough nylon and rubber shoes designed for beach and coastal use. Dad wore them regularly, but this was the first time I'd worn shoes to the beach in months. After the short spit of beach we were in the palm trees; I was pretty glad to have them, though. We found a distinct path that looked like it would lead across the width of the sand spit. The vegetation was almost exclusively palms, the only exceptions being the thick grass paving the path we found, and only the occasional shrub to push past. About halfway across we stopped to look around. We were in the middle of a lull in the palm continuum, with nothing to see except the disorderly arrangement of the coconut trees. With the almost perfect absence of sound, just the wind rustling the palm fronds overhead, it was the single most tranquil spot to stand, its rhythm and beauty utterly soothing. I looked at Dad. His face was partially illuminated with the dappled light pouring through the fronds. He too, was just looking about. I pulled the camera out of its case, and spun around several times to find the angle to capture the scene. The shutter snapped repeatedly, but the photos always missed revealing some crucial element. Some things are just not meant to be photographed.

The ocean's roar filled my ears as we made our way down the grassy path. The path dissipated and the palms parted to reveal the Pacific. The sun reflected off the sea, a blazing blue mirror. I took a slow step from the grassy sand to the dramatically different shoreline of Mopelia's outer edge. It was a shore of fruit-sized, smooth stones, worn after an eternity of grinding against each other. Another Pacific swell hurled itself onto the stones, sending spray up the width of the beach to us, following its attack with a hiss of water running over stones, and the rumble of it pulling them against each other toward the sea.

"Well, this sure is impressive," I murmured. After a minute listening to the thick, rumbling hiss of the stones and sea, I asked, "I'm going to get a close look; is that okay?"

Dad scratched his scalp before answering, "Just don't get too close and be really careful." He drew out the last few words for emphasis.

I picked my way across the stones, and tragically, the litter. Every few yards some plastic bottle had found its way from the ocean to nestle on dry land. Even here, hundreds of miles from the habitation of anyone other than eco-conscious pearl farmers, signs of humanity were present. The flotsam probably had been travelling hundreds of miles from Tahiti or Bora. After the stones, the shore's edge turned into an uneven ledge, dropping just a foot or two into the depths, where the water churned about boulders and coral in a bitter battle for survival. I stood on this ledge, my toes inches from falling. The water was receding, leaving the boulders below exposed, briefly. Then it rushed back in, quickly burying them and showering me in oceanic might.

I returned to the coast once again, this time with Mom. Dad's response had been a quiet assimilation of the scene, but Mom unreservedly sputtered her excitement for the beauty. On the way back through the coconut grove, Mom and I frequently diverged from the path in search of wildlife. Specifically though, we were looking for robber crabs. These bright red creatures were larger than bowling balls, and could scale a coconut tree, cut a coconut down, and crush it open with their claws instantly. It would often take me twenty minutes with a hammer, machete and several other implements to open one. Our prolonged trip back was fruitless; we did not find any full-grown robber crabs. Walking across the beach to cool down in the water, though, I stooped down and said, "Hey, check out this hermit crab I found." Spiny and bright red, he was one of the largest hermit crabs I had seen; he would have taken up the better part of my palm had I been brazen enough to hold him.

Mom's zeal continued as she gushed, "Oh! Look at him! Wait ... do you think he could be a baby robber crab?" We launched into a dialogue of informal, scientific conjecture. It seemed plausible, and our theory was that he was a juvenile since he did have the appropriate color and exoskeleton. Our theory continued to explain the shell, which was that he was still in possession of a softer shell, so he had adopted another shell in the manner of an actual hermit crab. It turned out, after later reading, that we had actually been more or less correct, and that he was probably a young robber crab.

That evening, I listened in with Mom to the SSB net. The weather prediction for Raratonga was worsening; we'd be getting company the following day. Mom said to them, "Just make sure, guys, that you have someone on the bow to watch for coral heads. Also, go starboard in the channel. Can't wait to see you all."

Again, around noon, our VHF crackled and the voices from *Contigo* made their way to us, "*Promise, Promise, this is Contigo,* come in please."

I grabbed the radio and depressed the speak button. "Hey, Chris, you guys here yet?"

His southern accent was unmistakable even through the VHF. "Yeah, we're just inside the lagoon, but don't see you . . . how far in the lagoon are y'all?" I replied, "Oh, you got to go all the way down the lagoon. The best spot's a few miles south of where you are now."

"Oh, thanks for the heads up, Alex," he said. "See y'all in a bit then."

In the afternoon we invited our comrades over, and they stayed for the evening. We had been baking much of the day, making bread of various types. There was no way to replenish those supplies when in remote places or at sea, so we had grown accustomed to making a batch every few days. With a preponderance of bananas easily acquired, we created and consumed many varieties of breads with bananas as well. To this day when I smell or see a banana, I instantly think back to the Pacific. That night, fortunately, we were having homemade pizza instead.

Over dinner Chris told me, "So, Alex, I went in to see some of the people on shore, you know, just to introduce myself, and I'm going to go free diving with them this evening. Apparently there's this great underwater cave in the channel, full of reef sharks and stuff. You want to come?"

Chris was an accomplished free diver who often spoke of his harpoon fishing. During his dives he would sit perfectly still on the bottom for three minutes so the big fish would get curious enough to come up and investigate, and consequently get harpooned. He was also an adrenaline junkie, so he did not have a problem hanging out in an underwater cave with a strong current to the ocean outside and sharks inside.

I thanked him profusely and politely declined. "I hope you have fun though!" I said. The following day, it turned out Chris and the guys he went with had survived, and only had to give the sharks the occasional hit on the nose if they got too curious. I would be returning to that channel one way or another, but not until we left days later.

We fell into a rhythm of life in the calm atoll with no visible signs of habitation, but in fact a few huts lay hidden in the verdant foliage. There were two families with pearl farms there, and they kept an outpost and a presence to guard their treasure vigilantly. Somewhat ironically, with only two clans on this pristine island, there was a feud between them, and they did not speak to each other. It was a solitary existence, much as ours was, although ours had a distinctly different feeling; we were mobile. Captain Jack Sparrow, when describing a ship, quips, "What is a ship, really? It is freedom." If a storm would come, or whim would change, we could alter our course and venture forth to almost anywhere connected to the ubiquitous sea.

Leaving made the assumption that we could traverse the lagoon safely, and exit the tiny pass we came through unharmed. As we sailed out, I stayed at the bow and vigilantly kept my gaze on the water ahead as we navigated the lagoon. "Starboard! Port! Okay, we're good ... wait, neutral!" I accompanied these shouts with wild gesticulations and hand gestures and the infrequent thumbs up in the off chance I had not been loud enough. Despite my hopes, as with last time, the concentration of coral only grew with our proximity to the channel. As we aligned our course with the channel, it became apparent that the current was much higher than when we had come in. Local wisdom said the current could exceed seven knots, just a bit over our maximum motor speed. Since steering comes from water passing over the rudder, if you are going the same speed as the water, steering does not happen. That is quite an inconvenience when you need to thread your way through a hundred-foot coral chute.

To either side of the channel surf broke on the reef, cresting ten feet high. We entered the delta at the channel's head, our speed increasing perceptibly. My job as coral spotter was complete, yet I remained on the foredeck. I was the first one in Mopelia and I intended to be the first one out. With coral and waves breaking on either side of us, we were in the water chute, picking up speed more and more speed as the throttle opened in strained attempt to outrun the current and maintain steerage. Whirlpools streamed across the water's surface dizzily, gaining and losing speed at random. With the water roaring and folding over the reef to either side, we shot forth from Mopelia onto strangely still water that resembled warped glass.

I started giggling. My attempts to stifle my laughter with my hand were futile, and I burst forth into a maniacal cackle as I ran back to the cockpit, crushing Dad with a bear hug. "We're alive!" I bellowed into his ear. Alive we were, and on our delayed way to the Cooks.

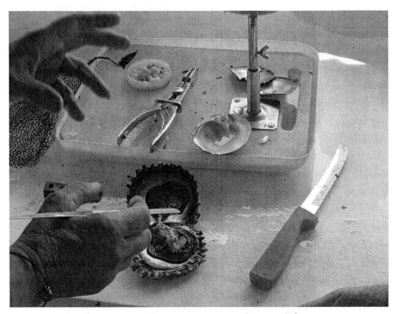

Grafting a mantle into an oyster for pearl farming

Mom watching for reefs as we enter Mopelia

Dramatic surf crashing on the reef's edge

Sheer euphoria in the aftermath of a tense exodus from Mopelia

Chapter 13

AITUTAKI, ALONE ON THE SEA

We were alone in the middle of the Pacific Ocean with no one for countless miles. Our last port of call had been French Polynesia, hundreds of miles to the east. The trip, although long, had been relatively uneventful. The weather had been fair most of the trip as my mom, the navigator and local meteorologist, always checked multiple sources before we headed out on a long passage. We always tried to keep as many variables as possible in our favor. Dad always says, "Luck favors the prepared." At sea, to be unprepared for almost any eventuality was, potentially, to perish.

It was three in the morning when a kind but tired voice woke me. Through my barely open eyelids, I looked up to see Mom. She wore a blue foul-weather jacket and a tiny lifejacket that inflated when wet. A dim red glow behind her broke the darkness. There was nothing I wanted to do more than drop my head to the pillow and retreat into sleep, but my family needed me; it was my turn to take control of the boat. In my tight bunk I donned a lifejacket similar to the one worn by my mom. I walked up the companionway from the shelter of below decks into the cool, black night. The relative coolness of being on deck shocked me into consciousness. Despite being so close to the equator, it was actually cold, compared to the day at least. Within a few minutes I was alert; after Mom had given me some basic information, such as our course and the weather, she went below to sleep. I was alone.

The blackness was complete but for the green and red lights of the instrument displays.

I sat down on the fiberglass bench, behind one of the two helms. I observed the small area that I would be confined to for the next three and a half hours, my shift. At the back of the boat, where I was, the railing was the sturdy metal framework necessary to keep the helmsman aboard should the seas become rough and break into the cockpit. I pressed the button that turned off the autopilot, and grabbed the helm with both hands. It was wide enough that my arms stretched away from each other, but not uncomfortably so. The surface was smooth leather, gone slightly sticky with its years in the marine environment. Occasionally one of the wheels made a rubbery squeak, or the rigging would grind against itself, making strange creaks and groans. Everything smelled, mostly of the salty breeze propelling us through the ocean, but there was also an odor of mustiness and of something mechanical.

As I steered, I constantly monitored the instrument displays. The wind was from our port aft quarter, calm, at most fifteen knots. It tossed my hair about as we coursed through the dark. When I was not looking at the instruments, I stared at the compass on the other side of the wheel, illuminated red, while making small turns of the wheel. It stared back at me; we watched each other's backs. It was easier to stay alert when the stars were out, but tonight the sky was cloud-covered. Every five minutes, I hit the autopilot button, and it beeped to notify me that the most diligent crewmember aboard had briefly assumed control. I looked in every direction from the boat, scanning to see if there were any tankers that could crush us. I leaned out of the cockpit, which was raised slightly off the deck, and scanned the blackness. The black of the abyss was unblemished; there were no other ships out there to provide a hazard. Whales and other large cetaceans were always a concern, since they (somewhat eerily, in my opinion) slept on the ocean's surface silently, and were undetectable by radar. Large cargo ship containers and other debris might also be floating along, waiting in our path to wreak havoc upon our hull. Large objects lost at sea could sink a ship in minutes, so vigilance and a little luck were our allies in the night.

I came back into the cockpit and moved across to the starboard side. Pausing, I repositioned the harness. This cable was all that ensured

I did not fall into the black ocean; fall away from my family asleep on a ship sailing itself away from me. As I moved, the harness was dragged across the floor, whispering. Again I leaned out of the cockpit, on starboard this time, to scan the blackness. With the billowing jib on this side, I lay flush with the deck to peer under its gentle curves. No lights above water. Scrambling back to the helm I saw a few green, underwater sparkles of bioluminescent plankton. I moved back to my original side of the cockpit, again unclipping and reclipping my harness. I turned off the autopilot and with another beep I resumed steering. About twenty minutes later, having performed one of my scans of the abyss, I went down below and look at the radar. The animated arm swept over a fifteen-mile radius. Like the night it scanned, the monitor was black. Mainly I looked for squalls; although small as far as storms go, on the radar they appeared as huge yellow lumps that dominated the monitor.

After about three hours, the blackness became a deep blue behind me, growing ever brighter. Eventually, the hue on the eastern horizon morphed into a pale pink. The wan light now shone down below decks onto a clock. It was 6:30; my time was up. Looking out across the breathing ocean, I sighed and hit the autopilot button again. It beeped in farewell. I descended the companionway to awaken my dad. He was asleep in the main salon, his normally neat hair rearranged by the salt and wind. It had retained its uncharacteristic shape, the dried saline serving as an unwelcome gel. Once he got up and took the reins, I curled up into a ball on the couch. Beneath a blanket, I left the lifejacket on. I was too tired to care. I needed to rest because the same thing was going to happen tomorrow.

Days later, sky and ocean were both gray. The ocean was darker, almost the blue it should have been. I sat on the wet teak; my hands clasped the helm. I rotated the wheel in a consistent pattern, one that let us slice through the swells. The four-foot wide helm was heavy in my grasp. I rotated her in a small cyclic pattern as we ambled through the waves. We were going about seven or eight knots, and we needed to do at least nine. My hair fluttered off to the right; I glanced at the sails. They luffed as they propelled us toward land, toward Aitutaki. I was forced to shift my stance slightly as a larger wave lifted us above the rough surface of the ocean. My favorite oceanography book said about every three-hundredth wave was abnormally large, up to five times the average height. That could turn a twelve-foot wave into a sixty-foot behemoth.

Mom climbed up the companionway, brows furrowed behind her shades. She looked a bit down as she crossed the cockpit toward me.

Raising my voice above the sound of the wind I asked, "What's your weather up to, Lady?"

Her earnestness was broken by a slight smile. "Scattered squalls throughout the area with a major front coming up from the southern ocean. We need to get to Aitutaki today to avoid it."

"Showers would be cool too," I added. We had not gotten water since Raiatea a few weeks earlier. We had four water tanks on board, and the two hundred gallons they held had to last four people for all their needs for about three weeks at a time. We had a watermaker aboard, which was a type of miniature desalination plant, but it was not functioning at that time. We also had water collectors, specially designed canvases to collect rainwater, but they could only be used when we were in port, and were subject to the whims of the rain gods.

Mom lightly shooed me away from the helm. I unclipped myself from the lifeline and moved toward the companionway before she could tell me, "Go below and help your father with the engine."

On the way I paused briefly at the chart desk where we kept all the nautical charts. I looked at Aitutaki, an atoll with a forty-foot wide meandering channel leading into a harbor smaller than a gas station. It was facing west. The winds were forecast to be thirty knots from the south, swells out of the southwest increasing to eight to ten meters. We were not getting in without a motor.

I asked Dad longingly, "Any progress?"

His face was covered in droplets of sweat and oil. He sighed, "I'm bleeding the fuel lines. I think there's air in there. But I'm out of ideas; it keeps on leaking."

We sat in silence for a bit, alternating between looking at each other and at the silent engine. The boat continued to pitch.

"Do you think Bruce would know?" I pondered aloud.

My dad waved a hand toward the radio. "Give him a call. See where he is. Let's find some solution."

Bruce, captain of *Blessed Bee* and veteran of many passages through the brutal Tasmanian Sea and the Southern Ocean, knew exactly what to do. He was already anchored in Aitutaki and suggested we use Teflon tape to seal the leak. He left us with the promise of standing by the radio in case further issues plagued us.

Teflon tape bound to the fuel line, the engine sputtered to life. Taking my turn at the wheel I guided us along at a sound nine-and-a-half knots. My greasy hair, streaked from almost a week without washing, was blown into my eyes. I shook my head but it found a way back. Lips pursed slightly, I concentrated on the pulsating blue vastness that lay in front of me. A gray, fuzzy thing on the horizon could be a cloud—but it wasn't. Aitutaki had broken the horizon.

As we finally drew close, the swells began to rise to their predicted height. We rushed down the sides of the waves, climbed back up, and then stalled briefly at the crests before dropping again. The surf attacked the shore audibly; it was especially easy to hear once the deep vibration of the engine faded away and the engine died, again. Pulling out the VHF we hailed any vessel that could pick up the signal, hopefully *Blessed Bee*. We knew that if we couldn't enlist assistance, we would simply set our storm sails and sail onward, which would delay our landfall by another week. We tacked up and down the length of the island; making short, frequent tacks in order to keep close to shore. Having abdicated the helm, I set the sails with each turn, which became more difficult as the wind strengthened to over thirty knots. We needed to buy time, walking a tight rope between a jagged reef and towering swells from the south.

After five or so cycles of this, Dad came up from below and announced that he could not contact Bruce. However, he had gotten in touch with the police, who acted as immigrations officers, fishing captains, and general services of all kinds on this tiny atoll. They were able to cajole a local boat to weave through the cut in the reef to assist us. We tacked. I set the sails. From across the growing swells came a small white craft. We pointed our bow into the wind, ceasing all forward motion to rise and fall with the waves as the small craft, now apparent to be a fishing boat, drew alongside. Pitching in the swells, we waited for this little boat to come alongside. I swayed on the deck, moving in an exaggerated rhythm to keep myself steady on deck and aboard.

As the petite wooden boat drew near, Bruce, a veritable tree of a man, stood with a coiled rope hanging like a whip from his hand.

Lashing his arm forward, he splayed out the rope; I frantically clasped it as it collided with my face. Wet and heavy, it could have been a dying eel. I wrangled it to the deck and lashed it to a cleat; then I looked toward the stern. Dad was imperious behind the wheel. Mom tied another rope between the two boats, and then the small craft began the sojourn to shore, us in tow. We were aboard a helpless twenty-three ton baby with no engine and her sails furled, since tacking within a channel as wide as *Promise's* length was not feasible.

The fishing boat entered the forty-foot wide pass between the coral jaws, with only ten feet of water or so between the sides of our hull and the menacing coral. Depth was another constant concern. The tip of our ship's keel was six feet below the waterline of our hull; this tiny opening only had six feet or more at a half-rising tide or above. The depth meter registered seven feet, but intermittently blinked to six or eight. Dad insisted we hold on to the boat, lest we hit unexpectedly and were thrust forward either onto the deck or, worse, into the tempestuous sea. The swells had only grown as we continued to be towed into the channel. The surf nudged us through the entrance. Moving with the water, we had no steerage and our normally sturdy vessel was totally vulnerable. There really wasn't much to do other than sweat, so I took pictures. The small fishing boat's engine buzzed ahead constantly. They guided us through a bottleneck and spun us around within the tight lagoon, stern toward the shore, bow toward the Pacific. We dropped the anchor ahead of us and tied our stern to two large coconut palms.

We relaxed for the first time in almost a week. I sat next to my dad, leaned into his shoulder slightly, and sighed. Although the wind still lashed, the waves pounding their fury on the edge of the reef could not reach us, and we floated on the calm surface of the lagoon. Across the harbor a crumbling jetty disrupted the glassy water. I ran my hand through my greasy hair, feeling both exhausted and filthy, encrusted with salt. A shower would be restorative. Normally we could find a dock hose to use for water, but not here.

I asked my dad, "How do we get water here?"

He sighed, his cheeks bulging with the exhalation, "We're going to have to jerry-jug it over, I think."

"That little five-gallon tank?" I groaned. "Ferry it back and forth?" He looked at me, so I added hurriedly, "Hey, whatever works. I mean, better than going to Raratonga. And I'm in no rush to leave the harbor."

A mere ten minutes earlier I had been happy to simply be alive and not churning in the giant swells of the South Pacific. Showers and cleanliness had been added to my short list of demands, too.

I felt a splat on my arm. In the tension that accompanied getting into a safe harbor with the impending storm, we failed to notice the thickening, moisture-laden clouds. The next second, the surface of the harbor churned with innumerable fat drops falling.

"The rain collector!" I shouted. "We need to use it!" Not listening for a response, I ran below and returned with the boat-sized canvas in tow. We suspended it above the deck, stretching it taught to the corners of the boat. The collecting canvas was like a snare drum at first; then, as it sagged with the weight of water, it sounded the same as the surrounding harbor. Plastic hoses dangled into filling ports in the deck. Water gushed through the clear plastic hoses like a faucet. I bellowed into the sky, spinning on the deck. I called below, "Mom! I need the big pot!" Beaming she clanked it down for me. Our water tanks aboard at full capacity held two hundred gallons. I had about twenty gallons in a canvas above me, spilling over the sides and down into the tanks. That was enough water to cook a meal and provide some drinks. I scooped the pot into the shimmering, liquid jewel and poured the world's purest water over my face. I did it again and again. The tanks overflowed.

The following morning I wandered out of my room late. "Morning, Chief. Time to get back to working on Bessie," said my dad.

I nodded my head and poured myself a bowl of muesli with a bit of long-life milk on top. I ate deliberately. Less than a minute elapsed before I finished and put the empty bowl in the sink. I motioned toward my bunk. We peeled the mattress back and lifted the boards beneath to reveal the red Westerbeke engine, streaked in grease. We tweaked every pipeline and nut on that side of the system until we hit one holding a certain cap down. I went to the cockpit to get a 7/16" wrench we'd left there and realized that it was totally overcast.

An hour or two later, Mom stuck her head in the door, "Hey boys, we're going to lunch with *Blessed Bee* in a bit; just a heads up." Dad grumbled at some mechanical object. I acknowledged her, "Thanks for the notice."

We all piled into the dinghy and traversed the 100 feet to shore. I tied it to a stationary barge that had washed ashore, mindful not to let the inflatable hull get too close to the jagged timbers. I followed my parents and Lara up the rocks and made for shore. Bruce stood by a beaten red pickup, and shouted "G'day!" in his cheerful Australian accent. He huddled in his foul-weather jacket, the rain running off it. He waved us over. Bruce, his shipmate, Gary, and my family over filled the cab. I peered through the windows and laughed. I vaulted into the bed of the truck not minding the fresh water shower and slapped the cab's roof. They cranked the engine, and after a few coughs it rattled to life. We ascended into the verdant hills, homes popping up sporadically. Each was a modest building with corrugated iron roofing and a few rows of crops alongside. We crested a hill; the expansive lagoon stretched away from the shore and had retained its electric-blue shade despite the driving rain.

I shook the water from my hair as we parked under the indigenous Norfolk pines. We walked into the restaurant, an octagonal pavilion with a kitchen in the back. Many locals milled about; the majority wore grass skirts and little else. A cluster of teens giggled off to the side, flowers adorning their hair, necks, and skirts, both boys and girls. Grabbing a table, we observed the preparations. "Hey, what exactly are they setting up for? Is it one of those dance shows?"

Bruce smiled in response, "Yeah, these kids are some of the best in the Pacific; they're going to the international competition in a few weeks."

Dad started to make some exclamation but was muffled by the voice through a microphone that announced, "Good afternoon, ladies and gentlemen. Tonight we're having a show by the Aitutaki Dancers, a gorgeous demonstration of some traditional dancing. But, of course, first we got a few buffet tables to the left if you're interested." The growing crowd gathered around the tables. I took a serving of nearly everything, Taro, a purple root vegetable, some coconut/seaweed coleslaw and a portion of every other food from water and land.

The last of the guests found their seats and the lights were dimmed. The dancers moved out solemnly, and stood for a moment in the dim lighting. The girls were in a row close to the audience, the men in a row behind them. A wave rustled over the sand. Then the drums erupted and the ukulele flew. The girls' hips swung, flinging their grass skirts in rippling waves. Behind them, the men's ankles stayed together as they moved across the sand stage, their knees swinging in and out at a cadence matching the girls' hips: fast.

The crowd and dancers passed through a few cycles of performance and ecstatic applause. At the end of one dance, as the audience roared, the dancers approached us. This was typical: the last dance of the show involved both the dancers and a randomly selected few from the audience. One girl walked up to me and extended her hand. In a moment of terrified reluctance, I professed a sprained ankle. Mom, sitting next to me, cried, "Are you kidding me? Get up there with her!"

Planting her feet in the sand, her hips swung into action as she spun around. I did my tentative best to imitate the male dancers I had seen, swinging my knees around like an intoxicated ant. I smiled at her as she came to face me. Looking beyond her blatant beauty, her features were coarser than those of French Polynesian girls. She was not as delicate; her cheekbones were higher and her jaw wider, stronger. Scattered applause began and I glanced back at her as I sat back down. The crowd stood in ovation. I smiled, staying seated. After bowing, all the dancers dispersed except for mine. She walked back to me and put her flower necklace and crown about my head, saying, "Thank you."

As she walked away, Dad burst out laughing, "Well look at you, Chief." He pointed the camera at me and gave me a swizzle stick. "Here's your scepter, Polynesian King; smile!"

Back in my berth, I hung the flowers on the same hook as the inflatable lifejacket, the necklace first and then the crown. The following morning I woke up and I pressed my face to the flowers, inhaling their overwhelming sweetness. Mom walked in, exclaiming, "Wow, those babies smell so good! But hey, are you ready to go on that tour to the nature preserve? It's leaving pretty soon."

Once ashore, we looked over to the huge jetty jutting into the channel. A few barges traversed the channel, transporting goods ashore from the monthly supply ship bobbing outside the barrier reef. Weaving through the coral heads, their slim aluminum hulls skimmed the surface of the lagoon. A team of marine engineers from New Zealand (the nation who oversees administration of the Cook Islands) worked nearby as well, surveying the artificial channel blasted through the coral. Although coral grows very slowly, sand can silt in from the sides and the modest depth of only six feet needed to be maintained for transporting the islanders' needs.

Our crew climbed into a small blue craft with our local guide and was on our way; for once, not having to worry ourselves about navigating through the serpentine maze of coral. We were all quiet, letting the sounds of the outboard motor and surging wake dominate our ears. I looked back at the main island of Aitutaki. Along the shore, palms and Norfolk pines bowed over the water. Denser, more verdant brush grew further inland.

Now almost at the barrier reef, the boat drew to a halt as we passed over the cline between the sandy shallows and the dark deep. Our tour guide, Captain Fantastic, cried, "Okay, everyone, this is a great little place for some sno'klin' if any of yous is interested," and he tossed the anchor off the bow. Virtually all the passengers scrambled to escape the confines of the boat and catch a glimpse of the Pacific in its prime.

With just a mask, I held my breath and traced the contours of the deepening seabed as I approached the coral metropolis. Clouds obscured most of the light, imbuing this realm with a ghostly beauty. My brain needed oxygen, but my mind needed to feast upon the vibrancy so rarely witnessed. The sparkling surface seemed distant as I surfaced. Having replenished myself, I returned. About twenty feet below the surface, the silky sand rested. Rising from this granular sheet were countless coral structures, edifice-like blocks of life comprised of a mesh of hundreds of corals penetrated by a plethora of fish drifting. Each of these coral mammoths rose far from the floor, leaving about five feet of open water above each—ample room for snorkelers to pass over. Not constrained by a snorkel, I continued to free dive on the coral. I wound around the outer corals and swam further into the labyrinth.

On the sand between the corals, several more static creatures lay, each about three feet across and mostly grey, highlighted with a blazing blue streak: giant clams. The grey shells were coarse and rippled, and between these hemispheres of armor were the fleshy blue lips. From one end of the lips protruded a little tube. I put my finger close to it, tentatively, and resisted the perceptible flow of water into it. That was the siphon feeder. As I surfaced, I felt a tap from behind. I whirled about, forcing myself not to scream; my minor phobia of sharks had continued to dwell in the back of my mind. Dad reminded me in pantomime that a giant clam was an amazing but surprisingly dangerous creature, one that had the power to literally suck in an entire arm if it got too close to the siphon. He then tilted his head off toward the left. I followed him in that direction, examining the coral in detail. As we drifted past, he pointed to a crevice in the coral. It was not too special, so I gave him a look. He pointed more fervently at the same spot. Then I saw it. A one centimeter, bright yellow, rounded cube, covered in black spots. Its disproportionately small fins spun perpetually, keeping it from drifting. Dad and I stuck our heads above the surface.

He spat his snorkel out to ask, "What is that little bugger?"

I responded, "No clue! He's pretty cool though."

Dad shrugged. "He's a pumpkin fish, then."

The tourists filed back aboard, each giving their limbs a shake to leave the excess water in the bottom of the boat. I was the last up, tossing the salt water from my hair. The process of losing that valuable cleanliness had begun. Captain Fantastic did a quick check to ensure we were all aboard before opening the throttle. Less than a minute passed before the aluminum bow nestled into the sand of a motu.

Fantastic called out, "I'm going to make us lunch. It'll be ready in about thirty minutes."

He went to an open shack to cook. As we paraded ashore, I traced a large SOS into the sand with my feet. We had learned from some of the islanders that this very spot had been used in the TV show *Survivor* the previous season. We hadn't known that, or ever even seen the show, since TV really was not a part of our lives.

I asked, "Hey, who has the camera?" Mom handed it over. I swiveled it across the sky in a vain attempt to capture a picture of an elegant white bird soaring overhead. It could have been a type of tern except for its tail extending a few body lengths behind it. Snap: another fuzzy shot of the overcast sky. The bird dove into the impregnable brush. Stumbling through the sand, I made my way toward where the bird landed. I gasped and, putting my index finger to my mouth, I beckoned my family over with the other. My mom peered into the brush and then spurted muffled exclamations. I smirked. Kneeling in the sand I pointed the camera at the bird and its fluffy offspring nesting on the ground, behind some branches. The adult bird peered at us and then back at its offspring, a compact white creature with tufts of white protruding from its head and neck. It resembled some lost Muppet creation of Jim Henson. Its jet stone eyes did not move. I looked at the pictures I had captured of the two and stepped back, trying to give them their space. It was too late. The adult bird hopped from the nest on the ground and began to limp away from the nest. "Oh, no! She was flying just a minute ago!"

Captain Fantastic handed us each a banana leaf with some fruit and parrot fish on top. "So, this is the food of my forefathers, and unless you brought your own forks, we'll be eating in the manner of my forefathers as well."

My foot twitched as a hermit crab clawed its way over it. I addressed Fantastic, "Hey, Captain? I didn't mean to hurt her or anything, but I was taking a picture of this one bird, big white bird, and its baby, and then the parent started to abandon the chick. It was limping away, but I had just seen it fly to the nest."

He laughed, "Yeah that's normal. She's pretending she's hurt so if you're a predator, you'll go after her, not her baby."

Pausing from her food, Mom smiled and commented, "Amazing what we mothers will do for you children."

Later that afternoon, after Captain Fantastic's boat docked, we made the short walk to the grocery store. I stopped beneath a ficus tree arching over the road. The majority of the mass was on the left side of the road, but the tree had grown over the road and its vines had grown down to the ground and formed another trunk on that side of the road. I wandered into the matrix of vines dripping down from above. The vines went into the sky indefinitely and formed a solid alcove around me. Running the thinner filaments through my fingers, I stepped back out to keep up with my family as we continued to get provisions.

We walked into the dank store. The lighting was poor, and the floor, dirty concrete. Although small, the refrigerated section was full of relatively fresh produce, the fridge stocked with frozen meats from the monthly surplus provided by the infrequent supply ship. My mom and sister, Lara, took a basket and scoured the aisles of packaged foods while my dad went next door to purchase oil for the dinghy's outboard motor. I took a bag to get produce. Although comparatively fresh, I still went over the whole rack, carefully turning all the fruit over and feeling them to determine which ones were the best. Of each fruit type, I took about five. Of those, two would be great and three closer to marginal. I searched for Mom and Lara. I found them debating over whether they should get cabin bread or sweet crackers, the two types of crackers available. "Why don't we get both?" I posed.

Mom shrugged. "Fair enough."

We walked up to the counter and greeted the girl behind it with, "Kia orana." She smiled, and Mom asked, "Do you guys have any toothpaste?"

The girl said, "I'm not sure; we might have some from the last shipment but we haven't finished unloading this month's yet." After a pause she continued, "But if we did it'd be in the aisle closest to the door."

I walked over and looked. There were a few faded bottles of shampoo, some bars of soap, and at the back of a shelf, a bottle of toothpaste. It was a foreign brand, but the exaggerated cartoon smile on the front could not have been an advertisement for anything else, so I brought it back to the register.

The cashier giggled, "Guess you got lucky then."

Across the square was a local market where we reconnected with Dad. He had been visiting with a local craftsman who procured a ukulele. We had a guitar aboard but had not added an instrument since our steel drum in the Caribbean, so the music teacher enthusiastically purchased it. Upon giving Dad his change, the Maori also gave us a good story. The Cook Island one dollar coin has a picture of Queen Elizabeth II on one side, and on the other a local deity, Tangaroa. The juxtaposition of the elegant monarch and the indecent nude god of fertility caused quite a stir back in proper circles in Britain when the coin was revealed.

That was our last afternoon in Aitutaki. A full week had elapsed since our dramatic arrival, and we all agreed that our time there had been far too brief. Aitutaki was one of the most scenic of the islands we'd seen recently, both above and below the water. Although we had taken an extensive tour of the lagoon and driven about the island twice, this left us with only a marginal understanding of the gorgeous and unique idiosyncrasies of the island. Each island has such unique features, in fact. However, in our brief time there, we were able to pick up some of the common trends. The most notable of these, by far, was the hospitality of the Maori people. This was evident in their readiness to assist if we ever needed a lift somewhere or even just the warmth shown in ordinary exchanges with them.

The very act of sailing the Pacific was a gamble—of precious resources, of time, and of our very lives. Of course, we wanted to play it safe, especially with the last article. The following day high tide was at eleven a.m., and we were anxious to hit the open sea for Palmerston Atoll. Wanting to get an early start and calculating the rise of water in the narrow channel, we left at 9:30. Even so, we scraped the bottom twice on the way out. Fortunately, the shallowest part of the egress we knew was sand not coral, and it merely cleaned the protective anti-fouling paint from the tip of our keel. With the weather about to turn foul, a massive front surging north from the Southern Ocean, we needed to move on and out of the way. Palmerston was scarcely better sheltered, but it was going to escape the temper of this storm.

Despite our reluctance to leave Aitutaki so soon, we possessed an undertone of zeal and excitement for the unknown before us. We shared an intense craving for the horizons yet to be crossed and the waves yet to be traversed.

Sunset at sea

In Aitutaki, cultural dancing starts at a young age

Happily stranded on a motu, Aitutaki

A fledgling red tailed tropical bird at nest on a remote motu, Aitutaki

A banyan tree engulfing the only road around the island

Alex under the rain catcher, Aitutaki

Chapter 14

PALMERSTON: A SOCIETY IN ISOLATION

$\mathcal{I}$ was asleep when we arrived.

"Allllllleeex!" The falling coo of my mother's voice woke me. I could just see a little, everything tinged with the blue of dawn. In an automated motion I rolled out of the bunk and went up on deck. I got to the cockpit and blinked at Palmerston. This was even less substantial of an atoll than Mopelia. The water broke over the barrier reef, flooding from the lagoon to the open Pacific. Only in three locations did the reef rise into land, small spits of sand bursting with palms and mahogany. The motu closest to us was the inhabited one, with an exact population of sixty-nine, all of which shared the last name Marster. The boat moved gently, as though the sea was breathing beneath us, not laughing raucously as it did on an open passage. Clapping his hands, my dad said, "That's it. Welcome to Palmerston, everybody."

We opened the hatches for the first time in days, letting both air and light into the living space below decks. The surf whispered in the background. My mom poured over a traveler's guidebook, a massive brick of paper that was her Bible for Pacific survival. It cataloged every cultural and linguistic nuance, as well as the geographic details of the islands. While she was intent on garnering further knowledge, I was content staring off into space, relishing the fact we were not moving.

The buzz of another boat's engine pierced the calm. With the exception of my sleeping sister, we all raised our heads. I clambered up the companionway onto the deck. A wooden dinghy wobbled over. The two dark, burly Polynesians aboard stared at us as they drew near.

"Dad! There're people!" I called.

They pulled alongside our hull. One of the men and I put out our arms to catch each other's boat. The other guy was wearing a faded Hawaiian shirt and khaki shorts, while the one who was directing the small craft quickly introduced himself as Ed. He wore a red mesh shirt and matching athletic shorts. Grease streaked his clothes. I passed them a rope, and soon they were aboard. The one in a Hawaiian shirt tossed his beaten briefcase onto the deck. It bore a placard saying "Immigrations." The sun rose above the horizon. I returned to my bunk, catching sporadic phrases from the discourse. The immigration officer, Pastor Terry Marster, said, "Ed will gladly host your family, Doctahs Ellison." Ed confirmed so, and Terry continued, "But is there anything you can do to help us back? Just pack a bag of stuff you could use to help. It'd be very appreciated." My mom's brick of paper mentioned something about this too, providing examples of mechanics who had repaired the small gas generator and the island's solitary truck.

Following Ed and Terry, my family tentatively got into their vessel and headed toward the reef. I climbed in after them, teetering with the weight of my full Swiss Army backpack. It was my favorite Christmas present when it came, filled with books, and the ruby nylon still shone, despite the few black streaks it had been blessed with. Lifted on a wave, I rolled backward into the bottom of the boat with my bag. Dragged from my position, I watched our boat shrink away as we drew up to the gleaming beach. When we beached, I lifted myself out, standing on my toes to keep my torso and bag dry. With my feet nestled in the sand, I licked my finger and scratched at the new smear on my bag. It blurred and spread. Ed hiked up the sand and pushed the brush aside as he walked inward. He kept a hand on a larger limb, keeping it out of the way as he waited for us. As I walked past him and into the engulfing foliage, Ed commented, "That's a beautiful backpack, guy." His face was blank as he stared at its little silver cross logo.

"I'm glad you like it," I said slowly.

Ed's voice was cheery as he said to my mom, "How're y'all liking it so far?" Before a response could be made he continued, "And your son has a really great backpack."

She said jestingly, "Yeah, but mine's better," and she pointed to an ambiguously colored and well-worn knapsack.

Ed pursued, "But his is just the best." He glanced around. We were all in the woods now. He sucked in a deep breath and said, "A'ight everybody. Follow me; my house is this way. We have a meal waiting for you, and can't let that go cold." With that he marched off, now on a dirt path that grew increasingly existent as we went. Above us was a layer of swaying palms, towered over by mahoganies, pillars of nature. These slowly parted as we reached a small, sandy clearing. A tarp was suspended between a mango tree, a palm and the small concrete bunker they owned. Beneath the tarp was a table, covered in fresh reef fish, scales still sparkling, and a grid of various fruits, most of which were orange in color. On no other occasion had my parents had such wide eyes and smiles. I mimicked them, realizing the magnitude of the effort this required of Ed's family, and the gratitude expected.

Ed looked on as we started the ceremonial gorging. He said to my dad, "So, Docta Ell'son ... when can you do the clinic for us?" I opened my backpack quickly to make sure everything was there. Rustling through it with my hands I felt the stethoscope, otoscope, and a little plastic thing that was probably a thermometer.

Running a hand through his hair, my dad replied, "Well, whenever works for you guys. We're happy to do anything for you after this gorgeous meal." He touched his stomach gingerly.

There was a brief silence. A chicken squawked and Ed used that as a segue. "Hey, can I have that backpack? That would be a huge help for me around here."

My mom stamped in before anyone could misstep, "Well, you would have to ask Alex since it's his." She tipped her sunglasses down her nose and fixated her eyes on me.

I zipped the bag shut and ran my hand over its silky surface. After feeling the silver logo I said, "I mean, of course you can have it. Uh ..." My voice trailed off. Ed sat taller and tried to say that it was fine if I really wanted to keep it. I professed that it was definitely his. He picked it up and held it to the sunlight.

"Can we just take our medical equipment out first, Ed?"

After passing the ownership of the bag, we reached the point where the adults had regressed into serious conversation and I was left sitting in their presence. That was when I received a tap from behind, and

Ed's older son, Dave, asked, "Hey, want to play football?" With that, I happily left the table. With the cruising community, a kid was a kid; there really were no subcategories. I stood eighteen inches taller than Dave, who was about two years younger than me, and towered over his younger brother Jon. Their friend Shaquina engaged in the game, too. They invited Lara in, but she declined, preferring to curl up in a sunny spot with a good book and watch, her fallback position in any situation that she was trying to assess before pushing herself into the unknown social abyss.

We grabbed a random assortment of objects, including buckets and chairs to form the boundaries and goals. It was Jon and me against Dave and Shaquina. They scored instantly as I tried to adjust my abilities, which I would have expected to be greater from size alone—or so I thought, but they showed me. We were about even when I tried my best. Five goals later, we switched sides, and my best kick propelled the ball high into a mango tree. Horrified, I sputtered an apology before I realized they were laughing hysterically. Dave proposed, "Hey, I'll race you up the tree to see who can get it first!"

He had home-field advantage, knowing each branch by heart. I, however, could cross between branches that he couldn't with his shorter limbs. We had attained considerable height, but we couldn't actually find the soccer ball. I grabbed the edge of a spiderweb and pulled it out of the way. The matrix of branches concealed that ball somewhere.

"I see it!" Dave cried. It was held in the highest of boughs, precariously perched, well beyond our climbing range. I reached up and shook a parent branch, hoping somehow it could be coaxed back to earth. From either that or the pulsating wind, it tumbled down.

As we resumed our game, Ed called out, "Dave! Have you fed the pig yet?" Dave dropped the ball and grabbed a reeking bucket from the side of the house. I followed him down the sandy path to the area behind his home. Beneath the mahoganies, and penned in by a thick barricade of stacked palm trunks, was their pig, slightly smaller than our dinghy. Dave grabbed a handful of the bucket's contents and held it above his head. The pig lurched forward, and putting his front hooves on the fence in a gesture of greeting, reached his snout up to grab the food. Dave and the pig, Mr. Big, were clearly fond of each other and had a trusting relationship. Somewhere in his heart, however, he knew not to get too close, since Mr. Big was slated literally to supply next Christmas's ham feast.

A brief bit later, we were given a tour of the island. We wandered down the paths, the kids and I taking the lead. Shaquina's mother, the island teacher, had joined us at this point, and was striking up conversation with Mom. Dave, Jon, and I idly passed the ball back and forth as we followed the shady path. Again, the path opened into a larger clearing at the school, on the edge of town. My family went inside the school as Shaquina's mom gave a tour. Lara was enthralled, since she loved schools in all their varieties, and this one was especially cheerful with colorful local crafts and art projects adorning the walls. The rest of us set up another soccer game. We played first to five goals. I was high-fiving Jon on our fourth score when Mom called, "Alex! Come inside and check this place out!"

It was a small operation, just one room housing kids of various ages. Despite being small, it was quite ornate, and I could see why Lara admired it; the walls were covered in posters of guidelines for writing, math, and general conduct, and the windows were open to the cooling breezes. The letters of the alphabet ran along the top of the walls, with corresponding images immediately beneath: Apple, Bear, Cheese, and so forth. Of course, none of which the children had seen frequently, if ever.

"We also have t-shirts for sale; we're trying to raise funds for a school trip to Raratonga." Mom was instantly endeared by the stylized sea turtle on the front of the shirt, and I adopted the role as the echo. Mom bought two, one for me and one for Lara. I may have been a hollow echo, but on a boat no clothing is ever unwanted.

We continued with our tour of the island, into the heart of the town. This was only a few paces away, and the difference was minimal. The houses were closer, and collectively they formed a loose grid. Their design was similar to that of Ed's home, the standard Pacific home: small concrete with a corrugated roof and palm thatch. It was conspicuously quiet as we tread between these houses; there was no one about or within them. A chicken ran across the main street. Why did the chicken cross the road?

As we walked toward the water I asked, "Hey, Dave? Where is everyone?" A response was unnecessary. We walked into a sandy area, a different sand, smoother, from being close to the beach. Some small camping tents had been pitched, and children squealed from within, one occasionally slipping out to breath before returning to the mayhem. The remaining sixty-nine residents milled about, talking, shouting, and bartering. Since the island and its population was so small, there was no real currency necessary. The island did belong to the Cook Islands, which shared the currency of New Zealand. However, in the same way people in most countries agree on the values of currency and subscribe to it, the people of Palmerston chose not to.

At the center of the group was a large, robust old woman weaving a hat from palm fronds. She beckoned us over and engaged us in conversation that seemed not unlike that of my grandmother. She finished sewing a piece of abalone onto the front of the hat and handed it to Mom, announcing, "For church on Sunday." Touching as the gesture was, I could hardly help smirking at the irony of the recipient. After excessive professions of gratitude, Mom put it on and we commenced our walk back to Ed's home, from where we would be ferried back to *Promise.*

On the walk back, Mom lent Shaquina the camera. She would not be able to keep the images since the camera was digital and there was no printer on island; she just wanted to play with it. She took a few dozen shots as we went, mostly of plants: flowers in her hand, shrubs, trees alongside buildings. She also recorded daily life, Jon hiding from his brother under the island's backhoe and Ed's brother holding a chicken—dinner—by the neck. We kept the pictures she took, and looking at them in the sequence taken, I saw a quick growth and even development of style. The first ones were merely efforts to close the shutter or macro shots. However, the last few possess a deliberate and artistic setup, capturing the homes and people better.

Had she not been a participant, I am sure she also would have adeptly used the camera to capture our last bit of time at the beach, a job no one filled unfortunately. As our parents all conversed by Ed's craft, Dave, Jon, Shaquina and I went into the water. A bit from shore, they scrambled onto a coral head, alive and vibrantly colored. I gaped, shocked by their audacious scrambling over the polyps, which every source in existence said not to do. It was also a brave assumption that there would not be any fire coral. They leapt into the water and carried on merrily. It was their island, so they probably knew what it could take in the ways of feet.

Something wet and slimy hit me in the face. I squirmed as it fell from me, and I realized it was a sea cucumber. I frowned at the black worm and flung it at Dave. Jon burst into laughter. War had broken out. Of course, the side that suffered the most casualties was the ammo: the sea cukes.

Ed piled us, the three island kids and finally himself into his boat. With the engine roaring to life, we zipped away toward the reef. Once we were back aboard, Ed and company stayed for a bit. The kids and I played various card games, we each taught each other a game. We also gave them some DVDs, which could be played on the communal TV system. This luxury was run from batteries hooked up to solar panels. Ed departed saying to us, "I'm so thankful for this all, really. What time do you want to be picked up for the clinic?" Mom responded, "How about seven?"

The silence of the early morning was broken by the whirr of an outboard engine humming its way toward *Promise*. My parents, considering the perils of being out of reach of medical equipment, travelled with enough medical provisions to take out an appendix, mend major injuries, rehydrate and treat shock, and—had we not lost the bag with the defibrillator—to resuscitate someone suffering from a heart attack. They also had acquired skills in medicine far away from the land of CT scans and million-dollar work-ups, as they had both worked as physicians in Africa and in Nevis, which is poor enough to have a Peace Corps presence. They both prided themselves on (and at one time had taught medical students) the art of physical diagnosis using only one's brain, body, and very low-tech equipment such as a stethoscope, blood-pressure cuff, and flashlights. As Palmerston was under the auspices of New Zealand, Mom and Dad also had had the foresight to bring copies of their medical licenses and professional documentation so that they could legitimately help pro bono in places where it was welcome and often necessary.

The island had a woman who was regarded as the local health worker, although she had not formerly trained as a nurse. Joaquin was indigenous to the island, understood the local customs and problems, and had a kind and gentle nature. She was always happy to share her small medical office with visitors who could help teach her things as well as share supplies. There was a very infrequent transport boat from Raratonga, but it only came every six months. For an acute injury or true emergency, help from an outside source was often not feasible. Just the week prior to our arrival, the islanders had buried a charming fifteen-year-old boy, who had slipped on the coral reef and hit his upper right abdomen. He bled to death slowly from a presumed liver laceration and was now buried in the local churchyard.

The islanders had been notified of the impending clinic, and by the time my parents reached the building, it was surrounded by curious children and ready patients. As it was early in the year and just past the worst of hurricane season, no formal medical help had been on island for many months; hence, almost everyone signed up. My mother, being a pediatrician, is always ready with a willing smile, stickers, and small books to dole out to her patients. Dave and Jon were eager to be her first patients, and then wanted to stay to be her assistants. This proved to be fortuitous as they knew everyone's name, likes, dislikes, and fears, and made everyone relax. Mom examined every single child on the island, twenty-nine in all. In addition to performing physical examinations, she diagnosed many chronic Otitis Externas, or swimmer's ear cases, to no surprise. Because of the narrow genetic pool there, she also noted several subtle birth defects and significant numbers of strabismus, or lazy eye, which without treatment can reduce vision. She reviewed use of the nebulizer on island with Joaquin and the patients with asthma, and requested a battery-operated version for the island in case the island's generator failed. She also ordered fluoride for all the children, since many had a significant number of dental cavities, and some had more significant infections. She marveled that although the island was a tiny dot in the middle of the Pacific, junk food and candy had found its way here and were hoarded when the rare ship came.

My father, who is a surgeon by training, but has also worked as a generalist in volunteer roles, saw all the adults who had complaints or previous problems such as hypertension. Joaquin was his assistant for a number of procedures and to help him observe local customs. When necessary, however, they helped however they could. When Mama Iti (a very large woman ironically named "Little Grandma") could not get up onto the exam table, my father and Joaquin examined her on a woven grass mat placed on the floor. It turns out Mama Iti also had a sweet tooth and a stash of candy, which was contraband with her diabetes. Joaquin would be left to try to implement the health policies and ferret out her great aunt's stash of sugar, as well as to monitor blood pressure, sugar in the urine, and other markers of illness.

After the medical clinic, the leaders of the island had a feast in our honor to thank my parents. Though they professed it was quite unnecessary, they graciously accepted the islanders' gratitude. My parents have always had the mantra, "It is not what you give but what you share that matters," and so were very glad to join endeavors to help people in any context. The local fruits and vegetables generously provided in overflowing baskets would sustain our stomachs, and hearts, for our next long passage to islands farther west.

Dave feeding "Mr. Big" leftovers from lunch, Palmerston

Main St., Palmerston

Joaquin weaving on the beach, Palmerston

On the steps of Palmerston Atoll School with new friends

Chapter 15

NIUE

The waves lapped at the hull gently. The marine night was as pure as ever, a black of infinite depth all around that was only broken by a fuzzy, flickering halo: the product of lights on a dock, seen through rain. Allegedly, there were moorings close by, but they were out of reach under the cover of darkness in a foreign harbor. We knew their general direction, but had to wait until the torrential rain stopped.

Reluctant to risk anything, we simply sailed in tight circles off the shore, waiting for the sun to rise. I huddled in the cockpit in a foul weather jacket. Dad and I alternated five-minute steering shifts; it was 6:00 a.m. and my shift was technically over, but it would require two of us to pick up a mooring. So, while Dad drove, I sought a place to dry out—an infeasible task. The bimini was losing its waterproof properties, locally reducing the deluge to a drizzle that still found a way in around the collar.

With the blue light emerging from under the horizon, the moorings became evident as did the topography of Niue. Dramatic and ragged cliffs rose around the perimeter of the island. Niue is one of the world's largest coral atolls, and is renowned for its incredible caves and chasms, as well as its abundance of sea snakes. Because it has no natural rivers or streams, the surrounding water is free of sediment; the water is so pristine that it is said that one can see 270 feet to the bottom of the harbor. Unfortunately, "harbor" is a relative term, as the main area is merely a dent in the western side of the island, affording little protection from swells and wind. It would be untenable in any storm or bad blow.

As the light improved, we ventured toward the mooring field, a few vessels of various kinds about; most looked like working boats for fishing the local seas. The lights on the dock were still glowing, starkly revealing the ordeal that awaited us prior to our getting ashore. Once moored securely, Dad and I went onto the foredeck. Kneeling on the fiberglass, I could feel the spiny traction grid dig into my skin. We unwound the elaborate system of knots trapping the folded dinghy to the deck, our ticket ashore, and began the tedious process of pumping air into it, deploying it, and heaving the outboard motor onto the back.

A few hundred yards of choppy water later, the dock loomed high above us. It was a solid concrete jetty, rising thirty feet out of the water. The only way up was a set of stairs projecting from the side; algae had grown to cover the surface, rendering it an opportunity for a slick fall into the surf that washed us up along the jetty's face, and then plummeted toward the bottom as it rolled back to sea.

"Okay, Boot, here's the plan." Dad said. "I'm going to take the helm, and you go up the steps, be really careful, and see if there's anyone around who knows what to do."

Timing was essential. As we rose with a wave, I threw myself against the wall. Step one was complete. The water was coming up around my ankles. On all fours, I scrambled over the algae and onto the jetty's top. It wasn't a rectangular surface, but rather a small triangular field of concrete pointing into the sea. A steel crane reached over my head; an arm sized lever with a local islander at its base.

"Hey! Excuse me!" I called, waving.

He raised an arm back, "Mo'ning! How're you doing today?"

I walked over and replied, "I'm well, thanks. Hey, is there a way to get a dinghy tied up or something?"

He chuckled and pointed to the lever he stood by. "Yeah, just gotta hook your dinghy up to the crane here, pull it up onto the dock, and you're good to go!"

I relayed this to Dad, and got back in the dinghy. We went to the boat, grabbed some harnesses, and returned to shore. Hooking the harnesses to the bow and pontoons, we attached the ropy mass to the crane; no midair passengers allowed. So, after introducing Dad to the helpful islander whose name was Ernie, we looked on as the crane groaned. The dinghy appeared after almost a minute of hoisting. Ernie grabbed a beaten rope dangling from the mid-section of the crane's arm and walked the dinghy over onto a solid surface before saying, "Okay, lower it slowly now." The crane did not have any mode other than slow, so obeying that request was easy.

After formalities and introductions had been run through, Dad asked, "Hey, Ernie, where is the customs and immigration here?"

In his loud, genial manner, he replied, "Oh, no need for directions, I'll drive you there!"

So we all piled into the beaten old Jeep and held on for dear life as he summitted the ramp up from the dock. The grade probably was too steep to be legal in most countries—not here though—and it was our treat to enjoy. The groaning engine, stressed beyond reason, hauled us upward precariously between the acacia that bordered the driveway and the frothing, grey-blue ocean beyond.

Crawling over the top of the driveway, we reached the upper limit of the plateau. We were in the capital, Alofi, a linear, one-street, utterly deserted hamlet. One car remained parked along the strip town, and no pedestrians patronized its street. Ernie spun the wheel to the right, knowing there would not be any traffic to worry about. He opened the throttle of his poor old four-wheeler and then spun into the parking lot of the police station, a concrete building larger than any other we had seen thus far.

Unbuckling my seatbelt from the forty-five-second car ride, I leapt out onto the cracked tarmac. I waited for Dad to emerge, and followed him onto the veranda of the station.

Dad paused, and said to Ernie, "Is there a car rental place on island by any chance?"

Ernie nodded, "Yeah, just down the street. Want me to book a car for you?"

Dad replied, "Oh, Ernie, thanks for offering but we can do that."

But Ernie persisted, "Oh it's nothing. A car for how many … two?"

Smiling, Dad said, "Thank you, you're the best. Anything with four seats would be perfect." Hearing that response, Ernie tipped his leather-brimmed cap and was off.

The customs formalities were virtually identical to those of any other island we'd been to. Police cleared us in, asked if we had anything to declare, how long we would be there, and then smiled and waved us out. As we walked out, Ernie's car came flying down the street. He rolled down a window saying, "I reserved a car under the name Lee. You can pick 'er up whenever you want." After Dad had professed his gratitude, Ernie continued, "Hop in, I'll bring you back to you the docks."

Ernie, like other industrious islanders, performed many functions in this tiny island nation, including being Commodore of the Niue Yacht Club, and he invited us all to visit it later that day. The people are hospitable and incredibly resourceful, often both seafaring and farming for their livelihood. Niue was colonized by Samoans in the ninth century, and invaded by Tongans in the sixteenth. Even on this tiny island there are two dialects, pooled together and called Niuean. These hearty souls are internally self-governed in free association with New Zealand. In an act of conscience, they were the first nation to universally ban smoking.

A few hours later, we returned as a family to the dock in the dinghy. Lara was not the most enthused with making the transition from the dinghy to the dock, as the relative heights changed frequently. Having completed the ordeal of getting into downtown Alofi, La was feeling altogether much more secure. Actually, I am sure that we all shared this sentiment. The town had awakened somewhat in our absence; the grocery store had opened its doors in hopes of a customer; and a truck rumbled past. The sky remained overcast as we piled into a car from the rental lot, one of five vehicles available. Traffic and business were slow. There is little commercial activity in Niue; most of the islanders grow cassava, squash, and yams for their sustenance, complimenting their diet by the bounty of the sea. Free-range chickens and pigs also dotted the landscape.

We were probably the only customers for the rental place, and then again for the Niue Yacht Club with Internet and ice cream down the street. With the overflowing bookcases of its nautical book swap, and overstuffed, somewhat mildewed chairs, it radiated a genuine hospitality offering a respite to any sailors weary of the constantly undulating sea. Lara adored this sort of comfort zone and snuggled right in. Like many small businesses in the Pacific, the front of the building was the business side (restaurant/store), and the back was the owner's residence. This was a charming teal cottage, and we were more than happy to patronize it. Mom went inside to check e-mail, in the event some urgent message had been sent. Dad went to the counter and ordered four hamburgers, and Lara and I sat on the picnic benches, painted to match the building and, incidentally, my t-shirt. Lara laughed at this ironic correlation, and in the middle of a fit of giggles, squeaked as she was leapt upon. She gasped, "A kitty!" The tabby nuzzled her and proceeded to curl itself into a feline ball in her lap and purr.

Dad came back with the food saying, "La, how do you manage to find every cat in the Pacific?"

She smiled. "I don't know, Daddy, I'm just really lucky!"

The road was not as flat as I had guessed from off shore, the top of the plateau did have a variable topography. Dipping, rising, and weaving over the typical, beaten island asphalt, we zipped alone through the elfin rainforest. Like Nevis, the island was round, with a main road running the perimeter. At some of the points we encountered archaic stone structures, those of the indigenous people, encircled by crumbling stone walls, weakened by the penetrating roots of the ficus towering above. This was an unusual structure for the old Polynesian population that had resided here; most Niueans had lived in coastal caves, close to the ocean that sustained them. Mom thumbed through one of her many guides, saying, "The Indatapa caves have some pretty phenomenal geological formations ... let's take a look; they're up on the right in a kilometer or so."

A precariously steep concrete strip was the way to these caves. Our little rental car crawled forth from the jungle, right on the coast. The concrete strip wrapped against the cliff, teetering on the edge of a two hundred foot drop into the raging Pacific, gray and, for all intents and purposes, infinite. It was at that juncture that we stopped the car, pulled the parking brake, and continued on foot.

Their voices urgent, Mom and Dad insisted on slow walking, closer to the inside of the curve preferably. While skirting the cliff I got a close look at the sedimentary façade. The rock existed in undulating layers more or less parallel to the sea that had formed them. I noticed a break in the pattern: segmented rods jutting against the grain, almost perpendicularly. This was a discovery that required the attention of the geology teacher.

"Mom! Check it out; I found some fossilized reeds!" After a few moments of excited jabbering, we moved on down the precarious slope toward the greater archeological site.

The concrete fell away, pieces hanging on the edge of the cliff, contrasting with the dark rocks that they rested on below. An indentation in the cliff led to a dank cave, burrowed only fifty feet or so into the stone. Surprisingly, the caves had occupants other than mold and bacteria: boats. Three outrigger canoes were stored in the first cave, and there were more in the others. These outriggers were dramatically different from the brilliantly-painted fiberglass ones from French Polynesia. Bare wood haphazardly nailed together and secured with hemp twine, each was equipped with a twelve-foot fishing pole. I looked from them to the swells and back to them. What could they be doing here? The answer lay on the rougher cliffs plummeting into the sea: a flight of rudimentary steps cut into the stone. Looking at the monstrous swells ravaging the cliffs, it seemed impossible that any mortal could get the boat down the cliffs, through the surf, and then do the process in reverse, with a boatload of fish. This was yet another testimony to the durability of these people; they are truly of the sea.

Niue is best known for its geologic phenomena, and our next destination was another cave. A tourist board had been posted at the head of the path leading to the caves, its vibrant colors proclaiming the history of the land and the way it was once lived upon. Mom stopped to peruse it but I eagerly surged past, down toward the reason we had pulled off the beaten road.

"Alex, wait for the rest of your group!" Mom called in her tour-guide tone.

I paused and looked uphill toward the trail-head. The bushes rustled, and I said, "There you guys are!" But instead of my family, I saw three local teens who grinned as they scrambled down the path, racing toward the cave beyond the bend in the path.

One called, "I think the ones you're looking for are back a few paces!"

Mom, Dad, and Lara all came along momentarily, in that order of appearance. Now that we were united as a group, I slipped around the lush corner of the path and found myself standing in a maw. The honey-colored limestone was stained dark further in, and into that dark throat I dove. I crouched to slip down the water-worn stone lip, the first step into the abyss. Mom was close behind; Dad stayed with Lara, who was reluctant. The tunnel was broad, forty feet across and half as high, and to my tremendous surprise, terrifically well illuminated, the golden stone bathed in blue light reflecting off the sea through the far end of the cave, a gaping cavity. The teen trio was slipping out the seaward end of the cave, relying strongly on local knowledge, the familiarity of a place gained only through residence. The air was exceptionally humid, and very salty. The surf hit, filling our view of the sea with violent spray. I started to wonder just what those guys were thinking, or if they were still alive to. They probably were, they were seafolk, Polynesian. Mom and I tread carefully through the tunnel; although the stone was smooth, it was greatly uneven, a veritable minefield of stalagmites. After a hundred feet of navigating the matrix of stalagmites in the tunnel, the walls and ceiling peeled back to form a vast cavern, pockmarked with sporadic wells and more stalagmites, the stalactites above completing the image of a closing pair of jaws. That was when Mom shrieked.

I whirled around. "Mom? You okay?"

She laughed, "The spray! It really surprised me."

I laughed back. I had welcomed the cool sensation of the aggressive surf bombarding the cavern's seaside entrance.

Another facet of the cavern's tremendous beauty was the mineral rainbow splattered across the floor. Splotches of green, purple, blue, and orange mottled the ground, mostly beneath the stalactites, where these vibrant minerals had landed after an eternity of dripping. The scene was epic: the vast space, intrinsically multicolored, enhanced by the dancing patterns of light from the ocean outside, which contributed its salty mist and potent roar.

Filled with a new appreciation for the planet's beauty, I wanted to continue exploring the island, maybe go spelunking with a local guide. That was not in the cards, though. Somewhere behind the stratus cloud covering, the sun was sinking, and we headed back to Alofi. The roads were still mostly deserted; we passed a car every five minutes or so.

Taking a different route home, we passed through a village, mostly devastated from a hurricane a few years before. Half the homes were caving in, one blackened from flame. The inhabitants had probably emigrated to New Zealand in search of a more reliable infrastructure. Not everyone, though, since Dad slammed the brakes, causing us all to scream, in order to let one cross the road. I peered over the dashboard to see who had not looked both ways before crossing. The pedestrian in question was a small dark bird, a scruffy chicken-like fowl: a kiwi. We knew how to recognize the bird from the New Zealand currency, specifically the ten-dollar bill. Lara collected every coin and bill she could abscond with from my parents' wallets; the currency was covered with flora and fauna, and the five-dollar bill even had her ultimate favorite bird, the fairy penguin.

After returning the car, it was our turn to make our own intrepid journey from land to sea. We rigged the harness back up, and hitching it to the dinghy, brought the rusty crane to life, letting the dinghy make its sluggish ascent next to the forty-foot coast guard speedboat it was parked alongside. There was no other way into the water safely except by way of the crane, but it seemed highly improbable the same creaking crane was capable of putting a boat of that size into the water. Fortunately, our concern was just our little inflatable.

After we returned to *Promise*, a slight drizzle began to fall. With the sky dark, the rhythmic sound of falling rain and the warm glow of our cabin lights, one of my favorite boat times arrived. Indeed, when safely in harbor, a fall in the barometer can be a gift, bringing a cozy day for reading, and filling the cabin with the aromas of the galley. An hour or so elapsed in this placid manner, the perusal of novels under yellow lights with the enticing smell of today's stew wafting about. Stone soup, as we referred to it, was a common dish aboard *Promise*, usually consisting of corn and various beans; it generally turned out to be some form of chili made from provisions that would keep. Today it had the added bonus of fresh squash purchased from an islander's small garden.

I was nearing the end of my book when a sharp thud resounded through the hull, followed by a shout, "Hallo? *Promise*? Might we come aboard?"

The accent was close to German, so I knew who it was before going to the cockpit to take their line. "Hello, Maryanne. Hey, Hanspeter," I called. There were a Swiss couple we had met in Bora Bora, when our hulls nearly drifted into one another in the middle of the night. Instead of it being a stressful event, we simply all laughed genially and set up our dinghies to keep our boats from "kissing in the night."

They handed me their painter and said, "Hello, Alex. How're you going?" their words laced with their European accents.

Tying a bowline, I replied, "Good, thanks. You're probably looking for my parents, right?"

Maryanne and Hanspeter, or Hansburger as I tended to call him, had just come from Suwarrow. Maryanne was wan and looking far from her normal, tan self. She said, "I know you guys are doctors and I was wondering if you could tell me if it's anything serious." She then proceeded to list her symptoms.

Mom asked, "You guys just came from Suwarrow, right?" They nodded.

"Hm," Dad said. "They did just have an outbreak of dengue there … you look a lot like me when I had dengue a few years back. I'll bet that's what it is." I actually thought she was looking pretty well for dengue, and since she had had it for some time, was probably starting to make a recovery. Regardless, Mom and Dad extended the invitation for further checkups should things take a turn for the worse. Unfortunately, due to its viral nature, there was no cure other than supportive care.

Then, in the typical symbiosis of cruisers, Mom asked, "Hanspeter, you're a computer guy, right? Could you try and help us with our Pactor modem? We've been having trouble getting Internet and therefore critical weather through it."

Hanspeter had been a computer engineer back in Switzerland, and was happy to try and resolve our issue with the Pactor. Unfortunately, he was not able to puzzle it out, and his analysis evolved into a conversation of computers. He said our laptop might have been the issue, and that led to discourse of his business in Switzerland, for which he had needed five languages: English, Spanish, French, German, and the arcane language of the land, Romansh—hence his unique accent.

We bade them good-bye and started the preparations for leaving harbor the next day. Niue had just been a stepping-stone in our travels, since we were being chased by a large weather front and Niue offered not the slightest protection from wind and wave. Still, our time there was strongly exemplary of the Polynesian reverence for the sea, and of cruisers' symbiotic relationships with each other.

Local outrigger canoe sheltered in a cave before the surf, Niue

Alex in one of Niue's many caves

Chapter 16

TONGA, THE KINGDOM OF WATER

We left at daybreak under a grey sky, heading westward toward the horizon. Most of this vast stretch of the Pacific was pristine and uninterrupted water. The Kingdom of Tonga, which was our next destination, was spread over 700,000 square kilometers, yet consisted of only 691 square kilometers of land. Of its 171 volcanic islands, only thirty-five were inhabited on a regular basis. Tonga is the last and only existing Pacific monarchy, and all the land there belongs to the crown. Each family, however, is allotted two parcels of land: one to live on, and one to farm. Outsiders can only lease land for a maximum fifty years, and this has discouraged commercial buildup of foreign enterprises.

To reach Tonga we had to sail over the second-deepest trench in the world, the Tongan trench, which runs like a vertical slice down the mid-Pacific. Tonga sits on the eastern edge of the Indo-Australian continental plate, which is working its way under the Pacific plate. The trench drops a staggering five-and-a-half nautical miles. We often wondered when sailing over such depths if we will encounter a rare, never-yet-seen creature of the depths such as a mutant giant squid. Our passage was boisterous but free of nightmarish creatures. The winds blew at a brisk thirty knots off our port aft quarter, and we rolled down the huge seas with ease at almost ten knots.

This realm of the Pacific is so remote that the charts we were going to use for Tonga, purchased recently from a marine supply company in New Zealand, were completed in the 1800s by a ship of her majesty's

British Royal Navy, the HMS *Penguin*. Despite most yachts' reliance on modern electronic navigation technology, we still plotted and checked every course by hand on a paper chart and used celestial navigation when feasible. Some remote areas are riddled with inaccuracies on the charts, both paper and electronic versions, in longitude especially and can be off by several miles. When in doubt, we tried to avoid reef-strewn areas at night, and always posted a bow lookout during the day.

The second night out the weather tempered a bit and we were able to have a feast of sorts: canned ham, canned fruit, and rice. Prior to living on a ship, I would have looked askance at the rubbery meal. On a ship, alone, in the middle of the sea, it was magnificent. We also were able to set the table in the cockpit and eat together, with our reliable friend Otto, our nickname for autopilot, at the helm. During our evening meal we calculated that we'd crossed the International Dateline, the arbitrary longitudinal line (running erratically around a few islands) that separated the days. We crossed it, and gained a day. The most significant consequence of this was for our celestial navigation, which required very precise date and time readings in order to calculate our position. We had jokingly rehearsed this moment many times before with our beloved professor at Mystic Seaport, Don Treworgy. Recalculations for the southern hemisphere, the International Dateline, and using other reference stars and the Southern Cross were all just theoretical considerations when we first studied the subject half a world away; now, they directly affected our lives.

As we had at Niue, we arrived at Tonga at about four a.m. In the beginning of my shift, the GPS that had failed us in Mopelia said we were close, and the more trustworthy radar was picking up an island-like mass. We were there. After activating autopilot, I went down below and awakened Dad, "We're here... now what?"

When we were less than a half a mile away, I got up onto the foredeck, and with both hands lifted the torso-sized flashlight and aimed it at the shore. It turned out to be a sandy beach, with some scraggly brush and then a blank hill rising up behind it. No signs of human presence, when a mooring would have been helpful. We motored in closer to shore, the depth about 300 feet until we were less than that far from the shore, so anchoring was not an option. Unable to come to a full stop, we dropped the sails, and bobbed in the lee of the bluff, giving the occasional turn of the wheel to keep us pointed into the wind. Dad and I sat in the cockpit silently after that. I put the light on the cockpit floor, and pointed it up so it shone on the bimini, illuminating the whole space eerily. I entertained myself with checking the pockets of my jacket. I found some Canadian coins and a pack of hand warmers: the last time I had worn that jacket was while skiing over New Years in Canada with the Forsons.

"Hey, Dad, feeling cold?" I asked, holding up the hand warmers, the side with the penguin outline toward him.

He laughed and then said, "If you're tired, you can go catch a few Z's. I'll be fine up here; it's not like there's anything to take care of really." My shift had been from one to four a.m. that night, and I gratefully saluted him and climbed down the companionway.

A few hours later, I lifted the pillow from atop of my head, which had muffled the quaking rumble of the engine. I stood on the bottom rung of the companionway so my head just poked above the deck. "Well, this place is sure unique," I commented.

We were weaving through a hive of motus—well, that may not be the correct term, but we were certainly surrounded by a great many islets, most of which were fairly high, some with sharp cliffs wreathed in dark foliage. The scene was dramatic in a more muted, almost stark way than Polynesia had been. The fiery sunrise above us reflected of the dark waters below.

These uninhabited islets, comprising a large portion of Vava'u, the section of Tonga we were in, gradually consolidated into fewer and larger bodies as we approached the main harbor, Neiafu. Tonga is part of the Ring of Fire, a band of volcanoes that circles the Pacific, and some islands, the younger ones, were still active, towering volcanoes. New islands appear sporadically in the region. This portion of the archipelago, the Vava'u group of islands, consisted of uplifted atolls covered with prolific coral growth.

Mom got on the VHF and hailed, *"Alana Rose, Alana Rose*, this is *Promise.* Come in, please." She repeated the call.

After a pause we heard John's Australian voice say, *"Promise*, this is *Alana Rose.* What's up, mate? Just getting in, are we?"

The largest and main island in the group, also named Vava'u, had a channel that spiraled in toward its center, round peaks forming the barricade around one of the best hurricane holes in the Pacific. Following the advice John had given us, we went straight to the industrial dock

208

at the mouth of the harbor. With all our fenders to port, we pulled up against the dock, a couple of dockhands emerging from the maze of containers to help.

Dad went up to fetch the customs officers, since they would come to the boat to perform an inspection. Mom reached into what we called the carbs cabinet, where we kept crackers, cereal, and cookies, and pulled out three packages of the latter. She opened all three and poured them onto a plate, the mound almost as high as the plate's width. She handed it to me carefully.

I took it, saying, "Gee, thanks. Is this a new diet reform for me?"

Tone serious, she said, "No, that's for the customs guys. Courtesy here dictates a snack."

I looked down at the plate in my hands and put it back on the counter. "This is more like a meal for a family … how many of them are coming?"

"Two." But any two people would not be the same thing as the two Tongan customs officials, who were tall, broad-shouldered, and rather rotund men, weighing a good three or four hundred pounds each.

Having snacks available was a relatively simple aspect of the Tongan culture. As it turned out, the culture is extremely conservative, and a few decades behind Western civilization generally. The first manifestation of this was Mom's own acting. The boat tipped slightly as the two officials cordially boarded and found their way to the cockpit, where they picked up conversation with Dad. After prolonged courtesies had been exchanged, Mom came up to the cockpit, bearing the cookie plate and wearing a little 1950s-style apron. Keeping her head slightly down she said, "I hope you like these, sirs." After putting the plate on the table, she retreated back below.

I had watched the show through the companionway, and as she stepped down below I collapsed onto the couch, muffling my laughter as much as I could. Mom—doctor, scientist, liberal, and firm believer in equal rights—had bowed down to the level of a 1950s housewife.

She threw her apron at me and said, "Shhhhh! It's a patriarchal society … and I'm trying to be politically correct here."

Meanwhile, in the cockpit, Dad was asked about his past career between mouthfuls of cookies. Dad explained, "Well, I used to be a cardiac surgeon, operating on people's hearts, fixing them if something went wrong. I spent most of my time working with children, fixing defects that they were born with."

One of the officials leaned forward and pondered, "I have often heard of this. I have also heard a story about changing or transplanting a person's heart, and I do not see how it is possible. A person's heart is who they are! How can you switch that with someone else or modify it? I respect you sir, but I simply don't believe that."

Dad took this all in stride, nodding gently and ambiguously explaining that it was complex and hard to understand.

Although many Tongans live a simple material existence with an average income of US $4,000, they are an extremely contented people. They have many phrases that illustrate their philosophy of life, which is intertwined with their identity; it is said by Tongans that if they lose their identity, they will die. Tongans offer wishes to others such as *mo'ui fiemalie*, a contented life; *nofo fiefia*, living happily; and *nofo fakalata*, making others feel at home, which they were certainly exceptionally skilled at.

The conversation between my dad and the officials went on for over an hour before they got down to business: five minutes of paperwork and then the inspection. Once down below, the first one commented, "This is a very pretty boat you have … I already asked, but do you have any firearms on board?" Dad shook his head.

They opened a few drawers, uninterested by the silverware in one and the assortment of string and small tools in the other, "Well, I don't think you pose any threat, so good day, and welcome to Tonga!" They'd eaten the entire plate of cookies.

Mom said, "Well, Dad and I are going to go ashore and grab some food, and maybe some more cookies too."

Following their departure, I flopped down in my berth, happy to pick up my book again. About thirty pages later I heard a thick voice call, "Hello, white American boat! Anyone aboard?"

I wanted nothing better than to feign absence, but went on deck to greet whoever it was. "Hello, can I help you?"

He said, "Hello, my name is Lofi. Are your parents aboard?" I shook my head and he continued, "Are you interested in any flags or jewelry? I have whale bone necklaces, and I make flags for all Pacific countries!"

I started backpedaling; if I expressed interest then this could go on indefinitely. "No, thanks. I mean, I don't really have much money and I don't know if my parents would be okay with it—"

Lofi cut in, "Well, take a look at these necklaces, they're really quite good."

Dissenting was not optional, it seemed. "Yeah, those are pretty cool … how much are they?"

He smiled. "Ten for the whale, fifteen for the other."

I asked, "Ten US?" He nodded. I said, "Hang on a moment, I'll see if I have that much money." I did. I put the whale necklace on and contrived a smile.

Lofi grinned. "So do you think your dad would be interested in a Tongan flag?" he asked.

This was my chance. "Yeah, maybe. He just went in to town that way." I gave him a brief description and a glass of water after he asked for that too. "Thanks."

A few days later, we headed back out the spiraling channel away from Neiafu to the outer islets. Rounding the first bend, I finished closing up the anchor well and looked at the beach off our port side. We were in an area where the water could not have had great circulation, and the brown water matched the dark, muddy sand. A big dog ran down the beach and started digging. I laughed at the universality of something as simple as a dog on a beach.

Then, *Oh wait*, I said to myself. I realized it was a pig. It dug ferociously, and starting gorging on some find. After reading further about Tonga, it seemed most likely that the pig had been digging for clams, and found some too. Both species were in abundance.

We wound most of the way out of the spiraling channel, stopping in a cleft between two islets, which framed a view of the seemingly endless network of smaller islands yet to be explored. We were almost alone in the harbor; the only other craft with which we shared the anchorage was a large raft, a houseboat if you will. Painted the blue of tropical waters, it blended in with the water. Once we left the main harbor, the water varied in hue from cerulean to a clear turquoise. Inspired by the gorgeous ocean, and the unique corals rumored to grow here, we wasted no time in deploying the dinghy to get to the snorkel spot. It was a swimmable distance, but with a slight cloud cover, it could be a cold hundred yards.

The tricky part was figuring out what to do with the dinghy once we were at the snorkel spot. The reef was tightly wrapped around the cliffs of an islet, the water about six feet deep right up to the cliff's base. Mom leapt into the water as soon as the craft's speed was low enough to do so safely.

I laughed and then said, "So, what do we do with the dinghy?"

We all looked around for a bit. Dad finally said, "There—we'll tie it to that bush." He pointed to a branch protruding from the rocky face. A bit of dirt fell onto the pontoons as we fixed it in place.

Having dealt with the ordeal of parking the dinghy, Dad and I at last we able to don masks and dive in after Mom. Most reefs lose a large portion of their beauty in the absence of a bright sun. However, this reef in Tonga, had a quiet splendor and a stillness, with few fish present, that was enhanced by the weak lighting. The even depth of six feet, covered in coral for the fifty feet of visibility, lent a sense of rhythm and pattern to the reef.

Across this silently magnificent reef splashed the occasional burst of the exotic. I saw a few brilliant blue starfishes, some pink ones, or in one scenario, both tangent and appearing to be "holding hands." Bonsai coral, a gorgeous forest green, rose from the seabed in a thin filament and grew wider exponentially, until it had formed the shape of an umbrella, or a bonsai tree.

Heaving myself into the dinghy I said, "Well, that wasn't your typical reef, but it sure was cool." Hardly dried, we zipped past *Promise* and approached the houseboat. We circled it a few times. It was clear no one was aboard, so there was nothing obnoxious about our inspection. One of the sides of the square had a verandah just above the water, with cleats for tying small craft to. We took that as an open invitation, and again Mom was the first one out of the dinghy.

She read the placard to the right of the door: "Sheri and Larry's Ark Gallery." The float was totally open, and we tentatively stepped in. An easel stood in the center of the room with a half-finished watercolor painting on it. The color of the wall was barely distinguishable; the walls were densely covered in paintings ranging from mere inches across to several feet wide.

"Hey, look, a cat," I said, stooping to scratch the head of the tabby that had appeared from nowhere.

Mom commented, "It's too bad it's just the cat, not the artist who's aboard; there's some great stuff here."

That night we sat in the cockpit before dinner, admiring the view in all directions. I was terribly thirsty, so I began to chug my entire glass of water.

"Look! Oh my God! Look over there!" Mom screamed suddenly, causing me to spray the glassful of water I had in my throat. She pointed to a true mammoth in the sky: a giant fruit bat, the slow beats of its wings causing its body to bob through the air.

Having overcome the inconvenience of spraying the table with water, my eyes bulged at the sight. "Whoa, that thing's huge!"

The bat landed on the crest of a tree, the top half of the plant swaying out of control. Even Dad, who never liked bats, started laughing, "That baby sure looks heavy!" The bat proceeded to emit a series of barks, and fell from the treetop, another bat having tackled it. Branches snapped and leaves floated toward the ground. We were silent with surprise. A minute of scuffling later, one took off into the purple evening sky, the other following suit. Almost every night, at one remote island or another in this archipelago, these flying foxes, or *peka* in Tongan, put on a magnificent show.

We returned to Neiafu several days later when fresh produce was running low. Having settled in, I got my first excursion into the town. Neiafu was a town with a few rows of streets parallel to the water, connected by a few sharp drops, which officially but undeservedly were considered a road. "Chute" would be more accurate. The hill Neiafu had been constructed on was incredibly steep; many of its buildings were on stilts. As we wove up the hill to a café, we often had to pause and wait for the disorderly stream of vehicles to pass by. Another bizarre element of Tongan culture pertains to cars, and especially hitchhiking, the undeveloped world's most common mode of transportation. If you are getting in the car with someone you are anything short of in love with, you ride in the front with them if you're the same sex, in the back if not. This was apparent in the cars rolling past: often a man would be in the front, chatting to a woman in the back, or vice versa, with all other seats free.

As for those without a car, there were many pedestrians about. To our wonder, despite the eighty-degree heat, many locals were in full-body draped black cloaks. These were held close to the body with a thick, intricate woven-grass mat, called the *ta'ovala,* which functioned as a belt and apron. These *pandanus* (leaf mats) are extremely important in their culture, often passed down from one generation to the next as prized heirlooms. Individuals as well as families have an entire collection of them for different occasions of importance, ranging from birthdays to funerals.

That was a morning of observational learning about Tonga. Although it was largely about culture, it was also a quick geography lesson. It was not until we sat on the deck of Tropicana, the hilltop café, that I appreciated the breadth of the harbor. It extended about a mile inland, the scattering of boats becoming less dense the farther from the town docks. Nor had I realized how far below they were; it must have been a few hundred feet. There were several rows of corrugated rooftops. We enjoyed the relative coolness of Tonga, as we were father south of the equator than we had been before; in fact, *tonga* means "south" in the Polynesian language. The ancient Polynesians reached Tonga from Fiji more than 3,000 years earlier. Tongans were once fierce warriors, and their dynastic kings, the Tu'i Tongas, were considered to be of divine origin. They controlled a huge area of the central Pacific region and travelled in enormous outrigger canoes called *kalia,* which could carry two hundred warriors at a time. Artifacts from this time in their history, including amazing war clubs, still exist. We visited several art galleries, small cultural museums, and bought a replica, which hopefully would never be used for anything more than smashing walnuts.

Having gotten lunch at what was supposedly the best place in town, Mom decided to call family. The timing was perfect. She was calling from May 1st in Tonga, to wish a happy birthday to her brother in Connecticut, where it was still April 30th and his special day. We then set out to explore the small town, the periphery of which had chickens and pigs that vastly outnumbered the humans.

A visit to an open-air market nestled under humungous trees revealed a group of woman weaving pandanus in the shade. Friendly in the extreme, they explained about the intricate process of weaving the various leaves they used and the exhaustive drying and staining processes passed down from generation to generation. *Tapa*, or dried bark of *hiapo* trees (paper mulberry), painted with natural inks, was also a revered local art, and we admired several in various stages of creation. Many of the pieces depicted animals, each of which had its own mythological prowess; the turtle ensured longevity, the whale, wisdom. They also reproduced patterns for decoration and gifts, with specific designs illustrating an important ceremony. They were wedding tapas, where red and almost black inks were interwoven in an overlapping diamond pattern, and one could imagine the two previously distinct families merging symbolically into one. Birthday patterns resembled large eyes in a backdrop of foliage peering out. The artists informed us that the first and the twenty-first birthdays were the most sacred, and required a feast sponsored by the family for the village. Often for important occasions such as weddings, large lengths of tapa, over fifty feet, were given as gifts from these generous and creative people. Their relationships and allegiance to one another bound them together; sharing their lives with family and close friends was paramount in their world.

As we wandered on, several irregular blocks later, we stood outside a large white cathedral trying to decide our direction. We bantered a good deal, and I finally pointed down the street saying, "Hey do you think that sign might be helpful?"

We approached it. It was a nine-foot pole, and like a mace, had spokes protruding from all sides, each tipped triangularly and each with a location written on it: Rome, New Zealand, Los Angeles, Mama Iti's Grocery, Tongatapu, Town Docks.

"Let's follow that one," said Lara. Dinner at a local waterfront pub followed, and we reconnected with the crew of *Alana Rose*, whom we hadn't seen since French Polynesia, and Bruce from *Blessed Bee*.

Since school was out, many children were fishing and swimming on the harbor's edge. We noticed that almost everyone, even those swimming, was fully clothed. Tongans, we learned, enjoy the water this way; in fact, there is a fine for swimming in a revealing swimsuit in some places. The cultural conservatism pervades the society; kissing or even holding hands in public is grossly inappropriate.

After dinner, one of the workers on the dock approached Dad and requested his help. He knew my dad was a doctor—word of mouth travels quickly on a small island—and the owner of the place was having medical problems. The local health center was dubious at best, even by Tongan standards, and an American physician was a rare and valuable find. (Given the gender division in the society, they would not even have considered asking my mother.) My father went off with a bag full of equipment and returned several hours later. When we tried to pay, we found that our restaurant bill had been waived. Captain Cook, who had visited this kingdom three times, named them the "Friendly Islands," and we understood why.

Late that night (late for sailors, so about 9:30 p.m.), we were sitting on deck, seeking a reprieve from the unusual yet oppressive heat below. After admiring the stars, Mom started singing "A Whole New World" from Disney's *Aladdin*. In the middle of the chorus, her voice was drowned out almost completely by the blare of brass instruments and the drone of singing Tongans. Tongans love tubas. It is an obsession they have nurtured over the last century, and they often have elaborate parades and performances simply for their own enjoyment. It was a Wednesday night, but there was some occasion to celebrate life in that big white cathedral on the hill. Even after such a short time in this country, we had no trouble looking at each other and knowingly saying, "Only in Tonga."

John from Alana Rose relaying information from shore

One the unique outer islands of Vava'u, Tonga

Promise at the customs dock, Tonga

Two Tongans in traditional dress in town

Lara on an beach abandoned but for a dog

A merchant in the Tongan fruit market, Tongatapu

Chapter 17

CHANGES

𝒫arents are good at hiding things when they want to. Having spent a few weeks in Tonga, Mom and Dad set out across the glassy harbor in the dinghy, hoping to clear customs and to settle what we owed to Sheri and Larry, from whose Ark Gallery we had bought several small paintings. I was hoping they would be able to find the corpulent customs officials; our sail to Fiji was pending, and I had read little else for the past week than travel guides (which I normally scorn) about the place, focusing especially on the Sri Siva Subramaniya Temple, a magnificently ornate building that is also the largest Hindu temple in its hemisphere. This passage also marked the start of a new phase to our Pacific journey; we would be leaving Polynesia and entering the generally more rugged Melanesia. That was a day or two away though, and it was still early.

The water and sky were a similar gray, the water rippling from the few somber atmospheric tears. Lara was still asleep, and I let her be. Picking up a workbook of mathematical puzzles, I flipped toward the end of the book; I had already done most of them. On my third puzzle, the drone of the dinghy broke through the rhythmic slapping of the ripples of the harbor against *Promise's* hull. The dinghy now had a third passenger, and all three aboard were in foul weather gear. I inferred that it was Larry, who had come into town to settle the issue of payment.

With one hand I took the painter, and with the other I shook Larry's hand as he came aboard, saying, "Hello again, Larry."

He responded from behind a graying beard, "Hey there, Alex."

It turned out that the issue of what we owed them had just gained another level of complexity. Mom said, "Hey, Alex, it's time to pack. We are going home." Seeing my confusion, she added, "I know we're home now, but I mean we're going to Connecticut. Larry is here for an overview of *Promise* before he sails her to Australia."

Our family usually has plenty of discussion before anything major happens. This was the largest event of my life, and it had just been cancelled. The shock and grief I felt then does not have a word aptly suited to describe it, so I wrote it simply as *Crunch!* in my journal a few days later when I came to my senses. My world had just been noisily crushed; I had been robbed of the greatest adventure of my life, and there was nothing left to think about.

Like an automaton, I crammed what clothes I could into duffel bags, and ferried various objects that needed to come home with us into respective bags. The packing was orchestrated and directed by Mom. Dad was showing Larry the ins and outs of the boat, focusing on the electrical systems without which the boat could do little other than float, which would be insufficient for crossing the remainder of the largest ocean on the planet.

An hour later, my entire family and all our worldly possessions were loaded into the dinghy. The rain was light as we crossed Neiafu harbor. Bringing our material world along in our arms, we boarded an archaic British plane, its propellers clicking as it roared to life. We flew south, to Tongatapu, the island home to the national capital and its king. We flew over the central cluster of islands in the archipelago, known by the administrative name Ha'apai. They were small specks of dirt in the vast, vast ocean, the kind of places I would not see again for an unknown number of years.

The airport of Tongatapu was poor even by the standards of the third world, its aging structure decaying: the rusty roof sagged, the concrete floor was sunken and cracked, potholed in some places. We had been on the last flight in, and the crowd was dispersing quickly. Before we could collect ourselves, we were practically alone in the airport. A goat walked across the main driveway, and a woman started getting into her Jeep under a tree. Dropping her bags, Mom ran over to her, flailing her arms to get the short Tongan's attention.

There had been no taxis, and there would not have been for quite a while either—not until the following morning. Sitting in this woman's old black SUV was a true gift, though it did smell of generic decay. We stopped at a gas station. Our fare was paying for a full gas tank, which seemed fair, even though it was almost sixteen dollars a gallon.

Mom asked, "So, do you know of any hotels nearby you could take us to, please?"

Our driver's English was fragmented, but she had a relative in the hospitality industry; she would take us to "he hotel." Driving through the worst poverty I had seen in quite a while, I began to panic, thinking we would be taken to some kind of hybrid hut and motel. I knew Tongans slept on the floor, and refusal of accommodations would be the single rudest thing we could do, especially after her altruism. As a sailor, I could sleep on just about anything, but the dirt floor of someone's open air home was not high on that extensive list.

The buildings grew closer, and the streets dirtier as we approached the capital, Nuku'alofa. Our road came in along the water, and we followed the gentle curve of the main harbor. In contrast to the town, the water looked startlingly clean. Our driver leaned toward the water and said, "Left be house of king." The royal palace was on the left, a modest, two story Victorian home behind a low chain-link fence. The fact that it was still standing from its time of construction in the 1800s by the visiting British is truly impressive; wooden structures do not last long in the tropics, especially without chemicals that would not have been in existence a century or so ago.

That was definitely on the upper side of the construction spectrum in Tonga, and to my immense relief, so was our hotel. Tall, concrete, ugly, modern, and air-conditioned, it was all I had hoped for. Mom hugged our chauffeur in deep, very genuine gratitude, ignoring the conservative culture of the land that probably would have discouraged the contact. The woman smiled, though, knowing how it was meant.

I could not sleep that night, even though I had a mattress. When I woke up, it was still bleak outside, and I turned on the TV, hoping for distraction. Channel two: Chinese news in Chinese. Channel three: a Chinese travel show in Chinese. Pushing the channel up button again, it looped back to channel two. This was not that surprising. The Chinese had done this in many third-world countries, including some in Africa: they invested heavily in the nation, and inserted their foot in the culture. Chinese merchants would play a large role in the economy, and apparently they dominated the television industry—not that there was actually any competition. Luckily, I was distracted by the sounds of brass slowly coming down the road. A funeral march consisting of several tuba players and a procession of people bearing pictures of the deceased ambled down the main road in both lanes. Only in Tonga.

Several hours later, my foot left the tarmac of Tonga for the last time as I shuffled onto the aluminum steps into a jet. We were on a small plane to Samoa, and would later board a larger New Zealand jet to the States. The flight back was even longer than the flight to Polynesia, a couple thousand miles more. It was night, and there was absolutely nothing to see out the window, just black—the same black we should have been traversing by the water.

The night turned to day and the sea to land. Making a connection in Los Angeles, we set out across the desert. It was the glorious antithesis of flying over islands like Ha'apai. The static folds of the land were waves frozen, undisrupted except for the rare peak capped in snow: islands of water in a dry, dry ocean. Having crossed back over both the international date line and the equator, it was four in the morning when we showed up at Grandma's house. We had given her no message in advance; we were just there. Surprise! It still caught me off guard too.

Finally I had to know what had happened. "Mom, so why did we just give up like that? What's going on?"

Her response was slow. "Well, your father and I thought it would be better if we had more time to settle in, find a home, find a school for Lara, and, you know, just get used to Connecticut again."

Incredulous, I asked, "You gave up in the middle of the dream of your—our—lives so you could spend more time in the America we have banished ourselves from for so long? We are never going to be able to do that, what we attempted, again." My voice had grown soft as I ended.

Mom looked at me and said, "Your father was also experiencing some medical problems, and we did not want to risk anything." Back when we had touched down in Raiatea, the only bag missing had been the one with the defibrillator. That was the one type of medical emergency *Promise*, an incognito ambulance provisioned to deal with any medical problem, was missing. It was not for a long time that I learned that defibrillator would have been the piece of equipment most likely to be needed.

It was ironic. Almost four years before, I had prevented the circumnavigation I had craved so badly by almost dying from a tropical disease. Now, in the middle of our partial completion of the endeavor, we were cut short again by a medical problem—one that fortunately was treatable.

So there I was in Connecticut. I would not be living on a boat again (not until I could buy my own at least), and I was three months away from starting high school, boarding school. I had sailed large tracts of two oceans, commanded a ship in the dark alone on a regular basis, seen countries few do, feasted with local hosts on remote atolls, danced with hula girls, been propelled down a tube of coral by fierce currents, and navigated natural minefields in atolls. I had learned what it meant to conserve, to be brave, and to value the very gift of life. What we had done was a calculated risk, one we had to be well prepared for merely to survive.

The Pacific is a vast, wild place, and one many people die in.

As we found out a few days later, *Blessed Bee* joined the long list of casualties. As we had prepared to go to Fiji, Bruce and his team had left to go to New Caledonia, and from there, the final thousand miles home to Australia. A mayday call had been made, reporting flooding and unmanageable conditions. Bruce had been a champion of the violent Tasmanian Sea, infamous for its storms, conquering its fierce conditions with flying colors. For it to be too much for Bruce, this must have been a beast of a storm. They had reported their coordinates and said they would be letting out their drogue, a sea anchor that would root them upright and stabilize the boat in the waves. Shortly after that message from their death squall, transmission was lost.

The coast guard sent extensive search parties, but in vain; only a few pieces of white flotsam were ever found. The most probable scenario was that they were caught in a microburst, fatally and accurately depicted in the film *White Squall*, and the weight of the drogue had been enough to tear the stern from the hull, from which point it would instantly fill with water and be swallowed by the sea. There would be no time to use the radio or even deploy the life raft. They were underwater just seconds after the sound of the hull being torn asunder echoed over the disinterested waves.

When I was told I looked at the rolling green lawn of my Grandma's house flowing into a small lake through my tearing eyes. We were all crying, not just for the loss of such a good friend and companion, but with the knowledge that it could have been us. We could have been the ones claimed by the water. That made it all the more poignant, though. We had survived, and not just that, we had lived. The quote printed on the journal I used in the Pacific is the words of Henry Miller: "The aim of life is to live, and to live means to be aware, joyously, drunkenly, serenely, divinely aware." This eye-opening experience was the archetype of awareness—awareness of the beauty and danger of the world, and just how far you had to go, and just how carefully you had to go there.

And how worth it doing so truly is.

CPSIA information can be obtained at www.ICGtesting.com
Printed in the USA
236945LV00001B/136/P

9 781462 018321